# A DANGEROUS KNOWING

# A Dangerous Knowing

*Sexuality, Pedagogy and Popular Culture*

Edited by

Debbie Epstein and James T. Sears

CASSELL
London and New York

**Cassell**

Wellington House, 125 Strand, London WC2R 0BB

370 Lexington Avenue, New York, NY 10017-6550

First published 1999

**British Library Cataloguing-in-Publication Data**
A catalogue record for this book is available from the British Library.

ISBN 0-304-33966-0 (hardback)
    0-304-33967-9 (paperback)

**Library of Congress Cataloging-in-Publication Data**
A dangerous knowing: sexuality, pedagogy and popular culture/
  edited by Debbie Epstein and James T. Sears.
      p. cm.
   Includes bibliographical references and index.
   ISBN 0-304-33966-0 (hardcover). – ISBN 0-304-33967-9 (pbk.)
     1. Sex role. 2. Gender identity. 3. Sex in popular culture. 4. Gays in popular
   culture. 5. Gays—Identity. I. Epstein, Debbie, 1945–  . II. Sears, James T.
   (James Thomas), 1951–  .
   305.3–dc21                                                    98-45040
   HQ21.D253     1999                                            CIP

Typeset by York House Typographic Ltd
Printed and bound in Great Britain by Biddles Ltd, Guildford and King's Lynn

# Contents

## Part Three: Sexualities as Identities

## Part Four: Interventions in Sexualities

# Contributors

**Dennis Altman** is Professor of Politics at La Trobe University in Melbourne and author of nine books, including *Homosexual: Oppression and Liberation* (1972, 2nd edn 1993), *AIDS in the Mind of America* (1986) and *Power and Community* (1994). He has also written a novel (*The Comfort of Men*, 1993) and an autobiography (*Defying Gravity: A Political Life*, 1997) and is currently writing a book on sex and globalization.

**Lori Beckett** works as a parent activist with the national and state organizations of parents with children in government schools. She represented the Australian Council of State School Organisations (ACSSO) on the MCEETYA Gender Equity Taskforce, and she represents the New South Wales (NSW) Parents' and Citizens' (P&C) Federation on the Department of Education and Training's Gender Equity Consultative Committee. Lori is also a research assistant and does some part-time teaching in the Faculty of Education at the University of Sydney. Her PhD research included a gender component in an analysis of the recent reforms in NSW education.

**Corrine Bertram** is a graduate student at the City University of New York, Graduate School and University Center. She is currently at work on her dissertation, an analysis of community building at an anti-violence education centre. Her interests include narrative, critical psychology, feminist psychology, memories of sexual abuse and scripts of sexual violence.

**R. W. (Bob) Connell** is an Australian sociologist, now at the University of Sydney after a period in the United States. He has worked on issues of social structure and social justice, and is author or co-author of *Masculinities* (1995), *Schools and Social Justice* (1993), *Rethinking Sex, Gender and Power* (1987) and *Making the Difference*.

**Vicki Crowley** is the Coordinator of Gender Studies in the School of Communication and Information Studies, University of South Australia. Prior to this she worked in the Faculty of Aboriginal and Torres Strait Islander Studies at the University of South Australia. She has researched and published in the areas of racism, post-colonialism, feminism, sexualities, schooling and education. This includes intersections of racism, sexism and homophobia, particularly in relation to policy formation and implementation. She is also interested in questions of identity formation.

**Barbara Crowther** is a senior lecturer at the University of Wolverhampton teaching Literary and Cultural Studies courses on the Women's Studies degree. Her chapter is part of an ongoing study of gender in popular representations of science, and the part played by television in obscuring and obstructing feminist ideas. She has also done research on young girls' diaries.

**Roger Deacon** teaches in the Education Department at the University of Natal, Durban, South Africa, and edits *THEORIA: A Journal of Social and Political Theory*. He has published in the fields of social theory, historiography, education and development, and his current research interest is the politics of postmodernism.

**Debbie Epstein** is Reader in Education at the University of London Institute of Education. Her research interests are in the interlinked inequalities of sexuality, gender and ethnicity in education and in popular culture. Recent publications include: with Richard Johnson, *Schooling Sexualities* (Open University Press, 1998); edited with Jannette Elwood, Valerie Hey and Janet Maw, *Failing Boys? Issues in Gender and Achievement* (Open University Press, 1998).

**Michelle Fine** is Professor of Psychology at the City University of New York, Graduate Center. Recent books include *The Unknown City* (with Lois Weis, 1998); *Becoming Gentlemen* (with Lani Guinier and Jane Balin, 1997); and *Off-White: Readings on Society, Race, and Culture* (with Linda Power, Lois Weis and Mun Wong, 1996). She has provided courtroom expert testimony for cases including Anthony T. Lee, *et al.* and the United States of America and the National Educational Association, Inc *vs* Macon County Board of Education; Shannon Richey Faulkner and the United States of America *vs* James E. Jones, *et al.*, for The Citadel, The Military

College of South Carolina; Ulcena *vs* Babylon School District, and the Board of Education of the Borough of Englewood.

**Sibyl Fisher** is a school student in NSW. She was in Mary Tweed's Year 6 class and worked on the anti-homophobia project in primary school. Now in high school, Sibyl continues to develop her commitment to anti-discrimination and social justice. However, she struggles with the heterosexist and homophobic cultures of the school and community. With the help of others, like her schoolmates and some friends, Sibyl works to realize a fair and just society.

**John Holmes** is lecturer in Drama and Drama-in-Education at the University of South Australia. His current research includes analysis of the continuity of successful drama teaching in primary and secondary locations, issues around race and sexuality and teacher sexuality in the education context.

**Robert Morrell** teaches in the Education Department at the University of Natal, Durban. An historian by training, he currently teaches and researches broadly in the area of gender studies but with a particular interest in the social construction of masculinity. In 1997 he organized the first conference in Southern Africa to focus on Masculinities. A special issue of the *Journal of Southern African Studies* based on conference papers is scheduled.

**Maria Pallotta-Chiarolli** lectures in the School of Public Health, Deakin University, Melbourne. Her research interests are the interweaving of ethnicity, gender and sexuality, particularly in relation to education and sexual health. Her publications include: *Someone You Know* (Wakefield Press, 1991), Australia's first AIDS biography; *Girls Talk* (Finch Publishing, 1998), Australian girls and young women writing about gender, sexuality and cultural diversity; the biography of five generations of Italian men and women in one family, focusing on migration and the constructions of gender and sexuality (*Tapestry*, Random House, 1999); and the forthcoming *Schooling Masculinities*, co-written with Wayne Martino (Open University Press).

**Rebecca F. Plante** is an applied sociologist and has taught at Tufts University and the University of New Hampshire. She has been a sexualities educator for over ten years and has done radio call-in shows. She writes a monthly magazine column for college students.

**Jeanne Prinsloo** is a lecturer in the Department of Education at the University of Natal, Durban, teaching courses in Media Education. A particular interest in the gendered nature of representations informs her work both in relation to media and the curriculum. Her current area of research is within the field of critical literacies.

**Kathleen Quinlivan** is currently working on her doctorate in Education at Canterbury University in Christchurch, New Zealand, which explores what is possible in terms of inclusion for lesbian, gay and bisexual youth in secondary schools in the 1990s. Previously an English teacher and adviser, she has completed research on the identity management strategies of lesbian teachers and students. She is also developing and running a mentoring programme for lesbian, gay, bisexual and transgendered youth.

**James T. Sears** is an independent scholar living near Charleston, South Carolina, and in cyberspace at http://www.jtsears.com. A Fulbright Scholar, lecturer and media commentator, he is the author of several books, including the critically acclaimed *Growing up Gay in the South* (1991) and *Lonely Hunters* (1997).

**Lisa Smyth** is a PhD student at the Department of Sociology at the University of Warwick. She is working on the relationship between abortion politics and constructions of identity in Ireland.

**Deborah Lynn Steinberg** teaches feminist and cultural theory at the University of Warwick and is an Associate Lecturer in Women's Studies at the Open University. Recent publications include: *Bodies in Glass: Genetics, Eugenics, Embryo Ethics* (Manchester University Press) and *Border Patrols: Policing the Boundaries of Heterosexuality*, co-edited with Debbie Epstein and Richard Johnson (Cassell).

**Shane Town** is a lecturer in the School of Education and a member of the Understanding Learning and Teaching Institute at Victoria University in Wellington, New Zealand. His research interests include sexualities and schooling, queer theories and pedagogies and their implementation in classrooms and in teacher education.

**Mary Tweed** was educated at Wells Blue Grammar School, and did her teacher training at the Froebel Institute College of Education, London, gaining a Primary Teacher's Certificate. She worked for an insurance company for a year before emigrating to Australia in January 1973. Mary taught in Sydney from 1973 to 1980. She moved to the south coast of NSW with her husband and three children in 1981, and has taught in two schools. Mary's interests have always been in student welfare, leading to establishing various student support groups such as 'buddies', peer support, child protection, school parliament and sex education for Year 6 students.

**Jeffrey Weeks** is Professor of Sociology and Head of the School of Education, Politics and Social Science at South Bank University, London. He is the author of numerous articles and a number of books on the social organization of sexuality. Recent publications include *Against Nature* (1991), *Invented Moralities* (1995) and (with Janet Holland) *Sexual Cultures* (1996). His current research includes a study of 'Families of Choice' in Britain.

**Mariamne H. Whatley** is Professor of Women's Studies and Curriculum and Instruction at the University of Wisconsin-Madison, where she is also Chair of the Women's Studies Program and Associate Dean in the School of Education. Her research interests include women's health issues and sexuality education.

# 1

# Introduction: Knowing Dangerously

*Debbie Epstein and James T. Sears*

## Knowing dangerously

Many kinds of knowledge are dangerous: dangerous because they destabilize established common-sense world-views; dangerous because they pull
the veil away from oppression, discrimination and suffering, making for
uncomfortable confrontation with these issues; dangerous because knowledge is, as Foucault has established (1980), a form of power. Such
dangerous knowledges range from the stories of Jewish survivors of the
Holocaust and of the survivors of other genocides, like those of Pol Pot and
of the Rwandan civil war (Karpf, 1996), to knowledges about racism and
acknowledgements of white privilege (as witnessed by the hostile reaction
in the media to Patricia J. Williams's 1997 Reith[1] lectures in Britain), to
knowledges about the oppressive nature of gender regimes revealed
through feminist and pro-feminist writings (as witnessed by what has come
to be called the 'backlash' against feminism).

Among these dangerous knowledges, sexuality has occupied a key
position. Not only does knowing about sexuality connote the loss of
innocence within the Judaeo-Christian–Muslim tradition, drawing on
stories about the fall from grace in the Garden of Eden, it also gives rise to
fears about the corruption of the young (see, for example, Dollimore,
1991; Epstein, 1997; Epstein and Johnson, 1998; Kitzinger, 1988; Rofes,
1998; Sears, 1998). In the story of Genesis, the fruit eaten by Eve and by
Adam was, specifically, from the tree of knowledge and it is clear that the
knowledge gained was knowledge about sexuality – hence their drive to
clothe themselves. Similarly, the story of Mary's virginity and the birth of
Jesus is imbued with fears about knowledges of sexuality.

## Perturbing pedagogies

This book is concerned with many different aspects of dangerous know-ledges around sexuality, but a particular focus is on the ways in which seemingly safe knowledges, or dominant common senses, are put into and held in place within hegemonic regimes of truth in relation to gender and sexuality both in the countries under discussion here and as part of a globalizing, and often commodifying, tendency. These processes are not simply about oppression or domination, of course. All such hegemonic knowledges are contested and the various contributions to the book show some of the sites of contestation.

As will be seen from the range of essays in the book, we have invited our contributors to interpret the term 'pedagogy' in an expanded sense, not restricting it to the application of 'the science of teaching: instruction, training' (*Chambers English Dictionary*, 1990) within formal settings such as schools, colleges or universities. In doing so, we wish to invoke something more than the formal 'pedagogics' often taught in European universities, on the one hand, something close to, yet differing from, Foucault's conception of 'discipline' or the 'disciplinary gaze' (Foucault, 1977) on the other, although our version of 'pedagogy' would include both of these.

We wish to think of pedagogy in terms of all the myriad ways in which we learn and are taught to position ourselves within the regimes of truth through which we understand our gendered, heterosexualized, racialized and classed world; the punishments for transgressions as well as the rewards for conformity. In this sense, pedagogy can take place through and within a number of institutional sites other than those, like schools and universities, which are formally concerned with education. As the articles in this book demonstrate, the law, the popular media and personal rela-tionships (among others) provide such additional sites, while large-scale processes of globalization and colonization as well as micro-processes of personal politics provide the means. Meanwhile, teaching is only some-times intended (even in schools and universities), and what is learnt is often different from that which is 'taught'. Indeed, as Elizabeth Ellsworth (1997) has argued, it may be useful to think of pedagogies as having a 'mode of address' in the sense in which this term is used within film studies – that is, to indicate that there is never an exact 'fit' between the intended audience (or student) and the person who actually sees, hears, reads or experiences.

We are taking 'sexual pedagogies', then, to include, at one end of the continuum, formal sex education and teaching in schools aimed at sustaining or undermining hetero/sexism and patriarchal gender regimes; at the other end we are concerned with the production of sexual identities in conditions not of our own choosing and always related to other 'differences which make a difference'. We are interested in tracing the means by which borders are policed (see also Steinberg et al., 1997) on the one hand, and people interpellated[2] into dominant forms of heterosexuality through the seductions of, for example, the popular media on the other – and always recognizing that these may be happening simultaneously. Policing may be seductive and seduction may be a form of discipline (Epstein and Johnson, 1998; Miller, 1990).

## 'Mastering' the narrative

If pedagogies may be simultaneously forms of seduction and forms of discipline, what, then, can we make of the notion of the 'master narrative', which constitutes one of the themes of this book? All pedagogies are historically located within the range of discourses of a particular time and place. Our formulation of the 'master narrative' is, in part, a reference to the ways that some stories of what sexuality (and, indeed, life more generally) is like come to be accepted as 'normal' or 'obvious'. However, we wish also to draw attention to the notion of narrative, or storytelling, as being in itself a key pedagogy and a key resource which people use in the construction of identity (see also Plummer, 1995; Sears, 1997). More than that, however, we want to explore which sexual stories have been made available in the processes of colonization, settlement and conquest which characterize the countries about which contributors to this volume have written.

The particular countries dealt with in this book are Australia, Ireland, New Zealand, the Philippines, South Africa, the UK and the USA. The history of each incorporates some aspect of conquest, domination and/or settlement, either within the context of the British Empire or, in the case of the Philippines, by the USA. As Connell (Chapter 6), Sears (Chapter 7) and Altman (Chapter 8) illustrate in their chapters, contemporary forces of globalization take many different forms. But, in the contemporary world, the economic, cultural, political and military power of America (both through the state and through the workings of capitalism) is a key element in the construction of contemporary 'master narratives' of sexuality as of so much else. For the most part, this power is not exercised through coercion (with important exceptions in, for example, Cuba, Nicaragua and the Middle East), but through seductive narratives of democracy and free speech on the one hand and of the 'fatal attractions' of consumerism and commodification on the other.

In *A Dangerous Knowing* we explore these 'master narratives' through the lens of the sexual. What can we learn about formations of nation and citizenship, about discourses of science, about formations of identity and about the roles of schools when we subject them to interrogation which highlights the sexual and, in particular, the compulsoriness of (white, able-bodied, middle-class) heterosexuality in countries which are very different, but which have similarities produced through their histories and in the contemporary world? How can we practise a pedagogy of sexualities that embraces desire while interrogating knowledge and honours the multiplicities of voice while challenging the master narrative? In short, how can we nurture a dangerous knowing?

*A Dangerous Knowing* arose out of a meeting between the two editors at the American Educational Research Association annual meeting in San Francisco in 1995 and the interest we had developed in each other's previous work (Epstein, 1993; 1994; Sears, 1991; 1992). It seemed to us that, as educators and researchers crossed borders (disciplinary and geographical) to think critically about sexualities and to break down conventional boundaries, there was a need to teach and think about sexualities with a particular focus on the 'master narratives' of sexuality inherited from a history of British and American imperialism and colonization. While there have been significant challenges to this tradition as it is variously incarnated across time and cultures (e.g., 'Westernism', 'Capitalism', 'Eurocentrism', 'Modernism'), its hegemony in moulding sexual discourse and mapping sexual boundaries is unquestioned.

Our plan was, therefore, to reflect on the many different pedagogies of sexuality – how sexualities have been constructed, reconstructed and imparted – within countries representing various Anglophone traditions on the one hand; and how sexualities have been imported and local sexualities constructed and reconstructed through neocolonization within other countries. To this end, we solicited contributions in as many different ways as we could: on the Internet, by letter, through word of mouth. The result is four distinct but interrelated metaphorical themes: Sexualities as Myth and Signification; Sexualities as Globalization and Commodification; Sexualities as Identities; and Interventions in Sexualities.

Each section begins with a 'discussant' essay which introduces the main themes of the section. A reading of these will show that some of the issues raised by contributors cut across the divisions we have made within the book. 'Sexualities as Myth and Signification' explores some of the myths which arise in three important sites for pedagogies of sexuality: science and the popular reporting of it (Steinberg), television (Crowther), and schools (Epstein). Jeffrey Weeks, in his introduction to the section, pulls the issues raised in the other three chapters together, adding his own concerns about what he has called 'families of choice', but which the Conservative government in the UK labelled as 'pretended families' (in Section 28 of the Local Government Act 1988). The myths and significations explored by these authors are key to the identity formation explored later in the book.

Part 2, on 'Sexualities as Globalization and Commodification', contains three chapters. The introductory chapter by Bob Connell and the chapter by Dennis Altman explore, in their different ways, the general impact of the globalization and commodification of sexualities, while Sears provides a detailed case study of the Philippines. These chapters touch on the internationalization of sexual myths and on the impact that this has on identity formations.

Part 3, 'Sexualities as Identities', begins with a chapter entitled 'Sexing the Globe' by Fine and Bertram which clearly indicates the links of this section with the previous one. The chapters in this section explore the complexities of identities in the USA (Fine and Bertram), Australia (Crowley, Holmes), Ireland (Smyth) and South Africa (Deacon et al.). Issues of race, religion, ethnicity and the law are themes which arise as key to identity formation in this section.

The final part of the book, 'Interventions in Sexualities', consists of an introduction by Mariamne Whatley which considers the effectiveness of the various interventions discussed and reflects on her own experience as a professor in a liberal US university. The countries covered here are the USA (Whatley, Plante), Australia (Beckett et al., Pallotta-Chiarolli); and New Zealand (Quinlivan and Town). Some of these accounts are more hopeful than others of the possibilities for progressive change within formal educational institutions. It is the premise of this book, however, that changes in sexual pedagogies are both necessary and possible, and that they are likely to come from within a variety of sites, including schools and universities, but not confined to them.

## Notes

1. The Reith Lectures are a set of lectures given annually on BBC Radio 4. They are extremely prestigious and were set up partly to carry on, and memorialize, the Reithian tradition of 'public service' and partly as an example of the 'best of British'. Patricia J. Williams was an unusual Reith lecturer in three respects: she is one of the few women to have given these lectures; she is one of the even fewer black persons (or persons of colour) to have given them; she is the first non-British Reith lecturer. The hostility of the reaction to her from some quarters was breathtaking, and ranged from comments in the tabloid press to aggressive interviewing by Melvyn Bragg on BBC Radio 4's programme, *Start the Week*.

2. The term 'interpellation' is used in Cultural Studies to indicate the ways in which people are 'hailed' or 'beckoned' by, for example, the cover of a magazine on a news-stand, and, by extension, how they are hailed by or pulled into particular discursive frameworks and, therefore, subjectivities (or, more accurately, subject positions).

## References

*Chambers English Dictionary* (1990). Edinburgh: Chambers.

Dollimore, J. (1991). *Sexual Dissidence: Augustine to Wilde, Freud to Foucault*. Oxford: Clarendon Press.

Ellsworth, E. (1997). *Teaching Positions: Difference, Pedagogy, and the Power of Address*. New York: Teachers College Press.

Epstein, D. (1993). 'Practising heterosexuality', *Curriculum Studies*, **1**(1): 275–86.

Epstein, D. (ed.) (1994). *Challenging Lesbian and Gay Inequalities in Education*. Buckingham: Open University Press.

Epstein, D. (1997). 'Cultures of schooling/cultures of sexuality', *International Journal of Inclusive Education*, **1**(1): 37–53.

Epstein, D. and Johnson, R. (1998). *Schooling Sexualities*. Buckingham: Open University Press.

Faludi, S. (1992). *Backlash: The Undeclared War against Women*. London: Chatto and Windus.

Foucault, M. (1977). *Discipline and Punish: The Birth of the Prison*, translated by Alan Sheridan. Harmondsworth: Penguin.

Foucault, M. (1980). *Power/Knowledge: Selected Interviews and Other Writings 1972–1977*. Hemel Hempstead: Harvester.

Karpf, A. (1996). *The War After*. London: Heinemann (paperback edition Minerva, 1997).

Kitzinger, J. (1988). 'Defending innocence: ideologies of childhood', *Feminist Review. Special Issue: Family Secrets, Child Sexual Abuse*, **28**: 77–87.

Miller, J. (1990). *Seductions: Studies in Reading and Culture*. London: Virago.

Plummer, K. (1995). *Telling Sexual Stories: Power, Change and Social Worlds*. London: Routledge.

Rofes, E. (1998). 'Innocence, perversion and Heather's Two Mommies', *Journal of Gay, Lesbian and Bisexual Identity*, **3**(1): 3–26.

Sears, J. T. (1991). *Growing up Gay in the South*. New York: Haworth.

Sears, J. T. (ed.) (1992). *Sexuality and the Curriculum: The Politics and Practices of Sexuality Education*. New York: Teachers College Press.

Sears, J. T. (1997). *Lonely Hunters: An Oral History of Lesbian and Gay Southern Life, 1948–1968*. New York: HarperCollins/Westview.

Sears, J. T. (1998). 'A generational and theoretical analysis of culture and male (homo)sexuality', in W. Pinar (ed.), *Queer Theory in Education*. Malwah, NJ: Lawrence Erlbaum, pp. 73–105.

Steinberg, D. L., Epstein, D. and Johnson, R. (eds) (1997). *Border Patrols: Policing the Boundaries of Heterosexuality*. London: Cassell.

Williams, Patricia J. (1997). *Seeing a Colour Blind Future: The Paradox of Race: The 1997 Reith Lectures*. London: Virago.

# Part One

## Sexualities as Myth and Signification

# 2

# Myths and Fictions in Modern Sexualities

*Jeffrey Weeks*

## Sexual myths and necessary fictions

Writing about sexuality, it is often said – indeed, I have said it myself – can be dangerous: to reputations, careers, peace of mind. I was once warned by a well-meaning head of department that my academic career would go nowhere if I continued to write about sex. Why not train as a social worker instead? I continued, more or less cheerfully, nevertheless, and for a while he was right, and I went nowhere very fast. My career was saved, if that is the right word, by an odd concatenation of circumstances, and by a tragedy. The circumstances made me eligible for a senior university post; the tragedy was the AIDS epidemic, which, equally unexpectedly, made it not only fashionable, but socially necessary, to research and write about sexuality in a serious manner. How else could one understand the complex relationship between desire, identities, histories, social networks, ideology, opportunity, chance, fear, stigma, pleasure, discrimination, power and love, that together with a host of other contingencies shape and constantly reshape the domain of the erotic – and determine the degree of risk we have to negotiate as best we can? Writing about sexuality seemed a little less dangerous than doing dangerous sex – and might even help us understand where the risks are.

The wider problem, however, is that a rational, judicious, would-be objective deconstruction of the ever-growing continent of sexuality might add to the sum total of human knowledge, but it does not necessarily reach the hearts and minds of individual human subjects. There is evidence aplenty that the injunctions of churches and kings and judges and doctors have not obliterated 'sin' or 'perversion'. It is doubtful whether more radical or libertarian writings on their own can change a culture, as many of the culturally conservative critics of the 'permissive moment' of the 1960s appear to believe. There is a limit to the potency of social engineering, or proselytizing. Even in the age of AIDS we now know how resistant people can be to simple messages about safer sex.

This is not because the erotic represents the Old Adam, that part of us most resistant to change. On the contrary, it is because the sexual is so much a mobile, changeable, culturally sensitive part of us, and our culture, that it is difficult to pin down. People absorb, or reject, the messages, wherever they come from, and then do what they can, in the circumstances in which they find themselves, calculating gain against loss, pleasure versus pain, risk alongside opportunity, to create themselves as sexual subjects. This is why in the end, despite the proliferation of discourses, the explosion of different voices, the normalization of sexual explicitness in much of the media and elsewhere, sexuality remains dangerous: because it is always ultimately subservient to the diversity of individual needs and desires, the complexity of social relations, the pluralism of cultural lives and the various possible ways of being human. Many have striven to pull all this together into a great discursive unity which attempts to unlock the truth of sexuality; but however protean it appears, there is always messy seepage as different truths contest the master narrative. The ultimate truth, if I may use the phrase, is that the sexual continues to be a battleground between different claims to truth. Each voice may proclaim its own rules for demarcating truth from falsity, be it religious revelation, scientific reason, historic justice, political correctness, self-expression or collective will. But in the market-place of contemporary sexual values, none of these has complete hegemony. The final truth may well be that there is no such thing; just us poor humans with our incommensurate goals, muddling along, doing our best, or worst, in the histories which entangle us. This is why the borders seem to require constant policing, and boundary disputes are all but inevitable (Steinberg *et al.*, 1997).

And yet, clearly, it is necessary to make distinctions and decisions. We may no longer live in a climate which permits us to say easily this is 'right' or 'wrong', but in everyday life we have to make pragmatic decisions all the time about what course of action is appropriate or inappropriate, better or worse. The general collapse of traditional forms of legitimation, whether religious or political, and the decay of traditional ways of life, from the family to familiar class-based social identities – what Giddens (1994) calls 'detraditionalisation' – have thrust more and more decisions back on to the individual. We are increasingly faced, as Bauman (1993) has put it, by the loneliness of moral choice. We live, as I have argued at length elsewhere, in an age of uncertainty, where good guides and firm guarantees that we can reach any particular destination are in short supply, and where the goals themselves are cloudy and indeterminate – particularly with regard to sexuality (Weeks, 1995). But that does not mean we cannot think about basic values. On the contrary, it makes it ever more imperative that we think what we can, and want, to be, how we should live. It is possible, I would argue, to find ways of being which combine respect for the irreducible diversity of individual and collective values with a commitment to certain basic minimum human standards. In fact, in everyday life many people, in an often messy, chaotic but vibrant way, do it all the time: strive to create ways of life which are valid for them without impinging on the validity of other, different ways of life. But to do that we need to free ourselves as best we can from the mythologies which pin us to the table like dead butterflies, exemplars of fixed types, patterned by destiny; and instead embrace some of the alternative 'sexual stories', in Plummer's (1995) phrase, or narratives which tell of 'a radical, pluralistic, democratic, contingent, participatory politics of human life choices and difference' in the making (Plummer, 1995, p. 147); that is, learn to live in harmony with diversity.

In his book *The Sense of an Ending*, the literary critic Frank Kermode (1967) made an important distinction, which is relevant here, between myths and fictions. Myth, he argues:

> operates within the diagrams of ritual, which presupposes total and adequate explanations of things as they are and were: it is a sequence of radically unchangeable gestures. Fictions are for finding things out, and they change as the needs of sense-making change. Myths are the agents of stability, fictions are the agents of change. (Kermode, 1967, p. 210; quoted also in Weeks, 1995, p. 99)

Adapting this comparison to contemporary sexualities, we can make a distinction between sexual myths, which elaborate an assumed naturalness, eternity and fixity about the body and its erotic possibilities, and those 'fictions' (stories, narratives, counter-discourses) which, when embraced by those who want, or have, to be subversive of the *status quo*, remind us that nature actually had very little to do with what we call sexuality. Plummer (1995) argues that:

> Society itself may be seen as a textured but seamless web of stories emerging everywhere through interaction: holding people together,

pulling people apart, making societies work ... the metaphor of the story ... has become recognised as one of the central roots we have into the continuing quest for understanding human meaning. Indeed culture itself has been defined as 'an ensemble of stories we tell about ourselves'. (Plummer, 1995, p. 5)

If this is the case, then the emergence of new ways of expressing basic needs and desires ('new stories') may be seen as vitally important. They indicate both changing perceptions and changing possibilities. New stories about sexual and intimate life emerge when there is a new audience ready to hear them in communities of meaning and understanding, and when newly vocal groups can have their experiences validated in and through them. This in turn gives rise to new demands for recognition and validation as the new narratives circulate. These demands may be the expressions of a minority, but they echo wider changes in intimate life.

The radical oppositional identities, such as lesbian, gay, bisexual, transgendered or 'queer', that have flourished in such abundance since the 1960s, can from this perspective be seen as equivalent to fictions: elaborate narrative forms which give shape and meaning to individual lives, and link us to a larger collective story, which tells of oppression, survival, resistance, transgression and claims to full citizenship. More: they are not just fictions; they are necessary fictions. Without them we would have no basis to explain our individual needs and desires, nor a sense of collective belonging that provides the agency and means of change (Weeks, 1995, p. 99).

Yet, as Crowther, Epstein and Steinberg show in the chapters that follow, the picture can get murkier than this theoretical model suggests. For conservative myths and radical fictions can become or remain hopelessly entangled. Radical television recycles traditional myths in soft and appealing focus (Crowther). Radical gay scientists 'discover' a gene for sexual orientation which conservative moralists greet as the possible magic bullet for the final solution to the problem of homosexuality (Steinberg). And even when the radical teacher opens up possible alternative ways of being to the young, these are rescripted in terms of mythic romance. Boundaries are broken down, and then reappear, apparently as intransigent, elsewhere. The resulting 'sex wars' (Duggan and Hunter, 1995) are seemingly endless. Can the deadlock be broken?

Three areas identified in the essays that follow show the possibilities for contestation, and change. The first (highlighted by Steinberg) concerns the dangers of certainty and the challenge of contingency when discussing sexual orientation. The second (a theme of Crowther's chapter) shows the difficulties but also the possibilities of new voices emerging in the discourses of sexuality. The third (raised in Epstein's analysis) relates to the new narratives of intimacy and love that can and do emerge.

## Dangerous certainties

The search for a gay gene – or the gay brain – illustrates the apparently incessant need, even within ostensibly radical, oppositional social movements, for certainty – for the revelation of the essential truth of our (homo)sexual natures. In another genre, the search for our real past, 'hidden from history', reveals the same imperative: to fix us in a true lineage denied us by our oppression and subordination (whether this be from sexism/patriarchy, heterosexism or racism, the need seems to be the same: redemption through discovery of the burdens of history). This dual move – scientific investigation and archaeological recovery – has been a dominant theme in the discourse of lesbian and gay politics since the 1960s, to such an extent that a critique of essentialism could also be conceived of as an attack on the very idea of a homosexual identity (for a recent effort, see Norton, 1997). This is why gay critics became so fiercely passionate at the arguments of those who emphasize the cultural variability, or 'social construction', of sexuality, seeing it as a fundamental challenge to their hard-fought gains and their claim to recognition as a legitimate minority group (see discussions in Stein, 1990). In a rights-based culture like the USA, it is often believed that the claim of lesbian and gay activism to recognized minority status may be boosted by theories of the gay gene or the gay brain (Rose, 1996). This ignores, of course, the painful lesson that, as in the 1930s, the idea of a genetic disposition towards homosexuality can as easily lead to hopes of eugenic engineering to eliminate it as to legislative reform to legitimize it – as Steinberg's chapter on contemporary debates underlines.

Anti-essentialist approaches, of course, do not forbid questions of the causation of homosexuality (whether genetic, psychological or social); they merely see them as irrelevant to the question of the validity of non-heterosexual ways of life. Michel Foucault (1979), often cited as the arch-priest of constructionism, himself remained agnostic about aetiology: 'On this question I have absolutely nothing to say' (quoted in Halperin,

1995, p. 4). One might have views, but that does not affect the more interesting questions. The issue of whether there is a biological or psychological propensity that distinguishes those who are sexually attracted to people of the same gender from those who are not can safely be left to those who want to cut up brains, explore DNA or count angels on the point of a needle. The really important debates are concerned with the meanings these propensities acquire, however or why ever they occur, the social categorizations that attempt to demarcate the boundaries of meanings, and their effect on collective attitudes and individual sense of self.

The complex relationship between societal definition, whether through medicine, legal processes, religion or various informal processes, on the one hand, and the formation of subjectivities and identities – self-definition – on the other, has in fact been the key focus of writing about homosexuality since the mid-1970s. The best historical work has attempted to hold these two levels together, though inevitably the stick has been bent one way or the other, depending on the biases or inclinations of the authors concerned. Sometimes the stick has snapped altogether under the strain, leading either to sociological determinism (you are what society dictates) or extreme voluntarism (you can be anything you want): neither is true (see discussion in Vance, 1989).

This is clearest if we look at the main focus of lesbian and gay studies until recently, the emphasis on identity, and the relationship between identity and community – between sense of being and social world. The most illuminating studies – summed up in George Chauncey's superb work of historical reconstruction, *Gay New York* (Chauncey, 1994) – have their roots in the commitment to lesbian and gay politics, but have demonstrated the complex interplay of elements that shape subjectivities. Chauncey's reconstruction of the class configurations of emerging categories of fairy, wolf, trade, invert, queer, gay, illustrates the intricacies of labelling, identity invention, social networking and regulation in a vibrant and living way. The main lesson I would draw from work such as this – and this is at the heart of the project of historicizing sexuality – is that pre-existing identities do not make communities or social worlds; they are shaped in and through those evolving social worlds (see Weeks, 1995). Identities are made in history not in nature, and often in highly politicized contexts. They are as much contingent as predetermined.

The lesson of this is that we need not be trapped in an endless cycle reproducing subordination or a constant minoritization of those who see themselves as different. On the contrary, the historical evidence is now very clear: what is made in history can be changed in history, not by simple act of will but in collective activity riding the rapids of social change. And recent experience, before our very eyes, confirms this. By the 1980s there was no doubt that the idea of a single modern gay identity had to be severely revised, largely because of a growing recognition of the diversity of possible sexualized identities. Now there are 'modern homosexualities':

> In scarcely a quarter of a century, same-sex experiences in the western world have been ruptured from the simplified, unified, distorting, often medical, frequently criminal, always devalued categories of the past. Instead, they have increasingly become a diverse array of relational, gendered, erotic, political, social, and spiritual experiences, difficult to tame and capture with restrictive and divisive labels. Crisscrossing their way through class, gender, and ethnicity, a stream of emerging identities, new experiences, political practices, and ways of living together have been firmly placed on the political agendas of the future. (Plummer, 1992, p. xiv)

Identities which once seemed categoric are now seen as fluid, relational, hybrid: we are not quite today what we were yesterday, or will be tomorrow. Identities are seen as narratives, built out of stories we tell each other in the various interpretive communities to which we belong. And there are many stories, most of which refuse to fit into the tidy slots that history has provided. The homosexual, as Plummer argues, is now 'both rigid scientific discovery and diverse signifier of potential, plurality, polymorphousness' (Plummer, 1992, p. 13). S/he is making her or his own history, not in circumstances freely chosen, not without opposition, but increasingly in narratives and voices that speak for different truths.

## New voices

As Barbara Crowther shows, these alternative truths are often occluded in popular representations about sex, in favour of a naturalized teleology. Yet, as Plummer (1995) has suggested, we live in a culture of storytelling, and at a different level of popular consciousness new voices are singing. What is startling about the last thirty or forty years is the ever-proliferating catalogue of new stories, new narratives, that have emerged, reflecting wider social changes and providing the language which makes change possible. The new stories about gender, sexuality and the body which have been told since the 1960s have been possible because of the emergence of new movements and communities that give rise to, circulate and rewrite these stories. The most common narratives are stories which tell of discrimination, prejudice and empowerment, stories which tell of coming out as lesbian and gay or as a strong, independent woman, stories of victimization and of survival, stories of difference and of similarity, stories of identity and stories of relationships. These new stories about the self, about sexuality and gender, are the context for the emergence of the claim to full sexual or 'intimate' citizenship (Plummer, 1995; Weeks, 1995). These stories telling of exclusion through gender, sexuality, race, bodily appearance or function, have as their corollary the demand for inclusion: for equal rights under the law, in politics, in economics, in social matters and in sexual matters. They pose questions about who should control our bodies, the limits of the body, the burden of custom and of the state. They are stories which spring up from everyday life, but in turn place new demands on the wider community for the development of more responsive policies, in economics, welfare, the law, culture. In some situations their influence has been significant, if not decisive.

In the case of AIDS, people living with devastating illness have taken the lead in defining both medical practice and caring relationships. In circumstances shaped in Western countries by the identification of a new syndrome of diseases with certain (homo)sexual practices or other exe-crated activities or groups, the marginalized found a voice and through a series of 'credibility struggles' (Epstein, 1996) established the importance of grass-roots knowledges alongside official, scientific discourses, both in defining the nature of the diseases, and in claiming access to forms of treatment:

> The AIDS crisis is a case in which the normal flow of trust and credibity between experts and laypersons has been disrupted. The autonomy of science has therefore been challenged; outsiders have rushed into the breach. (Epstein, 1996, p. 17)

At a time when politics was increasingly being seen as the domain of the experts, new forms of expertise have emerged, claiming their own validity. Self-help groups organized by the people most affected by AIDS, established in the absence of official support, became leading national agencies for service delivery and social care in most Western countries. Safer-sex techniques, pioneered in lesbian and gay communities, became the model for official health campaigns. The production of knowledge about homosexuality relied heavily on the knowledges produced by lesbians and gays themselves in the fight against AIDS and HIV. The process was not without its difficulties, prejudices, official silences – but new voices made themselves heard (see Berridge, 1996). The circumstances were unique: a deadly epidemic. But the particular example is representative of wider changes. Counter-discourses, oppositional knowledges, grass-roots politics and self-activity have begun to undermine traditional political forms, and to define new agendas. There has been an accumulation of new social and cultural capital, where new voices, new collective subjectivities have put forward their claims through a variety of social and political practices.

I am not claiming that these new social forms have swept all opposition away. Where there is power, there is resistance, while resistance in turn gives rise to new forms of power. Yet what is remarkable about the changes is the way in which, despite the various forms of hostility they have engendered, the transformations are still going on, working their way through the undergrowth, and opening up the possibilities for new stories about everyday life.

## New narratives of intimacy and love

Stories about intimate life – about relationships, desires, love – are at the heart of emerging discourses. As Debbie Epstein shows in her essay, the language for understanding these is often absent, especially among young people. Yet as her ethnography demonstrates, the young are having to confront new truths and questions, even in the most traditional of contexts, the school.

Modernity, Giddens (1992) has argued, is a post-traditional order in which the question 'How shall I live?' has to be answered in day-to-day decisions about who to be, how to behave, and whom and how we should love. The resulting 'transformations of intimacy', the product of the breakdown of traditional narratives and legitimizing discourses under the impact of long-term cultural, social and economic forces, are making possible diverse ways of life which cut across the heterosexual/homosexual dichotomy. It is in this context that we can begin to understand the significance of the new stories about non-heterosexual 'families of choice' that are now circulating (Weeks et al., 1999).[1]

These two quotations illustrate a broadening, almost metaphoric, use of the term 'family'. The first is from a black lesbian:

> I think the friendships I have are family. I'm sure lots of people will say this, but, it's very important to me because my family are not – apart from my mother, who's *kind* of important – on the whole my family's all I've got. And my family are my friends . . . It doesn't matter where I go or who I am with, I'm not going to just suddenly be given a family, or a history, or an identity, or whatever. You don't just get it on a plate. You have to create your own. (F02)

The second is from a white gay man:

> We call each other family – you know, they're family. I'm not sure whether that's family in the sense of being gay . . . I have a blood family, but I have an extended family . . . my friends. (M04)

For many self-identified lesbians and gays, friendship circles are like the idealized family (and infinitely preferable to the real one), offering 'a feeling of belonging to a group of people who like me' (M05); 'they support me . . . I socialise with them, talk about things that are important to me' (F01). Friendships provide the 'lifeline' that the biological family, it is believed, should provide, but often cannot or will not for its non-heterosexual offspring.

The most commonly used terms applied to such relationships by lesbians and gay men are 'chosen' and 'created'. For one gay man, friends are:

> more important than family . . . I take my family [of origin] for granted, whereas my friendships are, to a degree, chosen, and therefore they're created. And I feel a greater responsibility to nourish them, whereas my family will always be there. (M21)

The language is echoed by a young lesbian:

> In the last few years since I've come out I've learnt that family can be anything you want it to be, so I create my own family, basically, and that's been a difficult thing for me to get my head round, but I like it now. (F03)

The narrative of self-invention is a very powerful one, particularly in relation to self-identity and lifestyle. As a gay man in his late thirties put it:

> speaking from my generation ... discovering that I was homosexual meant having to invent myself because there was nothing there ... there weren't any role models. It may well be different for gay men coming out now ... But there's still that element of self-invention. (M17/18)

This story of creating your own life is widely echoed in the theoretical literature (e.g. Foucault, 1979; Giddens, 1992; Weeks, 1995) and reflects (as well as reflexively contributing to) the perceived reality in a postmodern world of fluid identities. It peculiarly relates, however, to the common discourse of many lesbians and gay men who see themselves as breaking away from the constraints of traditional institutional patterns which denied their sexuality and identity. Heterosexuals, a gay man suggests, 'slip into roles that are preordained and it goes along that route. Whereas we don't have any preordained roles so we can actually invent things as we want them' (M17/18). Or as a lesbian sees it: 'With my family of choice it's somewhere that, you know, it's an environment where I can be myself' (F15).

The dominant belief in the non-heterosexual world is that lesbian and gay relationships offer unique possibilities for the construction of egalitarian relationships. As a lesbian says:

> [in heterosexual relationships] there is an essential power imbalance that there are certain roles, which are backed up by economics and backed up by sanctions. And also ... men and women are socialised differently in terms of what ... heterosexual relationships are. Yeah, I think they're very different – very. (F34)

The assumption, amongst men as well as women, is that 'it's much easier to have equal relations if you're the same sex' (M31), because this equalizes the terms of the intimate involvement. Or as a lesbian says: 'The understanding between two women is bound to be on a completely different wavelength' (F33). Equal standing means that issues around, for example, the division of labour in the household, are seen to be a matter for discussion and agreement, not of preordained roles, because of 'being able to negotiate, being on an equal level to be able to negotiate in the first place' (M04); 'Everything has to be discussed, everything is negotiable' (F29).

Affirmation through involvement in the democratic, egalitarian relationship appears to be the dominant non-heterosexual norm, conforming closely to Giddens's (1992, p. 58) definition of the 'pure relationship':

> a situation where a social relation is entered into for its own sake, for what can be derived by each person from a sustained association with another; and which is continued only in so far as it is thought by both parties to deliver enough satisfaction for each individual to stay within it.

This does not mean that the privileging of heterosexuality has somehow diminished, or that the achievement of equal relationships is easy and without scars. The point I would make is a different one. Despite all the hazards, and the force and weight of institutionalized patterns, people do create relationships of mutual care, respect, responsibility and love (Weeks, 1995) which provide realistic alternatives to traditional forms of life which are now facing unprecedented stress. They represent the emergence of new narratives of everyday life and a genuine democratization of relationships.

## By way of a conclusion and introduction . . .

Myths, I suggested earlier, speak for a conservative order, fictions offer the possibility of change. Change can certainly be threatening; but so can staying as we are. The new narratives about sexuality represent the fruits of long-term transformations of patterns of life. They also provide examples of the emergence of grass-roots voices that are unlikely to be silenced, whatever the burdens of history, the power of experts or the numbing weight of traditional sexual norms. Perhaps that is why writing and speaking about sexuality still give off a whiff of danger.

## Note

1. This section is based on research conducted for a project funded by the Economic and Social Research Council, entitled 'Families of Choice: The Structure and Meanings of Non-Heterosexual Relationships' (Reference no.:

L315253030). The research took place between 1995 and 1996, as part of the ESRC research programme on Population and Household Change, and was based in the School of Education, Politics and Social Science, South Bank University, London. The director of the project was Jeffrey Weeks, with Catherine Donovan and Brian Heaphy as the research fellows. The core of the research involved in-depth interviews with 48 men and 48 women who broadly identified as 'non-heterosexual' (a term we use throughout the following discussion to encompass a range of possible self-identifications: as gay, lesbian, homosexual, 'queer', bisexual). All the first-person quotations in this article come from these interviews. All female interviews are denoted by 'F', and male interviews by 'M', each followed by a number. The numbers reflect the order in which the interviews took place. For a fuller discussion of the argument and a summary of the research findings see Weeks *et al.*, 1999.

## References

Bauman, Zigmunt (1993). *Postmodern Ethics*. Oxford: Blackwell.

Berridge, Virginia (1996). *AIDS in the UK: The Making of Policy, 1981–1994*. Oxford: Oxford University Press.

Chauncey, George (1994). *Gay New York: Gender, Urban Culture and the Making of the Gay Male World 1890–1940*. New York: BasicBooks.

Duggan, Lisa and Hunter, Nan D. (1995). *Sex Wars: Sexual Dissent and Political Culture*. New York and London: Routledge.

Epstein, Steven (1996). *Impure Science: AIDS, Activism and the Politics of Knowledge*. Berkeley and Los Angeles: University of California Press.

Foucault, Michel (1979). *The History of Sexuality, Volume 1: An Introduction*. London: Allen Lane.

Giddens, Anthony (1992). *The Transformation of Intimacy: Sexuality, Love and Eroticism in Modern Societies*. Cambridge: Polity Press.

Giddens, Anthony (1994). *Beyond Left and Right: The Future of Radical Politics*. Cambridge: Polity Press.

Halperin, David (1995). *Saint Foucault: Towards a Gay Hagiography*. Oxford and New York: Oxford University Press.

Kermode, Frank (1967). *The Sense of an Ending: Studies in the Theory of Fiction*. Oxford: Oxford University Press.

Norton, Rictor (1997). *The Myth of the Modern Homosexual: Queer History and the Search for Cultural Unity*. London: Cassell.

Plummer, Ken (ed.) (1992). *Modern Homosexualities: Fragments of Lesbian and Gay Experience*. London: Routledge.

Plummer, Ken (1995). *Telling Sexual Stories: Power, Change and Social Worlds*. London and New York: Routledge.

Rose, Hilary (1996). 'Gay brains, gay genes and feminist science theory', in Jeffrey Weeks and Janet Holland (eds), *Sexual Cultures: Communities, Values and Intimacy*. Basingstoke and London: Macmillan.

Stein, Edward (ed.) (1990). *Forms of Desire: Sexual Orientation and the Social Constructionist Controversy*. New York and London: Garland Publishing.

Steinberg, Deborah Lynn, Epstein, Debbie and Johnson, Richard (eds) (1997). *Border Patrols: Policing the Boundaries of Heterosexuality*. London: Cassell.

Vance, Carole (1989). 'Social construction theory: problems in the history of sexuality', in Dennis Altman, Carole Vance, Martha Vicinus, Jeffrey Weeks and others, *Homosexuality, Which Homosexuality?* London: GMP Publishers.

Weeks, Jeffrey (1995). *Invented Moralities: Sexual Values in an Age of Uncertainty*. Cambridge: Polity Press.

Weeks, Jeffrey, Donovan, Catherine and Heaphy, Brian (1999). 'Everyday experiments: narratives of non-heterosexual relationships', in Elizabeth Silva and Carol Smart (eds), *The New Family?* London: Sage.

# 3

# Sex Play: Romantic Significations, Sexism and Silences in the Schoolyard

*Debbie Epstein*

## Introduction

During the school year 1995–96, I carried out a small-scale research project in a primary school in north London which I shall call Edendale School.[1] I spent most of my time with one Year 5 class (of 9- to 10-year-olds) in the classroom, in the playground and at dinner. I was interested in how these children constituted themselves in relation to gender and sexuality both in class and through their play. I was already familiar with the school through the class teacher, Mr Stuart,[2] and prior to the project we had discussed what we both hoped to gain from it.

My purposes were partly to begin the exploration of gender and sexuality at this age, an area which is both unresearched and controversial because of common-sense assumptions that young children neither know about nor are interested in sexuality.[3] Indeed, the *Daily Mail*'s front-page banner headline on 6 March 1996, running across three columns and occupying $4\frac{1}{2}$ inches of prime space a third of the way down the page, which read '5-Year-Olds to Get Gay Lessons' (Halpin, 1996), is illustrative of this discourse of childhood innocence (which I have discussed at greater length elsewhere: see Epstein, 1993, 1997). For Mr Stuart, an out and politically active gay teacher, the opportunity was to have a researcher in the classroom to help him understand and analyse how children in his class made sense of and understood issues around gender and sexuality, and how they 'did gender'.[4] What, he wanted to know, did the texts he used in the classroom signify for the children in this respect?

Throughout the research, it was clear that, while these young children were not sexually active or aware in the ways that secondary school pupils often are, nevertheless they knew a great deal about (hetero)sexuality, which was part of the stuff of everyday life in their playground and classroom in a number of ways:

- through imagined futures, particularly as heterosexual women in couples and families which tend to dominate the fantasies of adulthood expressed by girls in their play and storytelling/writing;
- through traditional games and rhymes, particularly those associated with skipping and newer games based particularly on popular television scenarios;
- through versions of games involving running and catching which become transmuted into arenas of sexualized chasing;
- through the sexual/sexist harassment of girls by boys and sexually charged, frequently homophobic insult exchange between children, often of the same sex;
- through early attempts into the world of 'going out', 'dating', 'two-timing' and 'dumping' of some of the children;
- through the gossip networks of playground, staffroom and classroom.

Here my focus will be on the children's cultures, including the formations and significance of their quasi-romantic relationships, on Mr Stuart's use of particular 'alternative' texts about family and how the children read them, and on significant silences in which the children actively engaged around Mr Stuart's gayness. I will be arguing that the children had complex and contradictory responses to Mr Stuart's attempted normalization of homosexuality, sometimes rejecting and at others working with it, in ways which were strongly influenced by 'master narratives' of happy heterosexuality.

Shereen Benjamin (1997, p. 43), writing about her work as a feminist teacher and researcher challenging hegemonic masculinities in her class, comments:

Not surprisingly, one of my key challenges was in working with resistance. I found myself in a paradoxical situation. I was asking the boys to identify with me, an authority figure, probably perceived by them as middle-class, in resistance to a constellation of hegemonic and working-class masculinities that I had identified as oppressive. The boys could work out and choose from a variety of ways of working 'with me' or 'against me', but whichever way they decided to act they could not avoid being involved in resistance.

Similarly the pupils in Mr Stuart's class were required either to resist his push towards a counter-hegemonic discourse in which heterosexuality is not assumed and homosexuality is not condemned or to resist dominant discourses presumptive of heterosexuality and dismissive of or hostile towards lesbian, gay or bisexuality. This chapter will trace some of the strategies which the pupils and their teacher used in negotiating this particular discursive field. In so doing, I examine the ways in which a gay teacher like Mr Stuart may both embody possibilities, especially for the boys in his class, of different ways of being a man (or 'doing man') even before he makes any conscious intervention (see and compare Redman and Mac an Ghaill, 1997) and, at the same time, be constrained by dominant discourses of compulsory and assumed heterosexuality, whose myths pervade the spaces of both classroom and playground.

## A teacher and his class: a thumbnail sketch

Mr Stuart was in his early thirties. Over 6 feet tall, he appeared, at first sight, to exemplify the male teacher who can exert authority in class through his size and his voice. However, his body language and soft-spoken manner gave this the lie. Rather than standing over the children, he tended to crouch, to get down to their level. His voice was seldom raised in class[5] and he was more likely to display disappointment than anger in dealing with misbehaviour or poor work. He was well organized and prepared in detail for each day's work, with immaculate record-keeping, his pedagogic style mixing the formal and informal. For some lessons, he taught from the front, with the children sitting quietly in neat rows in desks which had been assigned to them. At other times they worked in small groups, chatting quietly as they did so. Barrie Thorne shows how:

> In managing almost thirty lively children within relatively small spaces, Mrs Smith, like other teachers and aides, drew on the general power of being an adult, as well as on the more institutionalized authority of her official position. She claimed the right to regulate the students' activities, movement, posture, talking, possessions, access to water, and time and manner of eating. (Thorne, 1993, p. 31)

Similarly Mr Stuart claimed the rights of the adult-as-teacher to control, regulate and survey his class and the children's individual behaviours. Foucault's description of the panopticon (Foucault, 1977), as a prison in which the prisoner can always be seen by the warder but cannot be sure

when he [sic] is under observation and therefore modifies his own behaviour, could equally be a description of any classroom and Mr Stuart's was
no exception. From his position at the desk or walking round the classroom, he could, at a glance, see any child, and there were certain children,
typically boys rather than girls, who drew his attention more frequently
than others. He was profoundly aware of gender relations in his class and
worked hard to encourage the girls to speak out, especially in 'circle time'
when every child had an opportunity to contribute to the discussion as a
selected small object (often a shell) was passed from hand to hand. Mr
Stuart took his turn in the circle, along with the children, and on the rare
occasions when he interrupted (for example, to reprimand someone) he
apologized to the class. Circle time was when class members could talk
about a range of events and, in particular, when feelings could be
expressed. Mr Stuart modelled this by speaking about his own feelings
whenever he felt it was appropriate. The children loved him, loved being in
his class and, when, in July 1997, he gave up teaching,[6] the parents in this
working-class, ethnically mixed, inner-city school set about raising enough
money to pay for him to work part-time at the school teaching music and
working with children who have special educational needs.[7] They had
raised over £300 within the first few days.

Edendale School had a large ethnic minority pupil intake. The area it
served had large, settled Cypriot populations, both Greek and Turkish,
although the Greek Cypriots seemed to be moving further north into more
suburban neighbourhoods. More recently, there had been an influx of
Kurdish and Somali refugees. There were also children whose families
originated in the Indian subcontinent, Africa, the Caribbean and children
of Travellers. In the UK emigration has exceeded immigration for at least
a dozen years, there is almost no primary immigration (as opposed to wives
and children joining men who had previously migrated and settled) and
very few young children who have migrated themselves, or even have
parents who have done so. Unusually, then, Edendale's roll included many
children who were, themselves, fairly recent immigrants (often refugees),
often with horrendous experiences of persecution and war. There were
over 20 first languages spoken at the school and at least 14 in Mr Stuart's
class. The biggest single ethnic/language group was Turkish. Classes were
kept quite small, usually between 20 and 25 pupils in each class, and many
of the pupils were transient, spending a few weeks or months in the school
before moving on to a more permanent setting, and their place taken by
others. The London borough where the school was situated is one of the

poorer boroughs/local education authorities in London and there was high unemployment within it. There was also a growing professional middle-class and mainly white population buying up houses (which are significantly cheaper than in some other areas of London) and there were a few middle-class children in the school, but there was only one in Mr Stuart's class at the time when I was doing my research.

The class was roughly evenly divided between girls and boys and I use the term 'divided' advisedly. When left to their own devices, the boys and the girls hardly ever mixed in the classroom (even though there was some mixing in the playground, which I will discuss in more detail below) and Mr Stuart made it a rule that, for circle time at least, boys must sit next to girls and vice versa. There was a small group of girls and boys who seemed to be positioned by the other children (and to constitute themselves) as the class leaders. These children were not necessarily the most successful academically, though they were all fluent in English. It seemed that, for the most part, the 'leading boys' were lively, quite noisy and often quite troublesome, even rough, in their behaviour. They were also the boys who were most likely to be at the centre of the daily football games during dinner play, who were most likely to become involved in physical fights to prove their toughness. Indeed, it could be said that these boys occupied subject positions of hegemonic masculinity within a school context in which it was definitely not the done thing for boys to be seen to exert themselves over their school work; they were much more likely to be working extremely hard at being boys/doing boy. At the same time, the boys were neither white nor middle-class and it may be that their dominant positions were contingent on being in a school which was both working-class and had a majority of pupils from ethnic minorities.

The dominant girls, in contrast, tended to be hard-working and eschewed the kinds of horseplay which the boys enjoyed. They were neither timid nor submissive, however, being strongly opinionated and ready to express themselves freely in front of the whole class. They were quite confident about school work and, during playtime, either chatted to each other in small groups or played in a mixed group with the boys in particular heterosexualized games, which I will discuss in more detail below. Indeed, one of the most striking aspects of the gendered dynamics of the class was that the children who seemed to be most attractive to the others and who, therefore, occupied the dominant positions, were those who engaged in considerable talk about boyfriends/girlfriends, dating, dumping, 'two-timing' and so on.

There were two particular children, one boy and one girl, who exemplify this group of leading children and were, indeed, at its centre:

*Elias* was an outgoing boy of Greek Cypriot working-class origin. He had significant problems with his school work, particularly reading, and Mr Stuart paid him a great deal of attention. He was often charming but was also often in trouble for fighting or otherwise misbehaving. He was often the first to voice an opinion which seemed to be prejudiced (for example, 'They're taking over London, the Turkish people are'), but was equally quick to withdraw such statements in favour of liberal sentiments (for example, 'They're just people. Like Greeks, some people think that's not nice. Turkish, some people think that's not nice. We're all the same people.'). He could be sensitive, even touchy, quick to take offence and quick to lash out when this happened, but was also eager to please and could be careful about people's feelings.

*Louise* was the only child in the class whose background could be said to be middle-class in terms of her parents' educational and professional qualifications. She was a tall girl of mixed Turkish/white English origin and was easily the most articulate child in the class, able to present an opinion with great fluency, a confident reader and generally academically able. She would frequently help other children with their work, particularly her girlfriends, but also Elias, with whom she had an ambivalent relationship. On the one hand, she found him irritating, particularly when he became involved in episodes of sexual harassment, invading the girls' changing rooms during swimming sessions when Mr Stuart was away from school on jury service and the class was being taught by a supply teacher. On the other, she found him attractive and the two of them declared themselves to be 'boyfriend' and 'girlfriend', although she had mixed feelings about this. She was an extremely perceptive child, both about other children and, as we shall see, about the adult world.

*Normalizing heterosexuality: the playground context* [8]
Barrie Thorne (1993) uses the term 'Gender Play' to describe the ways in which elementary schoolchildren in the United States insert themselves into gendered (and heterosexual) discourses. The playground was a major arena for this kind of play. Girls, particularly, are often enthusiastic in performing gendered, heterosexual parts through skipping and other rhymes. [9] Whereas boys' playground games often involve running and ball

games (usually football), the girls are much more frequently to be seen chatting or skipping to particular rhymes or playing clapping games which, more often than not, are about boyfriends, marriage and children. Of course, girls often indulge in verses of this kind without thinking of their meaning, enjoying the rhythm and the skipping. Nevertheless, it is an activity through which heterosexuality is normalized/naturalized (if not thought about reflectively). The fantasies developed through such rhymes, while not necessarily about sex as such, are certainly reproducing part of a culture of heterosexuality in which girls grow up to be women who marry men, go on honeymoon, have babies and otherwise perform their gendered, heterosexual female parts.

Other skipping and clapping rhymes performed by the girls gave particular pleasure to the players because they were sexually suggestive, somewhat risqué, and were normally performed to gales of laughter. While skipping and clapping were almost exclusively girls' games, there were other games which were played by both girls and boys. These were variants of chasing and catching games in which gender was very strongly marked and with sexual connotations introduced. One such game was a variant of the popular television show, *Blind Date*. In this game, three girls stood behind a wall and numbered themselves from one to three. The boy then chose a number (the question-and-answer session of the original show having been dispensed with). The game finished with the chosen girl coming out from behind the wall, the boy running away and all three girls chasing after him. When they caught him, which they invariably did, the 'chosen' girl would kiss him on the cheek. This game, like 'kiss, cuddle, torture' discussed below, could be seen as a reversal of the usual gendered power relations of the school playground. The fact that the boy was always younger and smaller placed him in a less powerful position than the girls he was playing with (and it is, perhaps, significant that no boy in their own year group would play this game with them). The chasing and catching of the boy by three girls provided the girls with an opportunity to display their own power, including the power to humiliate a boy. The fact that this took place literally on the margins of a playground dominated by bigger boys playing football is a paradox, as is the way in which playing this game can be seen as an activity which helps embed girls within the power relations of heterosexuality.

'Blind Date', as played here, was a version of the ever popular 'kiss-chase', usually seen in infant playgrounds (that is, amongst children from 4 to 7). At Edendale School, the children had evolved another version of 'kiss-chase' which they called 'kiss, cuddle, torture'. This was the subject not only of playground activity, but of much discussion in the classroom. When I interviewed the children, this was one of the key subjects of discussion. Samantha and Louise's account of the game was that the boys would nearly always choose 'torture', rather than 'kiss' or 'cuddle' when the girls caught them. The girls, on the other hand, were most likely to choose 'cuddle', since being kissed was embarrassing and being 'tortured' unpleasant. As in 'Blind Date', gender difference was strongly marked, indeed exaggerated by this game, as a binary and heterosexual opposition. Boys and girls, at least according to the girls, chose differently and, indeed, from my discussions with both boys and girls and from my playground observation, it seems that the girls literally never chose 'torture', whereas the boys frequently did.

It is interesting to reflect on the signification of these gendered choices by the girls and boys involved in the game. The choice of 'torture' by the boys seemed to signify that they were 'real men' who could put up with being kicked (which, the girls explained, was what torture entailed) rather than being soft enough to be kissed by a girl. Connell (1995) suggests that masculinities are, at least in part, achieved through a circuit of production in which bodily experiences (in his particular example, of same-sex enjoyment) are understood through the lens of what those experiences signify in the culture and then similar bodily experiences are entered into again with these culturally rich expectations. For both boys and girls, 'kiss, cuddle, torture' involved developing a repertoire of bodily experiences culturally interpreted. Rather than just being painful (which it is), the experience of 'torture' (being kicked, as Elias explained to me 'in some place that's not nice') is inscribed into the boys' 'boyness'. What is more, being tortured seemed to be more of a marker of 'proper' (i.e. macho) male heterosexuality than being kissed, which, because it was seen as feminized, became also an indication of being a sissy, which was immediately conflated with being gay (or, in the children's most common nomenclature, a 'poofter'). In fact, Elias appeared to be the only boy involved in the game who could get away with choosing 'kiss', possibly because he was well established as a 'real boy' and one who was heterosexually attractive. Indeed, within classroom and playground gossip, his heterosexual attractiveness was legendary – 'everyone wants to go out with Elias', as one girl told me.

Girls, too, entered into a circuit of 'bodily reflexive' experience. In the context of the game, they empowered themselves/were empowered through their ability to 'torture' and to choose not to be 'tortured'. Of course, the terms of their power were constrained by the more general relations of gendered power within the school. As pointed out above, the playground, especially during dinner play, was completely dominated by boys playing football and this was frequently a subject of complaint from the girls. Moreover, the choice of 'cuddle', rather than 'kiss', was definitely related to the potential for a kiss given in the playground to be mytholo-gized in classroom gossip, until it came to stand for excessive sexuality: the whore side of the Madonna/whore binary. Engaging in the game, but choosing 'cuddle', for the girls did establish their feminine/ized hetero-sexual credentials, but without the danger of being identified as, in some sense, 'loose'. Another constraint on the girls' ability to develop power in the gender dynamic of the playground was that the hetero/sexist harass-ment[10] of girls by boys was a constant presence, either in the girls' concerns and constantly retold narratives of what it meant to be a girl (a 'master' narrative, indeed) or because it was actively taking place.

## Signifying mothers/signifying heterosexuality

This was the context for the year group topic adopted by Mr Stuart and the other Year 5 teacher, Ms Allen (who, as it happened, was a lesbian) on 'Me, My Family and My History'. This topic was intended to be an opportunity for anti-racist, anti-sexist and anti-heterosexist work as the children explored different aspects of the topic, from their connections with other parts of the world, through their own family histories and differing family formations, to biology and sex education. It was Mr Stuart's intention that, should the opportunity arise within the topic, he would come out to his class (and, indeed, he hoped and intended that the topic would give rise to just such an opportunity). This was not a sudden decision; he had been out among the staff for a long time and had met with the school's governing body during the previous year and obtained their support for the idea that, should it be appropriate, he would come out to children in the school. I will discuss what happened when he did come out in the next section. In this section, I will focus on the way children used and made sense of two particular texts introduced for their potential to show alternative family formations to the nuclear, heterosexual family, which, in popular culture, if not in the children's lives, is usually white and middle-class. These texts were a Canadian children's picture book entitled *Asha's Mums* (Elwin and Paulse, 1990) and a photopack entitled *What Is a Family?* (Development Education Centre, 1990).

Bronwyn Davies (1989) shows how many children read feminist fairy tales in ways which recuperate them for the patriarchal gender order. The readings of *Asha's Mums* and the photographs from *What Is a Family?* were somewhat more contingent on the particular context than those of Davies's subjects. *Asha's Mums* tells the story of a little girl who is required to get the permission of her parents to go on a class outing to a science museum. When she brings the permission note back to school signed by two women, the teacher says that no one can have two mothers and the note must be signed by her mother and her father. The next day, both her mothers visit the teacher and explain the situation and Asha is allowed to visit the science museum. Along the way, there is a discussion amongst the children in Asha's class about whether or not it is possible to have two mothers. The book is attractively illustrated and, though it is a little 'worthy', it did hold the children's interest.

*Asha's Mums* was one of several books from which small groups of children could choose in order to do an activity in which they mapped the central characters' relationships to others in the story. Mr Stuart had given each group a sheet of paper on which he had already drawn a set of concentric circles. The task was to read the story, write the main character's name in the central circle and then the names of the other characters in a circle closer or nearer to the centre depending on the closeness of that character to the story's protagonist. He suggested that they start by writing the characters' names on small pieces of paper which they could move around on the larger sheet until the group was agreed about the relative positioning of each, when they could transfer the names to the big sheet. Mr Stuart moved round the classroom talking to the small groups as they worked. The group using *Asha's Mums* consisted of three girls (Christina, Aysegul and Nadia). Much of their conversation in relation to the book revolved around the question of how Asha came to have two mums and they decided to place the names of both mums equally near to her, followed by her baby brother and her 'best friend', then her teacher and the other children in the class. In this context, and in discussion with Mr Stuart, they decided that Asha's two mums loved each other and Nadia supplied the word 'lesbian' when Mr Stuart asked if they knew a word to describe women who loved other women. However, when, at the end of the session, each group of children was asked to explain to the rest of the class what they had done, this explanation of Asha's situation vanished from use and any number of other explanations, no matter how unlikely, were offered in preference:

| MR STUART: | So why d'you think that Asha has two mums? |
|---|---|
| LEVI: | [to laughter] They might have had, one of them might have had a sex change. |
| ELIAS: | Might have a step-mum. |
| LOUISE: | Maybe the kids are orphans and came to live with these two ladies. |
| CHRISTINA: | I think they adopted the children. |
| [General puzzlement in the class] | |
| MR STUART: | Do you think they might be two women who loved each other? |
| EDWARD: | [in a very shocked voice] Lesbians! |
| LEVI: | How d'you know which one's pregnant? |
| CHRISTINA: | No. Maybe they're sisters. |

(Conversation as noted in research diary, 29 September 1995)

It is worth noting, in this context, that neither Nadia nor Aysegul contributed to the discussion despite the fact that Nadia had supplied the word 'lesbian' when talking in the small group with Mr Stuart. Moreover, Christina, who had been involved in the previous discussion, offered a new explanation of Asha's relationship with her two mums which had been explicitly rejected by her small group earlier.

It seems that the presumption of heterosexuality within the class as a whole was overwhelming and that the explanation that there were lesbian mothers felt risky to the girls. The very term 'mother', in fact, signifies heterosexuality in common-sense terms (Kaplan, 1992; VanEvery, 1996). It may be that, in effectively defying the normative definition of mothers as heterosexual by offering the explanation of lesbian motherhood, the girls felt that they themselves might be seen as 'lezzies', a term sometimes used within the playground as a form of abuse. The group of three, in this context, operated as a kind of private space where transgression (or knowledge of transgression) of the myth that all mothers are, inevitably, heterosexual, could be allowed without the danger of contamination. But the whole class was a public space, no longer consisting of girls only, or of chosen friends with whom one could risk, as Nadia did, knowing the word and concept 'lesbian' in a non-condemnatory way. Edward, within the whole-class context, knew the word, but distanced himself from it by demonstrating his shock in the exaggerated expression in his voice.

When the children worked with the pictures in the *What Is a Family?* photopack there was also a resistance to reading a particular picture as being one of lesbian mothers. It shows two women, both smiling, with one of them holding a baby on her lap as a cat climbs out of her hand and the other, sitting very close and stroking the cat. Both women are, to my (adult, lesbian) eye at least, coded lesbian in their dress and self-presentation and, given the context of all these pictures being about 'families', the preferred reading of the picture would seem to be that it is of a lesbian couple with their baby (and their cat). The children were given several questions to address as they discussed their chosen pictures in pairs, including 'How are the people in the picture connected to each other?' Elias and Brendan, who had chosen this picture, were steadfast in refusing to admit the possibility of lesbian motherhood in their discussion of the picture, even when Mr Stuart suggested this to them. They insisted, instead, that the picture showed two mums who were friends and one had come to visit the other, even though there was only one baby in the picture. So, whereas the girls were prepared to entertain the possibility that Asha's mums might be lesbians while they were within the relative privacy and safety of their small group, the boys were not willing to do so even when working in a pair. It may be that this is an illustration of boys' greater unwillingness to take risks or to appear not to be 'real boys', even (perhaps especially) with their closest friends and allies.

## 'Some grown-ups aren't very grown up': coming out in class

In another activity for this project, Mr Stuart asked the children to work in small groups to write down three 'facts' about girls and three about boys. All the groups came to the conclusion fairly quickly that the only 'facts' they could write down would be biological ones like 'girls can have babies', and 'girls have vaginas'. When they came back to the whole class Mr Stuart went round the circle asking each child to offer one 'fact' that their group had written down. After a few along the lines of 'boys can stand up to go to the toilet' and 'girls can have babies', Aysegul offered:

AYSEGUL: [very embarrassed, looking down at her feet and whispering]
Girls can marry, girls can't get married to girls.
MR STUART: It's true that girls can't get married to girls because of the law, but girls can fall in love and live together.
EDWARD: Maybe they're lesbians.
[lots of giggles]

LEVI:          I know a man, I think it's disgusting.

MR STUART:     Well, I'm gay and I'm not disgusting.

[*lots of giggles*]

MR STUART:     The person I happen to love is a man.

ELIAS:         A man is a man and a woman is a woman.

LOUISE:        Everyone says you're not gay and Ms Allen is your girl-friend.

MR STUART:     Everyone is wrong. Ms Allen is a very good friend, but I don't love her –

SAMANTHA:      But we *saw* you and you were in the greengrocer's, laughing.

Clearly, the gossip networks had been active and the two teachers had been paired off in the children's minds. After all, shopping for fruit and vegetables is a very domestic act, and laughing while doing so may well signify romantic, heterosexual involvement! What seemed to be operating, here, was the development of a narrative around these two popular teachers whereby linking them romantically worked as a potent enactment of the myth of happy heterosexuality. The fact that the two teachers were evidently happy in each other's company (laughing while they shopped) was worked up into a kind of mythical, romantic, almost fairy story in which the two were destined to have the inevitable happy ending.

Much to my surprise (and, indeed, to Mr Stuart's), his being gay did not spread around the school. Two weeks later, for example, a child in the other Year 5 class was in trouble for using homophobic insults, and had no inkling that Mr Stuart was gay. When I interviewed Samantha and Louise, I asked them about gossip and they told me that, although they did gossip about and at school, they did not gossip about Mr Stuart because, as Samantha put it:

SAMANTHA:      Yeah. Maybe, if he told us and then he might not want the whole school to know.

LOUISE:        We wouldn't have done it.

Throughout this conversation (and the transcript of this section of it lasts for several pages), the girls refused to say that what they were not gossiping about was Mr Stuart's coming out to them. Neither they, nor I, used the term 'gay', and the girls were insistent that Mr Stuart would not want 'it' spread about:

| SAMANTHA: | Yeah, but, he doesn't want, really, everyone at the school to know. |
| LOUISE: | Maybe he does but, I don't know, I wouldn't really spread it because – |
| SAMANTHA: | Cos people go a bit funny in this school about – |
| LOUISE: | Yeah and then they'd go, they'd jump around and tell – |
| SAMANTHA: | Their mum and dad – |
| LOUISE: | – and then they'd say 'is it true?' or something. And maybe their mum and dad will think that he's a bad teacher and then they'll think that 'oh no, my son is going to be, like, um, don't want my daughter, he's going to be like that, so I'm going to take my kid away from the school' and tell Mr Snowden [the headteacher] about him and he could be sacked. |
| DE: | D'you think that would happen? |
| SAMANTHA: | No. |
| LOUISE: | No, not really, cos, most grown-ups are, um, grown-up about it but some aren't really. Some are. |

We all knew what we were talking about, here. It was, in Eve Sedgwick's (1990) terms, an 'open secret'. Furthermore, the children were absolutely aware of homophobia as a feature of society that they had to negotiate. They knew that 'most grown-ups are grown-up about it, but some aren't really' and seemed to have made a conscious (or semi-conscious) decision to build a kind of closet around the classroom in order to protect their teacher, but maybe, also, to protect themselves from the contamination of having a gay teacher. If being gay seemed to them to be dangerous because of the reactions of adults, then maybe being taught by a gay man was dangerous because of the reactions both of adults, who might remove you from the class of a teacher you liked, and of other children, who might tease you and accuse you of being gay or lesbian.

## Conclusion

In the context of Mr Stuart's teaching and, in particular, of his coming out to the class, opportunities were opened up for some radical shifts in the 'master narratives' by which these children had learnt to understand gender and sexuality. However, these possibilities were constrained in several ways. Talk about romance, dating, dumping and 'going out', in which the most popular children were keenly involved, was an important aspect of the way the class, as a whole, made sense of heterosexual gender relations. The involvement of this particular group of popular children in games in which both heterosexuality and gender were heavily marked took place in ways which reinforced the hegemonic gender order: macho men and cuddly, caring women were enacted through the conduct of 'kiss, cuddle, torture'. The way that motherhood is made to signify hetero-sexuality was difficult to shift, especially in whole-class discussions of the 'alternative' texts provided by Mr Stuart, although the girls (unsurpris-ingly) showed more signs of shifting the narrative than the boys. Finally, the mythology of happy heterosexuality was carried in the legend of Mr Stuart's romance with Ms Allen.

Nevertheless, the impact of Mr Stuart's attempts to shift the 'master narrative' and rewrite the myths of family and of happy heterosexuality should not be underestimated. Some of the girls in his class were able to articulate opinions about homophobia and heterosexism, even if they could not name them and, even for the boys, he offered alternative ways of being. Coming out to the class, in a context in which the very term 'family' was under consideration, constituted a radical challenge to these children, one which some of the boys initially responded to by making homophobic comments. However, even Elias and Levi were later (and, significantly, in private to me) moved to insist that they thought there was nothing wrong with being gay. In a way, it did not matter whether this was simply a version of trying to please the teacher, for as the boys took up an anti-homophobic stance, they momentarily inhabited this alternative world-view and thus created, for themselves, the possibility of inhabiting it again in the future.

## Notes

1. This project was a pilot for the ESRC-funded project on 'Children's "Rela-tionship Cultures" in Years 5 and 6', project no. R00023 7438, beginning on 1 January 1998 and lasting for two years.
2. All names have been altered to retain anonymity for the school. Participants in the study were asked to choose their own pseudonyms. In some cases, children chose names which do not reflect their ethnicity.

3. This common sense runs alongside the notion that if children do know about or show any interest in sexuality, they are somehow tainted and also the notion that they are seductive (and that their very innocence is part of the seduction). See Kitzinger (1988; 1990).
4. The phrase is Valerie Hey's (1997), used to indicate the performative nature of gender (see also Butler, 1990; 1993).
5. This is characteristic of the school culture at Edendale. I had spent three full days in the school before I heard any adult (including dinner supervisors) raise his/her voice to a child. Those who are familiar with schools will recognize what an unusual school it is.
6. The end of the school year 1996–97 saw an unparalleled level of resignations from school teaching in the UK. This appears to have been, in part, the culmination of years of what Jane Kenway, writing in the Australian context (1987), labelled 'discourses of derision' (see also Ball, 1990) combined with ever increasing pseudo-accountability through paperwork and punitive inspection by the Office for Standards in Education (OFSTED). It was also due to changes to pension arrangements introduced by the previous Conservative government, which made it the last opportunity for teachers to take advantage of early retirement. Edendale School was one among many which was very hard hit by this: the head and four other teachers (including Mr Stuart) left. For a small junior school (with a two-form entry) this constituted almost half the staff. It remains to be seen if the school can recover from this body blow.
7. This was Mr Stuart's original intention when he decided to leave full-time teaching in order to be able to write music for children to perform. However, the school's funding did not allow for them to retain his services part-time.
8. This section and the penultimate section of this chapter are drawn from an earlier paper (Epstein, 1997).
9. For a collection of children's playground rhymes see Opie and Opie (1969).
10. See Epstein (1996) for a discussion of the reasons for moving from use of the term 'sexual harassment' to using the term 'hetero/sexist harassment' and Epstein (1997) for a discussion of harassment at Edendale School.

## References

Ball, S. J. (1990). *Politics and Policy Making in Education: Explorations in Policy Sociology*. London: Routledge.
Benjamin, S. (1997). 'Fantasy Football League: boys in a Special (SEN) School constructing and re-constructing masculinities'. Unpublished MA thesis, University of London Institute of Education.

Butler, J. (1990). *Gender Trouble: Feminism and the Subversion of Identity*. New York and London: Routledge.

Butler, J. (1993). *Bodies That Matter: On the Discursive Limits of 'Sex'*. New York and London: Routledge.

Connell, R. W. (1995). *Masculinities*. Cambridge: Polity.

Davies, B. (1989). *Frogs and Snails and Feminist Tales*. St Leonards, NSW: Allen & Unwin.

Development Education Centre (1990). *What Is a Family? Photographs and Activities*. Birmingham: Development Education Centre.

Elwin, R. and Paulse, M. (1990). *Asha's Mums*, illustrated by Dawn Lee. Toronto: Women's Press.

Epstein, D. (1993). 'Too small to notice? constructions of childhood and discourses of "race" in predominantly white contexts', *Curriculum Studies*, 1(3): 317–34.

Epstein, D. (1996). 'Keeping them in their place: hetero/sexist harassment, gender and the enforcement of heterosexuality', in L. Adkins and J. Holland (eds), *Sexualising the Social*. Basingstoke: Macmillan.

Epstein, D. (1997). 'Cultures of schooling/cultures of sexuality', *International Journal of Inclusive Education*, 1(1): 37–53.

Foucault, M. (1977). *Discipline and Punish: The Birth of the Prison*, translated by Alan Sheridan. Harmondsworth: Penguin.

Halpin, T. (1996). '5-year-olds to get gay lessons', *Daily Mail*, 2 March.

Hey, V. (1997). *The Company She Keeps: An Ethnography of Girls' Friendships*. Buckingham: Open University Press.

Kaplan, E. A. (1992). *Motherhood and Representation: The Mother in Popular Culture and Melodrama*. London: Routledge.

Kenway, J. (1987). 'Left right out: Australian education and the politics of signification', *Journal of Education Policy*, 2(3): 189–203.

Kitzinger, J. (1988). 'Defending innocence: ideologies of childhood', *Feminist Review. Special Issue: Family Secrets, Child Sexual Abuse*, 28: 77–87.

Kitzinger, J. (1990). ' "Who are you kidding?" Children, power and sexual assault', in A. James and A. Prout (eds), *Constructing and Reconstructing Childhood*. London: Falmer Press.

Opie, I. and Opie, P. (1969). *Children's Games in Street and Playground: Chasing, Catching, Seeking, Hunting, Racing, Duelling, Exerting, Daring, Guessing, Acting, Pretending*. Oxford: Clarendon Press.

Redman, P. and Mac an Ghaill, M. (1997). 'Educating Peter: the making of a history man', in D.L. Steinberg, D. Epstein and R. Johnson (eds), *Border Patrols: Policing the Boundaries of Heterosexuality*. London: Cassell.

Sedgwick, E. K. (1990). *Epistemology of the Closet*. Berkeley: University of California Press.

Thorne, B. (1993). *Gender Play: Boys and Girls in School.* Buckingham: Open University Press (published in the US by Rutgers University Press).

VanEvery, J. (1996). 'Heterosexuality and domestic life', in D. Richardson (ed.), *Theorising Heterosexuality.* Buckingham: Open University Press.

# 4

# The Birds and the Bees: Narratives of Sexuality in Television Natural History Programmes

## *Barbara Crowther*

THE WAY THE natural world is presented to us on television makes it easy to forget how intensely constructed these packaged readings of nature are, and even that they are readings. As part of the legacy of the BBC's public service function, British wildlife films share the international reputation for objectivity and accuracy that attaches to the British documentary product, and provide a yardstick for quality productions in the genre. Yet – particularly important in today's competitive broadcasting economy – they also have a commercial function to provide entertainment, a remit to offer popular 'family' viewing with an accessible and exciting view of science, and here the premium on impartiality and strict objectivity is lower. The success of their populist style and format is evident from their consistently high ratings and remarkably wide-ranging audience, at home and across the world. Because of the respect they command, their manner of framing and talking about their subjects has been hugely influential on the popular understanding of animal behaviour, and of human behaviour too.

The point of this chapter is to expose the myths that underlie the view of nature conventionally found in these programmes, particularly those relating to gender and sexuality. It will suggest how the rhetoric of the genre constitutes part of a wider pedagogy governing human sexuality, implicitly signalling what is considered normal and natural in humans. By analysing two extracts from recent British natural history programmes (selected both for their typicality and for the range of issues they raise), the mechanisms and ideologies by which animal behaviour is commonly represented will be closely examined and discussed in relation to wider issues, focusing first on the use of anthropomorphism and narrative and later on their relation to scientific tradition.

Critiquing the genre is to mount a challenge not so much on the probity of wildlife film-makers as on science's fiercely defended claim to objectivity. Scientific researchers are not blank slates; however, popular science prefers to side-step the epistemological implications of this.[1] The history of science, as Donna Haraway has convincingly argued, is a history of storytelling, a succession of contesting stories that support different political positions regarding sex, race, class and so on (Haraway, 1988, pp. 79–80). Myths can appear to be validated by observation: deconstructing the stories and language of contemporary natural history films exposes something of the ideological grounding of these myths, including, as this study reveals, the androcentric bias that commonly informs them.

## Animals and storytelling

Wildlife films are part of a long tradition of mediating our understanding of human behaviour through animal examples. A legacy of Victorian prudishness has been to make parents and educators coy about human sexuality (Trudell, 1993, pp. 11–12) and this coyness is often dealt with by displacement onto animals. In formal education until recently, 'sex' was largely taught in biology lessons, where the behaviour of (say) frogs was made to substitute for humans, and where human sexuality is represented by section drawings of organs that bear little relation to anything a child is likely to see or feel. Pleasure, especially female pleasure, plays no part in this discourse.

Within families too, evasiveness often characterizes communication about sex and sexual feelings. Euphemistic phrases for human sexual intercourse such as the 'Birds and the Bees' or the 'Facts of Life' testify to the tradition of substituting animals for humans to discuss sexual issues. One spin-off of natural history films being scheduled at family viewing times is that it gives reticent parents the opportunity – for some the only opportunity they make – to raise the topic of sex and reproduction with their children, but vicariously, through the animal examples on the screen, thus avoiding the awkward area of human emotions and desires and, importantly, homosexuality, a topic conveniently (and not altogether accurately) excluded from the animal picture.

Using the behaviour of animals to introduce and explain to children the mechanics of reproduction (and signalling links to human sexual activity) seems appropriate and innocent enough. But habits of thought take hold early and encourage reductive and deterministic thinking about the roles of male and female. Moreover, when discussing animals casually it is difficult to avoid anthropomorphic speech (that is, describing animal behaviour as if it were human behaviour), and for film-makers anthropomorphism provides rich opportunities for making entertaining scripts, gender, predictably, being a favourite source. However, presenting creatures as having culturally shaped characteristics rather than just a biological sex is more than just playful; it can reinforce deep-seated ideological positions. Overtly sexist images like the notorious 'leader and his harem' are much rarer now,[2] but the legacy of drawing on conventional perceptions of gender is still maintained within a constant flow of metaphors around mothering and fathering roles, grooming, disciplining, jealousy, jilted lovers, coyness and so on.

The use of anthropomorphism has considerable implications for the science of natural history: for one thing, metaphors lose potency with use, and may be taken as literal description; for another, they carry connotative meanings which are far from neutral. There is growing recognition of the wider problems and power of anthropomorphic discourse in scientific writings (e.g. Birke, 1994; Harding, 1986; Kennedy, 1992; Tudge, 1995), but also widespread proof of its indispensability in popular products, not least in wildlife programmes.

The prevalence of so much anthropomorphic discourse in wildlife films suggests it is more than just gratification for the TV audience, but actually shapes the perception of the researchers themselves, the way they interpret animals' behaviour and the way they construct stories. It allows them to 'find' behaviour, roles and relationships among animals which (conveniently) have analogies in human behaviour. These 'discoveries' in turn validate them as natural to human culture as a whole. However, the paradigm for (apparently universal) human behaviour upon which so many of the comparisons draw and then comment is taken from the cultural world of the film-makers – overwhelmingly Western, white and male – which further reinforces their cultural hegemony.

It would be as simplistic to suggest that all male film-makers are unaware of the innate sexist tendencies in the genre, as it would to assume all females are aware of it. It is significant, however, that their development and training takes place in a very male-dominated sector of the industry, underpinned by an exacting work ethos that helps maintain its exclusivity (Crowther, 1995, p. 143). While technologically and artistically advanced, it is very conservative in gender terms, in both the relative scarcity and the status of women employed and in its scientific orientation. Researchers will, largely, have grown up using the male-oriented linguistic and cognitive traditions associated with the dominant paradigms of science.[3]

It is not surprising then that conventional (heterosexual) male attitudes to women, and male interests and perceptions, are regularly reflected in the way animals' behaviour is interpreted and represented on the screen. It impregnates the whole discourse.[4] It can be found in the phrasing of their scripts: males are regularly described in terms of their 'competitive behaviour' and 'territorial aggression', females in terms of their 'mothering instincts' and 'sexual receptiveness'. 'Sexual aggression' in males gets called 'initiation behaviour' in females. The stories through which they present their material tend to position males as the active subject and females as passive agents or in domestic or supportive roles. The most common stories are of survival, competition and family life; and the standard life-cycle story is generally presented in the orthodox biologically determinist birth-to-reproduction model, not a more encompassing birth-to-death narrative. These classic structures, supported by an authoritative narrative voice, establish and institutionalize particular agendas, determining what angles of animal life are shown and what questions are asked, disqualifying alternative concerns and interpretations.[5]

## Reading the texts

Two extracts from wildlife films, typical examples of those transmitted daily on British television – the first organized around a theme, the second a single species – will serve to illustrate how they contrive (mostly unconsciously) to organize and condition the audience's understanding of the different sexes' behaviour. While it is possible to adopt a 'resistant' reading position – if, for instance, we are mistrustful of the genre or other dominant discourses in society – the firm authority of the address in a science documentary (and the absence of specialist knowledge to debate the 'facts') militates against negotiating or rejecting the position constructed for us by the texts, making it hard to develop alternative readings.[6] Partly by denying their own ideological standpoint, they position us to accept the dominant system of beliefs about animal nature and sexuality, which in turn constitutes a normative way of perceiving ourselves and what is 'natural' behaviour in humans. The following analyses suggest how the 'preferred' meaning is produced through a number of interlocking aspects of the discourse.

### Continuing the Line (1990). Episode 12 of The Trials of Life, BBC Bristol. (Producer: Alex Rowe)

This extract comes from a major and very successful series, written and narrated by David Attenborough, probably the best-known and most respected figure in British natural history broadcasting. The series records the various ways different animal species deal with the common challenges of existence – here, reproducing.

> Crabs wear suits of armour which makes mating impossible; but this big male has detected a faint taste in the water which tells him that the little female is about to shed hers. As soon as she slips out of her shell while her new one is still pliable she and he can become intimate, and he's going to hold on to her so no other male will get the chance to claim her at that crucial moment.
>
> Her moult has begun. Her shell has split along the underside and he is helping her to disrobe. The empty suit of armour lying in front of her makes it seem as if he has two females in his embrace. The fact that one is merely the ghost of her former self is revealed only by its vacant eye sockets and the way the current blows it about.
>
> Now the female with her new shell still soft and leathery crawls beneath him. He fertilizes her swiftly before her shell hardens. She won't be able to mate again until her next moult. Soon he will abandon her, but he has already ensured that the eggs she will nurture for the next few weeks will carry *his* genes.
>
> A female wolf who's just become sexually receptive joins her howling pack in the Canadian north. All the males are interested in her but there's a ranking system in the pack and the senior male has priority in mating. Others who try their luck have to be reminded who's boss. [*Snarling face*] And he claims his rights. [*They mate.*]
>
> But he does not now leave her: indeed he couldn't even if he wanted to. His genitals have swollen so greatly inside her that the pair are locked together.
>
> This is no unfortunate accident. It's an important part of the male's breeding strategy. Remaining tied for so long gives his sperm time to reach her eggs before a competitor can displace him. It may be half an hour or so before they're able to pull apart.

The aftermath of such a genital lock may be slightly painful [*Male wolf licks his genitals.*] but the process has virtually guaranteed him his paternity. And animals that don't take such precautions can't be nearly so certain.

The narration of this film bears the genre's traditional hallmarks, a male RP voice (Attenborough's), calmly authoritative, delivering an apparently objective, merely descriptive account of creatures' lives and motivation, an impression reinforced by the filmic convention of selecting and editing images to 'prove' the truth of the script's assertions.[7] This decisive factual address positions viewers to accept its authority as incontestable. There is no window for reflecting on whose truth, and whose story, we are being told.

The story here, a common one, is about the male and his breeding strategy (not hers, not theirs; specifically so in the case of the wolf): the fertilization process is not presented as a mutually beneficial strategy.[8] Though the female crab '*crawls* beneath him' at the crucial moment, and though the female wolf '*joins* her howling pack', the active agency in most of the sentences, and in the overall slant, is male. The female crab must have emitted some fluid for the male to detect; the female wolf 'who's just become sexually receptive' is actually seeking a mate. Her post-coital comfort is not considered. The narrating consciousness is positioned with the male.

The efforts of the males to secure their succession is at the centre of countless contemporary wildlife programmes. As females are assumed to reproduce anyway, their selection choices are rarely touched on. This genetic survival is individualized, too: 'survival of the fittest' is repeatedly presented as about the fittest male – the concept of adaptive fitness hardly distinguishable from physical fitness. This story, after all, provides filmmakers with highly rated footage of dramatic and bloodthirsty sequences: aggressiveness, mating, fighting, even killing. Consequently we know little about the procreative chances of the weaker males, or patterns of rivalry or sexual arousal among females, or other preference factors besides strength.[9]

This narrative focus is consistent with the audience position constructed linguistically by the address. Though we may individually resist this construction, we are all assumed to share the experience of life and enjoyment of the tropes as if we had one common vantage point. The play around the crabs' seduction scene (from 'she slips out of her shell' to 'soon he will abandon her'), plus the fantasy of 'two females in his embrace', as well as the concern shown for the male wolf's painful genitals, constitute a kind of laddish macho talk ('[they] have to be reminded who's boss'). While it does not exclude the female audience, it still has a male reference-base, a male address; and while amusing, it also affects our understanding of the behaviour. This illustrates the problematic role of anthropomorphism, used overtly and largely self-consciously in the script of the crabs but integrated more subtly into the commentary on the wolves.

Usually, by virtue of the subject position offered us in the address, we accept the values and explanations signalled in the text. It is only when our personal emotional (or political) response is at odds with the 'preferred' interpretation, or we resist the dominant narrative identification, that we notice a conflict of interest, an absence, or a 'line'. The second example may demonstrate this.

### Queen of the Beasts (1989). Survival, Anglia. (Filmed and produced by Richard Matthews)

This film explores why lions live in groups. The stable members of a pride are related females, who show marked co-operativeness. Periodically, young mature males, unrelated to the pride, come and drive out the senior male(s) and any weaned male cubs, before killing all the sucking cubs.

[*Two lions sniff ground, raise heads, shake manes, bare teeth.*] The new masters of the pride have come for the females. One sniffs the spot where a lioness has urinated. Wary of these new and strange males, the females have wisely gone into hiding.

[*Plain with scattered bushes. Zoom in on one bush until cubs are visible underneath.*] But in this hide-and-seek game of life there is another and more immediate problem for these males. They cannot mate until the lionesses come into season. But the females already have cubs and so will not be ready to mate for another year or more. [*Close-up of cub's face.*]

The new males simply cannot wait that long for their chance to father some cubs of their own. [*Lion lopes, right to left, across grassland. Cut to cubs in long grass. Cut back to lion, stationary, looking back over his shoulder, then left again.*] They are in their prime now and may only have possession of the females for two years – just two years in which to ensure their genetic patrimony. [*Cut back to cubs – to lion looking left – to cubs.*] They cannot afford to look after another male's cubs; they cannot spend their short time at the top protecting another lion's young whilst waiting for their turn to mate.

[*Lion looks left, lowers head and moves off left at increasing pace.*]

They have done their waiting out there on the plains where they wandered for years in search of this opportunity; they can wait no longer. If the females lose their cubs they will come into season within days. The imperative for the new males is overwhelming: they must kill the cubs. [*Lion attacks one cub while a second runs off, and picks up and drops its limp body before moving off towards second cub who rears up before being attacked and killed; lion runs on to third, savages it and picks up body. Long shot of lion carrying body of cub as camera zooms out to vista of whole savannah.*]

Despite all the years of research into lion behaviour infanticide has rarely been seen and never before filmed. For all its apparent ferocity, the killing is only an expression of the urgent demands of the situation. But if the male's behaviour seems harshly pragmatic, perhaps the female's is even more surprising.

[*Male lion, lying beside river, is approached by female and whipped across the head with her tail. She repeats this on two others lying nearby. She settles near them, facing away from them; one male approaches and mounts her. Cut to head-and-shoulder shot of the pair, male licking female and showing his teeth. Female gets up and walks away followed by male licking her rump.*]

Bereft of their cubs the females now have exactly the same drives as the new males. They can expect around two years of stability. If they are to raise cubs they must start immediately. Within as little as 24 hours after losing their cubs the females come into season and start flirting outrageously with the new males.

The females are nervous at first, a bit scared of the new males; but the orgies in the first few months after a takeover are a good ice-breaker, and soon strong bonds are formed.

The levity of the script in the 'flirtatious' scene following directly from the horrific carnage is quite startling. The insistently defensive description of the lion's vicious attack on the cubs (five 'cannot' constructions, plus 'imperative', 'overwhelming' and 'must') betrays some unease; less understanding, however, is shown on the female's side: 'If the male's behaviour seems harshly pragmatic, perhaps the female's is even more surprising.'

Flirting and orgies have derogatory connotations when applied to women, which makes the presentation of the female's 'drives' almost lascivious, and not 'exactly the same' reproductive programming as the males' drive to kill. Moreover, while the males' motivation is drawn as calculating ('they wandered for years in search of this opportunity'; 'they cannot afford to look after another male's cubs'), females are ascribed emotions (they are 'wary' of the new males, then sexually 'nervous'). This different treatment of the sexes and its latent anthropomorphism – partly concealed behind the self-conscious irony of 'flirting' and 'orgies' – mirrors similar patterns across the genre and illustrates the subliminal mediation of our under-standing of the natural world.

There would be other ways of telling the lions' story. To use the terms of French feminist literary theory (e.g. Irigaray, 1985), where 'feminine' writing is defined as fluid, open-ended and disruptive, and 'masculine' as end-oriented, linear and cohesive, this script carries many of the markers of a 'masculine' text. We see this in its narration (the way it tells the story: we are positioned to identify with and vindicate the perpetrator) and its address (the attitudes it assumes or wants us to share), as well as its language. There is no recognition of the shock or sentiment we feel after that emotionally very powerful and savage scene (whose impact is deliber-ately heightened by the suspense technique of rapid cross-cutting). It is followed instead by an acknowledgement of the unique skill of the photo-grapher: 'Despite all the years of research into lion behaviour, infanticide has rarely been seen and never before filmed.' Then, with an indecent haste, rivalling that of the lioness, it turns immediately from the ferocity of the male to amusement at the 'surprising' spectacle of her 'outrageous flirting'. The recoil that many people feel is not legitimated, but is rendered inappropriate.

Interestingly, and somewhat disturbingly, a female voice, that of actor Rula Lenska, narrates this film, possibly to soften the savagery, possibly because a pride is organized around lionesses. In fact, it does not change the substance of the film at all; but it serves to throw into relief certain related issues. The script's acceptance of the lionesses' 'wise' absence during the attack on the cubs, and the recruitment of our sympathy for the male, sit uneasily with the female speaking voice. One might expect a woman to question at least the mother lion's reaction. The lionesses have shown marked solidarity and shared care of the young, and their collective strength in hunting is impressive, yet their teamwork fails to protect the cubs from a male predator (indeed, we do not even know if any resistance or concern was shown). This begs important questions about the bound-aries of female co-operation and relations within the pride, areas of knowledge which remain disturbing lacunae in the text. How females of other species interact, in single-sex as well as mixed-sex conditions, might be of considerable interest to many, especially women, to broaden popular understanding of 'the natural'. But co-operative behaviour does not make for such dramatic narratives as the conflict model, and cannot guarantee success in a competitive film market.

## Scientific models: sociobiology

Female and single-sex behaviour is marginal, possibly even damaging, to sociobiological thinking, the dominant strain of scientific 'knowledge' which informs most wildlife programmes, some very heavily. *The Trials of Life*, for instance, a very influential series (which contained the clips of the crabs and wolves), was organized and premised on sociobiological prin-ciples.[10] Scientists know it is a theory; mediated through popular television it emerges as truth. In sociobiology, human behaviour is seen as animal behaviour, all of which is seen as genetically programmed for adaptive selection. Ultimately, human social evolution is seen as part of biological evolution. Thus studying animals provides the key to understanding all human social activity. This model has generated interesting research hypotheses and sophisticated variants have developed, but its reductivism and determinism have understandably earned it a reactionary reputation as Social Darwinism.[11]

Sociobiology, with its conceptual merging of animal and human, encourages anthropomorphism, and allows neat equations to be made between animal and human behaviour, which makes it a gift to popular television, offering a version of science that suits its entertainment brief and a rationale for all the 'blood-and-bonking' footage. Because reproduction is so central to the sociobiological thesis, it not only constructs heterosexu-ality as an imperative, but tends to overemphasize the differences between male and female behaviour (predictably along male:active, female:passive lines) and to universalize behaviour patterns. This assumes a consensus around the meaning of human behaviour and denies the importance of individual variation, seeing it as deviant instead.

Sociobiology, in the hands of male scientists, has served patriarchal interests well.[12] Its discourse, organized around the concepts of inheritance and blood lineage, monogamy and polygamy, territory, competition, domination, and investment and return, are the concerns of the male Establishment, which are (gratifyingly) found mirrored in the animal world. Part of the danger of popular biologism is that it can be manipulated to 'prove' and justify almost any human behaviour.[13] It is used to vindicate adultery, racism, xenophobia and homophobia.

Diversity in sexual and social behaviour within a species, even within a group, and inconsistent behaviour in an individual, undermines the generalizations popular (and polemical) science likes.[14] Its disruptive potential makes primatology and other ethologies (studying animals in the wild) particularly attractive to feminist scientists, but their interpretive work challenging conventional categories and telling different kinds of stories will be slow to percolate to wider audiences. Stories that do not support the primacy of the patriarchal macro-story (with its heterosexual imperative and its adversarial potential) remain largely untold: in television natural history the infertile or post-reproductive females, the less aggressive males and other substandard individuals are virtually invisible.

The genre, then, because of the specific identifications between animals and humans encouraged in its very structures, represents yet another pocket of cultural practice where the Other in the audience – the old, the odd, the weak, the unaggressive, the female and the non-heterosexual – have their interests displaced onto the strong male subject. Those viewers who are positioned, socially and sexually, furthest from the male heterosexual culture that dominates both broadcasting and science are perhaps best able to recognize the absences and biases in wildlife television programmes, and to see how much of a myth their claims to objectivity are. But so secure is their position in the schedules, and so authoritative and convincing their address, it is unlikely that any demonstration (like this one) of their influence in supporting the wider sexist and heterosexist ideology will modify their material or format. Scientifically informative as they are, ultimately their purpose is to entertain; and even classed as 'edutainment' they still need to meet the demands of the market-place (however supply-led this concept of demand is). The 'if it ain't broke, don't fix it' attitude lies behind a recent off-the-record comment by the (male) Head of Development of one commercial wildlife film company: 'We don't have internal debates here! We tell a story we think will be popular; the scientists among us keep us on the straight and narrow . . . I don't think we consider how our gender or our attitude to gender affects our work.' Popular filmmakers may think of their programmes as ephemera, but they carry more responsibility for social attitudes to human gender and sexuality than they may realize.

## Notes

1. The belief that scientific observation and deduction can be objective is increasingly being challenged, particularly in the life sciences, and feminist science is at the forefront of this challenge. The neutrality of the observer's perception has, in the patriarchal West, a history, grammar and vocabulary based on a male norm. Researchers' procedures and their personal and cultural histories, including gender, can produce substantial differences in their findings (Haraway, 1988, p. 79). Wildlife television still largely denies this: according to producer Alex Rowe, only about four centuries ago 'was true science – based on objective observation and free of preconceptions – able to break free and start to discover why things *really* are as they are' (Rowe, 1990, p. 11). See also Martin (1991) and Haraway (1992) – particularly her essay 'Teddy-Bear Patriarchy' on the patrio-imperialist ideology behind the animal dioramas in African Hall at the American Museum of Natural History in New York City.

2. At the prize-giving ceremony of Wildscreen 1996, David Attenborough, amused by its unreconstructed 'relish for anthropomorphism', showed a clip about Galapagos sea-lions from a 1967 documentary *The Enchanted Isles* (*Survival*: Anglia), for which the Duke of Edinburgh provided the commentary:

   > The cows are delightfully feminine creatures with melting eyes and sleek figures; and like so many humans they obviously enjoyed basking in the sun. They are also polygamous, which means that the harem can sleep peacefully; but the lord and master has to keep up a constant offshore patrol, lest some covetous intruder should attempt to snitch one of his more flighty wives.

3. For a brief discussion of these see Crowther (1995, pp. 136–7); also Birke (1991), Sperling (1991). Shirley Strum's reflections on entering a well-established scientific research field, primatology, offer a useful commentary on interpretive 'truth':

   > Adult males are viewed as the core of the troop, affording protection, asserting discipline, and providing cohesion through their leadership. The role of females is merely reproductive ... I had my doubts that even baboons could be so easily explained. I questioned that the adult males, a

small percentage of the troop, could be responsible so totally for its social life. (Strum, 1975, p. 679)

4. Discourse, throughout this chapter, is used in the Foucaultian sense of the rules governing how a subject is talked about and practised, rules of exclusion and of definition which 'determine who speaks, what is or is not discussed, what questions may be asked, and what is "true" or "false"' (Bleier, 1984, p. 194). A useful discussion of feminist discourse analysis and science can be found in Warren (1988, pp. 47–50).

5. The grip of the discourse is not so tight as to prevent film-makers pushing out its boundaries, even working against its innate rules, but the major commissioners tend to back variations on safe formulas and demonstrations of technological innovation, rather than projects that attempt a radical change in the way animals are viewed and discussed.

6. Reader-response criticism recognizes that people's allotted place in the gendered (and otherwise segregated) world affects the meanings that readers find in a text, and they are able to negotiate the 'preferred' meanings through identifying their relationship to the dominant 'voice' of the text.

7. The process of matching image to script, or of constructing a script from available footage so that a minimum of supplementary library footage needs to be bought in, are post-production skills concealed from the audience in accord with the conventions of the realist mode. Job advertisements, like the following from the *Guardian* (June 1996) for producer/directors at the BBC's Natural History Unit, Bristol, indicate how highly constructed nature programmes can be:

> You'll be working with state-of-the art graphics and editing systems, on specific projects. You must be capable of structuring innovative programmes on the basis of available footage, and identifying any additional footage required. You may do this in conjunction with a writer, but you'll still need a firm grasp of storylining and dramatic structure . . . Experience in working with animals, or similar actuality situations would be an advantage.

8. This orientation in the discourse of reproduction, betrayed through the imagery in formal scientific texts, is the subject of Emily Martin's (1991) article 'The Egg and the Sperm' whose subtitle summarizes her observations: 'How science has constructed a romance based on stereotypical male–female roles.'

9. Films with a female orientation tend to use this 'difference' as the hook, and may speak of relations as matriarchal (countering patriarchal) rather than seek out terms free of the traditional scientific paradigms which are, in Donna Haraway's phrase, 'penetrated by the principle of domination' (Haraway,

1978, p. 35). Moreover, as Ros Coward has pointed out, if females express preferences, their behaviour tends to be described as 'selecting their mates as "good" parents, either for their genetic endowments or their ability to provide' (Coward, 1988, p. 212). Again, the focus is on male, not female, fitness.

10. The producer confirms this:

> Humans made it, a human presents it, and a whole lot of humans will watch it – yet nowhere are humans mentioned. But by adding a touch of anthropomorphism to the narration and the titling, Sir David Attenborough, the writer, and Peter Jones, the executive producer, have made it obvious that it is about us too. Sociobiology, *The Trials of Life* is saying (without saying anything about it), is simply one branch of ethology. (Rowe, 1990, p. 11)

The effect of the sociobiological permeation of nature films is described by Ros Coward:

> While appearing to confine themselves to the life of beasts and plants, the programmes offer consistent comment on human society ... [and] draw often unstated analogies, leaving the viewer to make the connections. (Coward, 1988, p. 210)

Moreover, as some practitioners admit, it makes it easy to pander to audience partiality for clichés.

11. Sperling (1991) and Haraway (1988) outline how sociobiology has been used by feminist researchers like Sarah B. Hrdy. The study was formalized by Edward O. Wilson's book *Sociobiology: The New Synthesis* in 1975. The dubious methodology of crude biologism, from which sociobiology developed, was criticized soon afterwards by Evelyn Reed as 'the determination of society and culture through the genes'. 'Indeed, once human society is biologised, anyone can play the game by inventing a fanciful hypothesis equating us with animals' (Reed, 1978, pp. 51, 48).

12. See Stephen Jay Gould's essay, 'Potentiality versus Determinism' (1991), and Evelyn Reed's essay, 'Sociobiology and Pseudoscience' (1975) in Reed (1978).

13. Thus, for example, the perception of penetrative sex as an uncontrollable genetically programmed urge among male animals has conveniently been recruited to 'justify' aggressive sexual behaviour in the human male. Such Social Darwinism is criticized by Shirley Strum:

> Unfortunately many popular writers ... [have] used animal behaviour as a justification for what the authors *like* to think about human behaviour

... We can't use animal behaviour to justify human foibles, and decide we're destined to behave with violence or force or male dominance because it's an irrepressible part of our 'animal nature'. These are misleading and dangerous assumptions. (Strum, 1977, p. 76)

14. See Sperling (1991, p. 18). The diversity-within-species approach is reflected in Jan Aldenhoven and Glen Carruthers's important film *Kangaroos: Faces in the Mob* (1994: Cape Green Wildlife Films, Australia).

## References

Birke, Lynda (1991). 'Science, feminism and animal natures II: feminist critiques and the place of animals in science', *Women's Studies International Forum*, **14**: 451–8.

Birke, Lynda (1994). *Feminism, Animals and Science: The Naming of the Shrew.* Buckingham: Open University Press.

Bleier, Ruth (1984). *Science and Gender.* London: Pergamon.

Coward, Ros (1988). 'The sex-life of stick insects', in *Female Desire.* London: Paladin.

Crowther, Barbara (1995). 'Towards a feminist critique of television natural history programmes', in Penny Florence and Dee Reynolds (eds), *Feminist Subjects, Multi-media: Cultural Methodologies.* Manchester: Manchester University Press.

Gould, Stephen Jay (1991). *Ever Since Darwin.* London: Penguin.

Haraway, Donna (1978). 'Animal sociology and a natural economy of the body politic', *Signs*, **4**: 21–60.

Haraway, Donna (1988). 'Primatology is politics by other means', in Ruth Bleier (ed.), *Feminist Approaches to Science.* London: Pergamon.

Haraway, Donna (1992). *Primate Visions: Gender, Race and Nature in the World of Modern Science.* London: Verso.

Harding, Sandra (1986). *The Science Question in Feminism.* Milton Keynes: Open University Press.

Hrdy, Sarah B. (1981). *The Woman That Never Evolved.* Cambridge, MA: Harvard University Press.

Irigaray, Luce (1985). *This Sex Which Is Not One.* Ithaca, NY: Cornell University Press.

Kennedy, J. S. (1992). *The New Anthropomorphism.* Cambridge: Cambridge University Press.

Martin, Emily (1991). 'The egg and the sperm: how science has constructed a romance based on stereotypical male–female roles', *Signs*, **16**(3): 485–501.

Mills, Stephen (1989). 'The entertainment imperative: wildlife films and conservation', *ECOS*, **10**(1): 3–7.

Reed, Evelyn (1978). *Sexism and Science*. New York: Pathfinder Press.

Rowe, Alex (1990). 'All us animals', in 'Life of Trials' supplement, *BBC Wildlife*, 8(10).

Sperling, Susan (1991). 'Baboons with briefcases: feminism, functionalism, and sociobiology in the evolution of primate gender', *Signs*, 17(1): 1–27.

Strum, Shirley (1975). 'Life with the Pumphouse Gang', *National Geographic*, May, 147(5): 672–91.

Strum, Shirley (1977). *Westways*, March.

Trudell, Bonnie Nelson (1993). *Doing Sex Education: Gender Politics and Schooling*. London: Routledge.

Tudge, Colin (1995). 'In praise of anthropomorphism', *Biologist*, 42(1): 8.

Warren, Carol (1988). *Gender Issues in Field Research*. Newbury Park, CA: Sage.

Wilson, Edward O. (1975). *Sociobiology: The New Synthesis*. Cambridge, MA: Harvard University Press.

# 5

# Pedagogic Panic or Deconstructive Dilemma? Gay Genes in the Popular Press

*Deborah Lynn Steinberg*

## Introduction

The 'gay gene' story broke on 16 July 1993 in the journal *Science* as a report from Dean Hamer and his research team, based at the National Institutes of Health in the USA. On the same day, the story was picked up in the British context by *The Times* and the *Independent*. On 17 July, all of the main British broadsheets and tabloids carried the story. Discussion continued in *The Times* and the *Independent* until 24 July and 19 July respectively, while disappearing from the tabloids after the first day.[1] It is worth noting that Hamer's investigation into the possible genetic basis of homosexuality grew out of his research on AIDS-related cancers, a point which some of the news reports picked up. Thus AIDS was the immediate conceptual frame and referent for both the gene research and its coverage in the popular press.

Hamer's alleged findings of genetic links to homosexuality were based, as Ewing (1995) notes, on a two-part study of 40 pairs of gay brothers. The first part involved drawing up family trees with the aim of identifying other gay relatives – the result of which appeared to show more gay relatives on the maternal than on the paternal side of the family. Hamer and his team inferred from this a pattern of maternal inheritance (that is, that homosexuality was passed down as a recessive trait on the X chromosome). The second part involved an analysis of the DNA of the gay brothers 'to see if they had inherited genes in common that could, by inference, be linked to their sexuality' (p. 2). In addition to his reported findings, Hamer concluded the *Science* article with a plea that the research should not be misused to intensify stigmatization of and discrimination against gay people (p. 5). Some discussion of the research methodology, albeit with varying degrees of detail,[2] and acknowledgement of Hamer's caveat were also picked up by all the papers.

On the face of it, and as Hamer's team seemed to be uncomfortably aware on evidence of their caveat, the very notion of a 'gay gene' would seem entirely consistent with the underpinning assumptions of both scientific and common-sense homophobias. Its plausibility, for example, is dependent on the presumption of 'gay' not only as a unified social category, but as a singular, organic *problem* from which can be inferred biological origins. Such assumptions have underscored sexuality sciences since the nineteenth century where '[h]omosexuals were one of a number of . . . *internal others* explored for stigmata of degeneracy within the West – alongside criminals, prostitutes, the feebleminded – whose bodies were believed to carry the germs of ruin' (Terry, 1997, p. 274).[3] More recently, biomedical AIDS research has constituted a dramatic site for the reconstitution of such 'languages of risk'[4] in which germs and gays elide as 'deviant', dangerous and deadly bodies (Patton, 1985; Watney, 1988; Redman, 1997). Against this backdrop, 'gay genes' inevitably resonate with, indeed seem simply to offer an alternative, hereditarian version of, pre-existing venereological common senses surrounding homosexuality and (and *as*) sexually transmitted disease.

The 'gay gene' also fits with the by now iconographic parade of organic and social conditions which are said to have genetic origins. Gene discovery stories, from cancer to crime, from schizophrenia to anorexia, have become a commonplace feature of both scientific and popular discourse. Typically, it is those conditions or characteristics already construed as medical or social problems that become candidates for the seeking of 'candidate genes'.[5] 'Treatment', 'cure', 'prevention', 'solution' are all implicit in the diagnostic framing of both the science and the objects of its inquiry. In this context, the ascription of genes, with their inevitably pathological connotations, to homosexuality is hardly surprising.

The neo-essentialism implicit in genetic science itself has its adjunct in the dominant pathologized 'otherness' characteristically ascribed to lesbians and gays in the popular press. As many commentators[6] have noted, social conservative moral panic at the presence or possibilities of lesbians and gays in schools, making families, forging (organized) claims for civil equality, have appeared over recent years with clichéd regularity. Debbie Epstein's (1997) analysis of the myriad antecedents to the Jane Brown panic provides a salient illustration.[7] If such notions constitute the dominant conceptual field in which an imperative search for 'gay genes' was imaginable in the first place, its putative 'discovery' would seem only further to entrench them.

Given the ways in which 'gay genes' seem to embody the homophobic trajectories that have broadly characterized both sexuality science and popular reportage, one might therefore expect that the press treatment of the 'gay gene' discovery would have inevitably followed in similar suit – just another homosexual monster story. Yet as we shall see, when 'gay genes' hit the popular press, a replay of such familiar ground is what *did not happen*. Indeed, if anything, the 'gay gene' stories marked not only a moment of *departure* from, but a significant *destabilization* of the familiar phobic narratives of homosexuality.

This chapter will attempt to account for the surprising displacement of these narratives. Through a close examination of British reportage, I shall trace the ways in which the 'gay gene' stories marked a point of convergence for a number of discourses, in particular those of science, homosexuality and abortion, whose interplay served to rupture dominant homophobic common sense.

## On the horns of a moral dilemma: (im)partial science?

If the 'master narratives' of homosexuality are predominantly framed through the horror genre, those of science are rather more ambivalent. Press take-up and treatment of scientific discourse characteristically occupy three competing narrative conventions. Perhaps the most salient and familiar of these constitutes science as a reservoir of natural facts, an objective, transcendent endeavour beyond politics and even meaning, a society of experts and body of expertise whose due is deference and celebration; a sweeping tide of progress, intrinsically progressive, rushing toward Disney's Tomorrowland in all its incipient wonder.

Yet science also has its monster narratives, coexisting contrarily, and yet in obstinate synchronicity with the presumptions of its objectivity and rational benevolence. The notion of science in the service of an evil agenda, for example, is deployed in the various genres of 'Hitler horror', with their spectres of human experimentation, genocidal apocalypse, reproductive slavery, clones and (sub)human–animal hybrids. As reference point or spectacle, such dystopian mythologies bespeak both an elaborated cultural recognition of and latent anxieties about the disproportionate powers of contemporary science. Yet if the figure of the mad scientist embodies such anxieties, it also, through its baroque grotesquerie, neutralizes them. Against such a yardstick, science-as-usual can appear banalized, easily recuperated, reconfirmed.

The interplay of these narratives can be seen to be played out graphically in the ambivalent rumblings of celebration and disquiet that have greeted contemporary genetics. As suggested above, we are fast becoming accustomed to the 'discoveries' of an ever-widening array of genes. Yet if heroic promises of rescue, cure and resurrection seem embodied in the mastery of molecular space, so too do dispossessions and annihilation. Indeed, the gene has quickly become embedded in popular vernacular as the quintessential metaphor of origins, the protein (and protean) medium of destiny, a higher order as marvellously mundane as an architectural blueprint, and yet a weapon, in the wrong hands of course, of mass destruction.

When genetic discoveries seem to bespeak noble motives, the prevention of 'serious' disease, for example, the science goes largely unproblematized. Announcements are made, embellished with wishful extrapolations about treatments and cures for the future, the only caveat that this is only an early stage; more work needs to be done. The reported 'discoveries' of oncogenes,[8] genes for cystic fibrosis, Duchenne Muscular Dystrophy and Huntington's chorea, for example, are classic examples.[9] Indeed, just recently, as I was sitting down to breakfast, the radio announced the 'successful' genetic engineering of mice with three times the normal muscle mass. This research, it was asserted, would lead to greater understanding and possible cure of muscular dystrophy. End of story.

On the flip side, it is no accident that of all the new reproductive technologies on the horizon, it has been the prospect of cloning – the interbreeding of human and animal, and germ-line experimentation on human embryos – that has generated the greatest public consternation. Not only do these practices seem most to fit the clichéd iconography of fallen science/scientist, but their perceived extremity produces a permissive space in which the powerful can momentarily be identified as 'other', the mighty brought low, the insider revealed as outcast. The fears invoked in the recent moral panic about the cloning of the sheep 'Dolly' played precisely to the conventions of a modern Frankenstein story. It was the scientist, the hubris his creation embodied, who was taken to presage disaster. The quaint appellation of 'Dolly' provided the point of identification, for an innocent and vulnerable 'us', the potential human objects of the morbid, metamorphic fantasies of the scientist-who-would-be-God.

More often than not, however, it is a third narrative, the *moral dilemma*, rather than the moral panic, which greets the perceived slippages of science from its moral high ground. The moral dilemma posits that while science itself is a neutral, objective practice, it none the less in particular instances generates difficult ethical questions. These questions typically focus on the uses and potential abuses of the science. Fears tend to be displaced on to other, 'biased' interests (commercial, governmental or 'society', for example), rather than those of scientists themselves. Thus the 'moral dilemma' is, in this sense, a narrative frame in which both the benevolent and monster narratives of science can be simultaneously retained, even as the former is delicately questioned and the latter apparently disclaimed.

*Mapping moral minefields*
Broadsheet headlines marking the discovery of 'gay genes' explicitly framed the story as a moral dilemma:

Gay Gene Raises Host of Issues (16 July 1993, Connor, *Independent*)

'Gay Gene' Raises Screening Fear (17 July 1993, Hawkes, *The Times*)

Scientists Claimed This Week That Homosexuality in Men is Influenced by Genes. But Who Does the Discovery Help? Tim Radford Reports on the Moral Minefield of Genetics. (17 July 1993, Radford, *Guardian*)[10]

The tabloids also announced the 'gay gene' discovery with notable ambivalence. The *Daily Mail* headline read: Genes Gays and a Moral Minefield (Jones, 17 July 1993). The *Sun* (Watson, 17 July 1993) juxtaposed three bold-print headlines for the same story:

Mums Pass Gay Gene to Sons Say Doctors [main headline]

Parents may demand abortions after tests [sub-headline]

'Don't try to eradicate us' [bottom line, credited to Gay Rights Group Stonewall]

The *Daily Mirror* (Swain, 17 July 1993) similarly juxtaposed:

> Battle Looms over Scientific Discovery [top of the page]
>
> Men Inherit Gay Genes from Mum [main headline]
>
> Inherited link is proved [inset mid-story]
>
> Seek out and Destroy Fears [inset sub-story headline]

Encapsulated in these headlines are a number of contestations about science – its rational precision, its claims to political neutrality, its (disinterested) moral agency.

### Tentative truths

Ambivalence around the notion for example that there *is* a 'gay gene', that scientists 'proved' the link, emerged in both the tabloids and the broadsheets, albeit in quite distinct ways. In the tabloids, as suggested by the *Mirror* inset mid-story headline, the 'fact' of gay genes seemed to be taken as a given. Indeed, as Steve Jones[11] himself asserted (but did not explain) in his article for the *Daily Mail* ( 17 July 1993):

> There have been many earlier claims of a 'gay gene'. All were rubbish. This one almost certainly is not. The gene has been tracked to a short section of DNA. Although there are hundreds of genes hidden in there, the one for homosexual behaviour is probably among them.

The literal text of the passage is, in fact, an optimistic rather than absolute reading of the factual existence of 'gay genes'. Yet, Jones's own media prominence as a genetics expert would seem to render the 'probably' and 'almost certainly', juxtaposed with the 'all were rubbish' of prior claims, as more a statement of scientific modesty than one of doubt. In both the *Mirror* and the *Sun* very brief summaries of Hamer *et al.*'s research methods were presented without comment (or explanation); the 'dilemma' instead, as I shall discuss further below, centred on the implications of the 'find'.

The broadsheets, by contrast, provided much more pointed equivocation both on 'gay genes' as facts and genetic science as a stable body of expertise. Terms such as 'precisely located' or 'pinpointed' juxtaposed against 'theory' or 'claimed' suggested a more resistant relationship to the science. In an article appearing in the *Independent* for example, reporters Connor and Wilkie state:

> Scientists can now locate the *precise position* of a gene and find out what it is responsible for, and what variations of that gene exist. (18 July 1993, emphasis mine)

Yet, later in that same article, 'gay genes' appear to be disclaimed from this narrative:

> It is easier to say what has not been discovered: the researchers in the United States whose findings were announced last week have *not* found a gene that causes homosexuality and they have *not* proved that homosexuality is heredity. They believe they have evidence linking a region of the X chromosome, which men inherit from their mothers – with the sexual orientation of some gay men ... (Ibid., original emphasis)

These passages are significant for their validation of the rational precision of genetic science on the one hand and, on the other, the instability of the 'gay gene' as a *particular* fact. At the same time, the attribution of 'they believe' suggests, as did Jones's comment discussed above, that grandiosity is a product not so much of scientific claims but of their misinterpretation (for which this article is presumably intended as a corrective).

Yet both the *Independent* and *The Times*, in addition to providing considerably more detail about Hamer *et al.*'s research methods, also raised tentative questions about their validity.

> Research has found a common genetic pattern in 33 pairs of homosexual brothers, but other scientists say the evidence so far is only inferential and *the statistical basis of the study is weak*. Evidence has been growing that there is an inherited component in homosexuality. It occurs more often, for example, in identical twins ... (Hawkes, *The Times*, 16 July 1993, emphasis mine)

> The scientists do not know why seven of the 40 pairs of gay brothers do not appear to have the same genetic markers. Dr Hamer said these gay

men may have inherited other genes that are associated with homosexuality or they might be influenced by environmental factors or life experiences. (Connor, *Independent*, 16 July 1993)

In both of these passages, however, the caveats about the weaknesses of the study are immediately recuperated through the flow of the article: in *The Times* article by an abrupt, *non sequitur* (and empty) reassertion of the evidentiary basis for the claim of a 'genetic component to homosexuality'; in the *Independent* by an alternative genetics-led explanation of homosexuality in the brothers who lacked the expected 'markers'.[12]

The fundamental premise of the claim of a 'gay gene', i.e. that 'gay' can be treated as a 'factually' unified identity/behavioural category, was also questioned – albeit in only one editorial, again in the *Independent*:

> Um, but it's absurd isn't it? This notion that homosexuality, or the predisposition thereto, has been genetically located … For a start, homosexuality is an abstract noun, a cultural construct with a short historical life, as was famously pointed out by Foucault …
>
> Genes decide this. Genes decide that. Genes affect this. Genes affect that. It would be extremely odd if they didn't affect sexuality, since that would rather imply that our sexuality had no basis in our physical being. But it is cultures that decide what constitutes homosexual behaviour or a homosexual disposition. Indeed, one could argue that our own culture has yet to make its own decision on this point. (Fenton, *Independent*, 19 July 1993, original emphasis)

Here the perceived absurdity of a universalized (and transhistorical) *inference* of 'gay genes' underpinned a radical destabilization of the guiding assumptions about the truth values of genetic science and expertise that otherwise, at least partially, constituted the 'gay gene' reportage. In the balance of broadsheet reporting, however, the 'dilemma' about scientific accuracy was framed more tentatively, and relegated to the background of more urgently deployed concerns about the moral status and potential (mis)use of the science.

*A balanced morality*
Despite the fact that it may rarely be carried out in practice, the notion of *balance* is central to common-sense claims of both journalistic and scientific integrity. The distinction between broadsheets and tabloids as high and

low culture respectively rests largely on the extent to which they are taken to participate (or not) in the liberal rationality of *giving both (or all) sides*. The very framing of the 'gay gene' stories as a moral dilemma would seem to signal such balance, indeed to function as a prescriptively recuperative metaphor for scientificity itself. Thus the interests of journalistic balance were contiguous both with concerns about a possibly unbalanced (i.e. biased) science and with an imperative to recover a middle (i.e. neutral) ground.

> Steve Jones, professor of genetics at University College, London, said 'What I overwhelmingly hope for is that this research will not be used to make moral judgements. The findings are scientifically fascinating, but socially irrelevant.' (Connor and Whitfield, *Independent*, 17 July 1993)

> Discovering that homosexuality may have a genetic component tells us nothing about the moral or social status of homosexuality. If we choose to classify homosexuality as a disease, we have made a moral choice: it does not follow from the science of molecular genetics. There are no values to be discovered in the double helix of DNA. (Connor and Wilkie, *Independent*, 18 July 1993)

As these passages suggest, the association of genes not only with homosexuality but specifically with *homophobia* problematized the notion that the science was morally neutral. The impetus to recuperate scientific integrity seemed to require several rather paradoxical disassociations. For example, the notion that 'the findings are scientifically fascinating, but socially irrelevant' suggests that in a science of homosexuality, the science can none the less be disaggregated from the object of its scrutiny; the meaning of 'gay', prerequisite to the notion of its genetic inheritance, can nevertheless be disaggregated from the gene/tics. Jones resolves this tension in a claim for a homosexuality science which has no moral meaning; Connor and Wilkie argue that the science has, in itself, no moral implications.

Significantly, the neutralization of the moral *status* of scientific knowledge depends here on a disaggregation of scientific from moral *agency*. The 'we' of Connor and Wilkie's claim articulates a displacement of moral agency on to those ('us') who, specifically, do not exercise scientific agency. Since scientific problem-solving is disassociated from problematization, scientists cannot be held accountable either for the social consequences of their practices or for their own take-up of common-sense problematizations. Moreover, even as moral agency is dislocated from scientific agency, so too is the *moment* for moral considerations. As Jones states in his *Daily Mail* article: 'Scientists cannot evade their responsibility; they, after all, have provided the opportunity for [moral] choices, but they must not be the people who decide. Society must do that' (17 July 1993). There is a rather stunning sleight of hand here, from an assertion of scientific responsibility followed by its immediate denial – projected instead, *post facto* on to 'society'.[13] Jones's perspective both here and in his statement quoted in the *Independent* (above) is significant for the way it seems, on the one hand, to locate science within a social context while, on the other, posits that its *use* (or misuse) is an extra-scientific phenomenon. Implicit here is the rather odd suggestion that scientists, indeed scientists *alone*, do not 'use' the artefacts of their own practice.

The idealization of this displaced '*post-facto*' investment of scientific moral agency in 'society' emerged in several articles as a call for a (legislatively drafted) 'gene charter' to control the 'misuse' of genetic information. In the *Daily Mirror*, for example, this call for a 'gene charter' emerged specifically as an antidote to the potentially *monstrous* implications of genetic science:

Patrick Dixon, author of *The Genetic Revolution* says a 'gene charter' was urgently needed to avoid abuses.

'Every new gene discovery brings closer the horror of eugenics, designer families with embryos selected for intelligence, hair colour or sexual orientation' says Dixon. (Swain, 17 July 1993)

The 'gene charter', invoked here as the mechanism for the achievement of scientific balance, also bespeaks journalistic balance. The rational, democratic, public interest connotations attending the notion of a 'charter' not only discursively neutralize the horror *narrative* but, in so doing, offer a symbolic containment of the material possibilities of an horrific science. It is significant that neither the *Mirror* nor any of the other stories taking up the 'gene charter' question saw the need to provide substantive elaboration on what such a 'charter' would constitute or how it would work. The invocation alone seemed to be taken as enough to signal the containment of a safe genetics.

The final foreclosure on the attribution of moral meaning to scientific agency emerged in the reassertion of a characteristic element of both

Utopian and dystopian narratives of scientific progress – that, good or bad, it is inevitable:

> The question then is where and how to draw the line. Some would argue that scientists should stop meddling with our genes, that their research should cease immediately. *This, even if desirable, would be almost impossible to enforce.* But critics may well ask why 26 nations are contributing a total of $2 billion to attempt to map the entire human genetic make-up when their governments have not, apparently, given more than a second's thought to possible safeguards against *the results being misused.* (*Independent*, 18 July 1993, my emphasis)

The notion that even the undesirable activities of science are ultimately outside social control significantly undercuts calls for social regulation of scientific products. The pessimism of this passage is notable for the way in which it offers a critical recognition of science *as* a social/moral practice only to characterize that recognition as futile.[14]

## Abortive anxieties: mothers make/break gay sons

As many of the passages quoted above suggest, it was specifically the fear of eugenic applications of the 'gay gene' science that constituted its perceived monstrous possibilities. Indeed, implicit in the 'gay gene' as a diagnostic 'fact' is the notion of a 'therapeutic abortion'. Here the seemingly easy slippage between 'gay genes' and those for 'other diseases' could not but evoke both the material and conceptual terrain of prenatal diagnostic technologies. Juxtaposed with a scientific monster narrative (only partially contained by the displacement of moral agency onto 'society'), it was perhaps inevitable that abortion, with its own distinctive monster myth-ologies, would become a central discursive resource for the articulation of the 'gay gene' moral dilemma. In this context the spectre, as many papers had it, of 'gay genocide'[15] became a point of convergence for a network of anxieties around diagnostic imperialism, women's reproductive choice and, saliently, the power of mothers to make and break sons.

*Mothers make gay sons; recessive narratives and the Freud connection*
> The researchers concentrated on the X chromosome which men inherit only from their mothers, after studying family histories that tended to show that homosexuality was passed down through the maternal side. (Hawkes, *The Times*, 16 July 1993)

Until these findings began to surface, it was generally assumed that homosexuality was a matter of free choice conditioned by upbringing. Parents may have been held to play a large role in this shaping of their children's sexual orientation. Freud and his followers have pointed accusing fingers at over-loving mothers and inadequate fathers. But parents were not thought responsible for actually passing on a tendency to homosexuality, like one to left-handedness. It is unfortunate that once again mothers seem likely to take the main blame. (*Independent*, 16 July 1993)

The preoccupation with pathological and pathogenic mothers in the face of 'deviations' from conservative familial discourse is as endemic a feature of popular representation as it is a cliché of psychoanalysis. The take-up of this discourse in the search for 'gay genes' is precisely suggested in Hawkes's note of the scientific concentration on families where a maternal line of inheritance could be inferred.[16] Simon LeVay, whose research on 'gay brains' set the stage for Hamer *et al.*'s study, was also quoted as being influenced by the 'Freudian view of the origin of homosexuality' (Connor, *Independent*, 16 July 1993). The notion of homosexuality as a recessive, maternally inherited predisposition or trait both reinvests in and reifies the psychoanalytic narrative of homogenerative mothers. Indeed, 'gay genes' would seem to confirm the impossibility of true Oedipal separation.[17] Here the 'inadequate father' becomes redundant as maternal influence appears to be singularly 'to blame' for the compromised masculinities of gay sons – mama's boys truly, after all. 'Gay genes', maternally inherited, also recapitulate the embodied effeminacies – limp-wristed, feminine-voiced – of popular stereotypes of gay men, intrinsically flawed through their direct corporeal links with femaleness.

*Mothers break gay sons: endangered embryos and gay genocide*

The research published in the learned American journal *Science* raises disturbing ethical issues. Could, for example, this discovery eventually lead to ante-natal tests being offered to pregnant women who might choose to abort a foetus carrying such a gene? The very idea fills me – and I suspect most people – with revulsion. (Jones, *Daily Mail*, 17 July 1993)

Now Mums-to-be may be offered tests to discover if their boy is going to be homosexual and doctors fear parents could decide on abortion rather than have a gay son. (Watson, *Sun*, 17 July 1993)

A programme of screening foetuses for the relevant gene and then offering mothers the possibility of abortion (as is done with major congenital defects like Down's Syndrome) would come up against rival claims of civil liberties. A woman's right to abortion on her own chosen grounds would have to be weighed against the potential right of a foetus to develop in its own way and by implication the right of other adults to live in the way they prefer without stigma. (*The Times*, 17 July 1993)

A House of Commons Early Day Motion was put down yesterday by pro-life Liberal Democrat David Alton, and signed by 30 MPs, calling for a gene charter to tackle the problem.

A Spokesman for the Campaign for Homosexual Equality warned: 'Once you start offering the facility to choose babies of a certain hair colour, skin colour, sexual orientation etc., you are on a very slippery slope. Gay people have as much right to be born as anyone else.' (Swain, *Daily Mirror*, 17 July 1993)

Monstrous mothers are stock characters in both master narratives of homosexuality and anti-abortion discourse. In both contexts, endangerment is constituted as intrinsic to the maternal body and will. As these passages illustrate, the take-up of anti-abortion discourse in the 'gay gene' stories signals a number of startling narrative shifts. For example, mothers, in this context, become responsible not only for homosexuality, but for homophobia. The investment of 'society' in eugenic selections and the incipient homophobia of the 'gay gene' science itself are thus displaced on to women who, given the choice, would choose, it is asserted, to annihilate gays. This construction of homo-destructive mothers is entirely congruent with, indeed foregrounded through, the anti-abortion common sense of pregnancy as an adversarial condition – 'two people in one body, one of whom is about to be murdered'.[18]

There is, in this formulation, a latent problematization of the 'gay gene' science for its provision of what is perceived to be yet another (illegitimate) rationale for abortion.[19] As a consequence, the 'fact' of gay genes is implicitly recuperated. However, it is a woman's right to choose, rather than homosexuality science (or institutional homophobia), that is constituted as the harbinger of gay genocide, the threat to gay rights 'to be born', 'to live the way they prefer, without stigma'. Hence the call for a 'gene charter' which pits gay freedom against women's choice and reconstitutes gay rights struggle as a function of anti-abortion politics. Gays, here, elide with endangered embryos, claimed as point of projective identification for the genocidal potentialities of diagnostic genetics. Indeed, in the face of such abortive anxieties, gays, even for the iconographically right-wing, gay-bashing *Sun*, become momentarily transformed from repressed 'other' into the rest of 'us'.

## Here there be (no) monsters: (re)defining homosexuality

Amidst the narrative oscillations between 'good' and 'bad' science and the displaced anxieties surrounding eugenics-minded mothers, the 'gay gene' stories appear to destabilize the characteristic disease-association of dominant discourses of homosexuality. Steve Jones, for example, stated baldly: 'Let us dispose of one issue straight away: the fact that homosexuality can be coded for by genes does not make it into a "disease" or a defect' (*Daily Mail*, 17 July 1993). Two articles from the *Independent* rather amusingly posited that gays ('gay genes') might even carry an evolutionary advantage:

> One suggestion [as to why the 'gay gene' did not die out through natural selection] is that a genetic predisposition would somehow confer an advantage to sisters of the man, because in primitive societies he would be less likely to set up his own home and more likely to help raise his sisters' children. But Professor Jones said there is 'absolutely no evidence of this'. (Connor, *Independent*, 17 July 1993)

> Some genes do give rise to what is inherently a disease, such as sickle cell anaemia. It might seem tempting to eliminate this gene, but it turns out [it] ... also protects against malaria. What other functions might a gene for homosexuality perform? We have no idea. (Connor and Wilkie, *Independent*, 18 July 1993)

The 'great gays' argument, so characteristically prominent in the wake of Section 28 debates of the late 1980s,[20] was also reinvoked in resistance to the prospect of gay screening:

> Leaving aside the Hitlerian eugenic attitudes implied, only a glance is required at the list of homosexual geniuses down the ages – from Michelangelo to Britten, Bacon and Nureyev – to show the catastrophic loss that [screening] would inflict on mankind and not just by

eliminating geniuses. The contribution of homosexuals to making society more civilised and less brutal can hardly be overestimated. (*Independent*, 16 July 1993)

Yet, as both the evolution and 'great gays' positions illustrate, the destabilization of the homosexuality-as-disease narrative was highly ambivalent. Not only are disease referents explicitly retained as analogies, as for example with cystic fibrosis, but homosexuality as a problem or abnormality, albeit benign, is reasserted. The evolutionary picture of 'successful' masculinity measured in terms of heterosexual dominance and reproduction is only rather dubiously liberalized with the possibility of gay men as helpful 'sisters' to their heterosexual sisters. The projection of the modern notion of homosexual identity into 'prehistory' has an interesting double movement suggesting homosexuality as, on the one hand, original to the human condition and, on the other, as an intrinsically and transhistorically subordinate form of humanity. In this context, even 'natural selection' takes on an ambivalent meaning with the implication that if nature did not eradicate this 'abnormality' (even if 'we have no idea' why), then neither should we.

### Minor monsters: from disease to 'minor ailment'

Within the framework of liberal resistance to eugenic screening of gays, then, notions of homosexuality-as-disease were largely retained, but in reconstituted forms and demoted in their importance. This was played out in a number of ways. For example, even Steve Jones, in the very same article as his stated rejection of the association, went on to make an analogy between the genetic predisposition to homosexuality with disease conditions such as diabetes, cancers, haemophilia and with the minor and correctable condition of myopia. Of the latter, which he himself suffers, he stated: 'Now I am old and know that [myopia] is genetic. It makes no difference to the treatment. I just carry on wearing the glasses' (Jones, *Daily Mail*, 17 July 1993). Indeed, the lateral associations in the flow of most articles placed homosexuality in the framework of serious disease, even where there were graphic rejections of that formulation. There is, moreover, an interesting series of slippages in Jones's reference first to a 'gay gene' (where gay is not a disease) to the slight abnormality to the notion of (small, adjustive) treatment. This extraordinary reconstruction of homosexuality as a 'minor ailment' was a consistent theme across the 'gay gene' reportage:

A British expert on medical ethics warns that should the theory prove correct and a prenatal technique become available to test for the gene, new laws may be needed to prevent the abortion of foetuses carrying it. 'We are testing foetuses in many ways in the womb and are aborting them if they have sometimes *relatively minor abnormalities*' says Richard Nicholson, editor of the *Bulletin of Medical Ethics* ... We must have a wider public debate about how much difference we will accept in society. (Swain, *Daily Mirror*, 17 July 1993, my emphasis)

Richard Nicholson, editor of the *Bulletin of Medical Ethics* said he hoped the debate would highlight the fine line between *minor abnormalities in the foetus that should not lead to termination* and more serious problems that did. 'I don't regard homosexuality as an abnormality that needs to be changed back to heterosexuality.' (Connor and Whitfield, *Independent*, 17 July 1993, my emphasis)

It is here that we begin to understand that this is not an issue for homosexuals alone. One in 30 children is born with a genetic problem of some kind – blindness, deafness, mental handicap for example. Perhaps we can accept the rights of their parents to decide that these are handicaps with which they would rather not cope. But what of a gene that predisposes to cancer or heart disease? ... And that leaves aside all the other things that cause children to disappoint their parents. (*Independent*, 18 July 1993)

The emphasis in these passages on tolerance (or, at the greatest extreme, treatment) of homosexuality is clearly underpinned by a construction of abortion as the greater social ill. It is also possible that a more general liberal shift in popular sensibilities around homosexuality might have foregrounded the possibility that screening out homosexuality could be perceived as 'not an issue for homosexuals alone'. Whatever the case, the demotion of homosexuality to 'minor disease' was widely perceived as a key basis for the invalidation of eradication as an answer to homosexuality. It is, perhaps, not surprising that treatment (including gene therapy) emerged in the tabloids to resolve tensions between competing monster narratives of eugenic science, homgenerative/destructive mothers and abortion:

We are not prisoners of our genes. Science can reveal what is in them, but it can also treat and cure what it finds – if society decides that it should. Genetic research is only the beginning of that process, not the end. (Jones, *Daily Mail*, 17 July 1993)

Recent advances have made gene therapy a reality. The treatment has the potential to help thousands of sufferers of genetic diseases caused by single gene defects. Doctors hope one day to treat cancer by manipulating genes. (Watson, *Sun*, 17 July 1993)

Dr Tony Vickers, former head of Britain's work on the Human Genome Project, says the ethical issues involved in gene therapy are not only which problems should be tackled but also ensuring that any successful therapies become widely available. He says most countries resist any genetic engineering that would result in permanent and inheritable changes to genes, as opposed to therapeutic work. (Swain, *Daily Mirror*, 17 July 1993)

The 'treatment' option, though only laterally associated with but not explicitly linked to 'gay genes', clearly reinvests in the master narrative of homosexuality while disclaiming its most extreme implications. Indeed, against the possibility of 'gay genocide', the invocation of treatment represents the possibility of (if not the call for) a more tolerant view of homosexuality as well as a more balanced, even anti-homophobic science. In the broadsheets, by contrast, 'treatment' was more likely to be characterized in similar terms as eradication. Connor, writing for the *Independent*, for example, stated: '[a] principle concern is that people who perceive homosexuality as an abnormality will call for attempts to diagnose it, perhaps by a pre-natal test, or attempt to "cure" it by developing so-called treatments' (16 July 1993).

If anti-abortion discourse framed a highly contradictory articulation of resistance to homophobic selection (and to the disease-construction of homosexuality), so too, at moments, did forms (or disclaimers) of racism.

Does this mean being gay is a disease? No, this discovery merely means that the variation in human behaviour mirrors to some degree the variation in human DNA . . . Some variation is completely determined by the genes; whether someone has blue eyes or brown. But no one suggests having brown eyes is a disease or that being blue-eyed has greater moral value. (Connor and Wilkie, *Independent*, 18 July 1993)

Different societies have always held different beliefs about some or all of these conditions. In India, thousands of abortions are carried out each year for the simple genetic reason that the foetus is a girl. To me, this is absolutely wrong, but I say this as a human being, not as a scientist, and my views represent those of the society I come from which, thank God, had advanced way beyond that. In modern Britain, homosexuality is a legal, acceptable preference. Science neither can, nor should, alter that. (Jones, *Daily Mail*, 17 July 1993)

The disingenuity of the references to and rejection of racial hygiene ideology implicit in both these passages is striking. While it may be true that blue eyes, for example, have not been associated with disease, brown-eyed people have frequently been subject to pathologized discourse and blue eyes have most certainly been invested with notions of both moral and racial superiority. Connor and Wilkie's ill-chosen metaphor (and wishful thinking) here seems to reinforce rather than disclaim the very embedded-ness of moral discourses that accrue even to seemingly innocuous physical characteristics. Moreover, the attempt to redefine homosexuality as a morally neutral behavioural variation is significantly compromised by its reinvestment in biological discourse. Perhaps more disturbingly, Jones's explicit anti-homophobia, claimed as a modern British common sense, is articulated through a graphically colonialist (Orientalist) evolutionary discourse. In this formulation, science is characteristically relocated within civilized sensibilities; monstrous 'othering' is, reassuringly, produced only by (other) monstrous 'others'.

*The discrimination debates*
The partial destabilization of the disease discourse of homosexuality was perhaps most emphatically illustrated in the preoccupation in all the papers with the question of homophobic discrimination and gay rights. Aside from (although also incorporating) the question of eugenic screen-ing, significant attention was given to debates about whether the gay gene discovery would intensify the social stigmatization of homosexuality or, alternatively, would provide a 'natural' basis for the extension of civil rights protections.

The happiest outcome of the latest research would be to reduce the intolerance that homosexuals encounter in virtually all fields except show business and the rag trade. Religious fundamentalists would find it harder to label homosexual behaviour a sin. Parents could cast aside fears of their children being corrupted by gay teachers. More importantly, homophobes might come to appreciate that sexuality is an infinitely complicated matter, in which nature and nurture play roles that are likely to remain hard to unravel. (*Independent*, 16 July 1993)

Michael's reaction to news of the gay gene was double-edged. On the one hand he fears there could be some lunatics who would take this discovery as an excuse for arguing foetuses carrying the gene should be aborted. On the other, it should make no difference since homosexuality ought to be accepted as natural anyway. But if the scientists prove their theory, it could make a profound difference to family relationships. 'It might encourage young people to tell their parents. They should know they haven't done anything wrong.' (Swain, *Daily Mirror*, 17 July 1993)

Even among gay activists there is disagreement about whether proof of a biological tendency would result in more, or less, discrimination. On the one hand, the fact of genetic basis would undermine the idea that homosexuality is a form of moral turpitude . . . In these terms, demonstrating that a homosexual life is not chosen in free will would result in more protection and less vilification. But those who defend the idea of homosexuality as an alternative lifestyle . . . reject such biological determinism. They do not wish to be excused their sexual orientation on the grounds that they cannot help it, but to be accepted as they are. There is a fear that those who regard homosexuality as inherently deviant and unacceptable could use such a scientific breakthrough as a way of eliminating the tendency altogether. (*The Times*, 17 July 1993)

Whatever the ambivalence surrounding the causes and status of homosexuality (and in part made possible by it), the discrimination debates emphatically constituted *homophobia* as a problem – which the finding of 'gay genes' would either ameliorate or add to. In all three passages, it is the homophobe, rather than the homosexual, that emerges as disclaimed 'other' – 'lunatic' at worst, irrational at best – who embodies the threat of gay discrimination. Indeed, the homosexual monster narrative itself, with its characteristic themes of 'sin', 'corruption by gay teachers', doing 'wrong' to one's parents, is graphically reconstituted as a *homophobic* monster narrative. In this context, gay rights activists (or their supporters) are discursively relocated, both in terms of victimhood *and* affirmative social agency, on the moral high ground. Moreover, although displaced on to the putatively non-scientific figure of the homophobe, homophobia nevertheless constituted a more or less implicit yardstick against which the 'gay gene' science was, in the immediate sense, to be judged, and a symbolic index of judgement about the multi-discriminatory potentials of genetics more generally. Connor and Wilkie take up this point directly:

> Gay activists in Britain, however, are suspicious of any scientists who make a study of homosexuality, they fear they are being singled out and labelled as a problem because of perceived abnormality. They fear that homophobic elements in society will use the genetic research to 'diagnose' or 'treat' homosexuality as if it were a disorder to be cured or eradicated. (Connor and Wilkie, *Independent*, 18 July 1993)

At the same time, in their consideration of the potentially beneficent, anti-discriminatory effects of the 'gay gene' discovery, these debates effectively recuperated the science. For example, for the purpose of both sides of the debate (i.e. the claims of a natural basis for the extension of rights or of a dangerous knowledge), 'gay genes' had to be taken as 'fact'. The emphasis, moreover, on the (mis)use of the 'gay gene' science by 'homophobic elements in society' also reinvested in the notion of a disinterested science even where the (justified) suspicions by gay activists of scientific motives in the study of homosexuality were noted. Finally, the ascendancy of anti-abortion discourse with its attendant stigmatization of monstrous mothers, was implicitly reconfirmed. Whether 'gay genes' were seen potentially to fuel a 'final solution' to the 'gay question' or to reinvigorate gay rights struggle, a woman's right to choose always remained on the wrong side of the debate.[21]

## Discursive displacements

Lisa Smyth has traced evolving social theory on the phenomenon of the *moral panic*. As she has noted, the notion of a 'moral panic' is generally taken to signify 'the mass media's involvement in maintaining and policing definitions of [certain] social behaviours [or groups] as "deviant" or problematic' (Smyth, 1996, p. 1). The role of moral panics in shoring up and recuperating the hegemonic grip of social conservatism on popular common senses of 'law and order' and 'family values' has been widely examined.[22] Indeed, it can be argued that they constitute, in this capacity, key *pedagogic* strategies of the Right. Moreover, as Epstein and Johnson (1998) have argued, moral panics are perhaps best understood as *defensive* responses to perceived or actual erosions of the fragile hegemonies of conservative philosophy, or, to borrow from Raymond Williams (1977), moments where the recuperation of the dominant is staged on the terrain of the apparently emergent.

Yet both the reportage on the Case of X, discussed by Smyth in this volume (Chapter 12), and the 'discovery' of a 'gay gene' depart from the characteristic narrative sequences of a moral panic, even as their meanings and forms seem to be animated from within its popularly recognizable conventions. In the Case of X, we see, as Smyth notes, a seemingly reverse trajectory, a moment where the tensions of social conservatism seemed to become unbearable, where the dominant common sense broke down and the emergent resistances of the liberal left appeared not only to defeat the right-wing consensus on both abortion and Irishness, but indeed generated a significant (though only partial) reversal of constitutional law. As I have traced in this chapter, the press coverage of the 'gay gene' in Britain also represents a moment of emergent liberal rather than dominant conservative sensibilities. Here the familiar moral panic about homosexuality gave way to the *moral dilemma* where competing narratives of homosexuality, science and abortion became enmeshed in what might be termed a *circuit of displacements*.[23] The continuous slippages between the problematization of homosexuality on the one hand and of homophobia on the other were embedded in further narrative oscillations pitting gay rights, for example, against abortion rights, monstrous science against monstrous mothers, scientific against moral agency. Yet even as homophobia emerged as a key object of critical focus, conventional constructions of homosexuality were retained. The notion that homosexuality is abnormal, for example, was reasserted in its representation as a static biological/social category, a statistical minority and, particularly, a recessive trait. While the view of homosexuality as a natural disaster was refused, it remained, at best, a sociobiological idiosyncrasy that required tolerance both from 'society' and science. The presumption of heterosexuality as normative, normal (and even an inherited characteristic) went unquestioned.

Moreover, the possibility of this liberal-resistant reframing of homosexuality/homophobia was grounded in both the ambivalent status of gene science (including its associations as monster science) and the power of anti-abortion common sense. In this context, the reconstitution of gays as points of projective identification relied precisely on the displacement of monstrous anxieties (about gays, genes and eugenics) on to women. Thus, contained within (and productive of) the moral *dilemma* about 'gay genes', was a residual moral *panic* about monster mothers. Ultimately, the gay gene stories represent not so much an encouraging shift in popular sensibilities around homosexuality (though I think they do suggest this possibility), but rather that in a clash of monster stories, some monsters might become, if not heroes, then at least not quite so monstrous.

## Notes

1. Although breaking the story on 17 July, the *Guardian* carried out most of its reporting on the 'gay gene' in the final week of July.
2. Unsurprisingly, the broadsheets had somewhat more elaborated descriptions of the research than the tabloids. Indeed, what did appear in the tabloids generally appeared to be excerpted verbatim from the broadsheet reporting.
3. Terry notes that there have also been resistant strands of sexuality science, for example, the sexological approach of Magnus Hirschfield, which have tended to regard homosexuals as 'benign natural anomalies, afflicted not by biological defects but by the social hostility that surrounded them' (Terry, 1997, p. 274).
4. Elsewhere (Steinberg, 1996), I have used the phrase 'languages of risk' to describe the ways in which women have been constituted as dangerous bearers, carers and (disease) carriers in medical discourse.
5. When a condition is assumed, in the first instance, to have sole or partial genetic origins, the term 'candidate gene' is used to refer to the particular genetic material suspected to confirm that hypothesis.
6. See, for example, Stacey (1991) and Epstein (1993).
7. Jane Brown's refusal of subsidized (though still expensive) tickets to a ballet of *Romeo and Juliet* in the summer of 1993 hit the headlines in January 1994, developing into a protracted media hysteria of homophobic panic. Epstein traces the interplay of (anti-)homophobic and (anti-)racist narratives deployed in the Jane Brown reportage.
8. 'Oncogenes' are understood to cause, or be implicated causally, in cancer.
9. Elsewhere (Steinberg, 1997), I have examined the professional discourse which significantly underpins pervasive expressions of popular optimism about such 'discoveries'.
10. This appeared in bold print over the main headline 'Your Mother Should Know'.
11. Steve Jones emerged as perhaps the foremost 'popular' geneticist in Britain in 1991, when he gave the Reith Lecture series on Radio 4. Since then, he has been involved in various forms of popularization/popular education around

genetics including television, the popular press, radio and in books intended for a lay readership (including Jones and Van Loon, *Genetics for Beginners*, 1993).

12. It might be added that seven seems a rather significant number in a sample of 40, a point which was implied in *The Times* article, but not explicitly noted.

13. Connor and Whitfield (*Independent*, 17 July 1993), both validate and problematize this expectation of 'the public' to handle scientific knowledge by raising three issues: (a) whether 'piecemeal' announcement of the results of genetic science fuels public resistance to confusion with respect to the science; (b) the need for there to be a debate on 'what *we* regard as "normal" genetic information otherwise scientific results might be used to further polarise opposing factions still further' (emphasis mine); and (c) quoting 'Paul Nurse, professor of biology at Oxford University' that delay in announcing scientific results was illegitimate: ' "It won't help if there is a restriction [on science]", he said.'

14. The assertion that a ban on genetics (or indeed any form of scientific 'progress') would be 'unenforceable' is one typically used to foreclose any further discussion. Yet, given the vast infrastructures of labour-power, training, economic investment , sites and resources for genetics research, it is hard to imagine how a widespread genetics 'black market' would be able to operate in the face of a ban that took these factors into consideration. Furthermore, it does not logically follow that an impossibility of absolute enforceability negates any possible value in partial enforceability.

15. For example, a passage from the *Independent* reads 'Peter Tatchell, spokesman for the gay rights group Outrage, said that aborting foetuses that carry a genetic predisposition to be gay "is tantamount to prenatal genocide of homosexuals" ' (Connor and Whitfield, *Independent*, 17 July 1993).

16. Ewing (1995) specifically critiques Hamer *et al.* for discarding subjects from the study who did not fit the pattern suggesting maternal inheritance.

17. In Lacanian terms, gay genes would seem to posit a son whose claim on the phallus is compromised, who can never fully enter the realm of the symbolic, tied as he must be to the Imaginary through unbreakable biological connection to the body of the mother.

18. This characterization of pregnancy was asserted by Bernard Braine and other parliamentary supporters of the 1988 Alton Bill, which attempted to lower the upper time limit for legal abortion to 18 weeks' gestation. For further discussion see Steinberg (1991).

19. Within anti-abortion discourse, all rationales for abortion are illegitimate.

20. Section 28 of the Local Government Act 1988 is a vaguely worded proscription against local authorities' support of the 'promotion of homosexuality' or the validation of gay families (termed in the Act as 'pretended family relationships'). See Stacey (1991) for further discussion of the 'great gays' position

taken up amongst activists and in the popular press in the wake of the Stop the Clause Campaign.

21. Connor and Wilkie do suggest another danger in this context: 'But what would happen to the child if its parents decided not to abort after a "positive" test? It might grow up knowing that it had been labelled as genetically gay, a burden of knowledge that would inescapably affect his future life and choice of sexual partner. It could become a self-fulfilling prophesy' (*Independent*, 18 July 1993). Interestingly, this passage recuperates the homosexual-as-problem narrative (as well as the science-as-problem narrative), by introducing a twist on the anti-abortion theme – the danger of prenatal diagnosis when abortion is refused. It is significant here that common-sense assumptions of heterosexuality are not perceived as a 'burden of knowledge', though such assumptions as we all know are often (wishfully) regarded as 'self-fulfilling prophecies'!

22. See, for example, Cohen (1972); Hall *et al.* (1978); Epstein (1993, 1997).

23. I am borrowing here from Richard Johnson's concept of a 'circuit of production' which refers to the continuous interplay of productive-interpretive moments (authorship and readership) in the making of meanings within particular and competing discursive fields (Johnson, 1986). The 'circuit of displacements' is intended to describe the continuous discursive slippages produced through the specific narrative convergences in the 'gay gene' stories.

# References

Birke, Linda (1994). 'Zipping up the genes; putting biological theories back in the closet', *Perversions*, 1: 38–51.

Cohen, Stanley (1972). *Folk Devils and Moral Panics: The Creation of Mods and Rockers*. London: MacGibbon & Kee.

Connor, Steve (1993). 'Gay gene raises host of issues', *Independent*, 16 July, p. 3.

Connor, Steve (1993). 'Homosexuality linked to genes', *Independent*, 16 July, p. 1.

Connor, Steve (1993). 'Elusive answers to Darwin's riddle', *Independent*, 17 July, p. 3.

Connor, Steve and Whitfield, Martin (1993). 'Scientists at odds in "Gay gene" debate', *Independent*, 17 July, p. 3.

Connor, Steve and Wilkie, Tome (1993). 'The gay gene', *Independent*, 18 July.

*Daily Mail* (1993). 'Scan fears', 16 July, p. 8.

Epstein, Debbie (1993). *Changing Classroom Cultures: Anti-Racism, Politics and Schools*. Stoke-on-Trent: Trentham Books.

Epstein, Debbie (1997). 'What's in a ban: the popular media, Romeo and Juliet and compulsory heterosexuality', in Deborah Lynn Steinberg, Debbie Epstein and Richard Johnson (eds), *Border Patrols: Policing the Boundaries of Heterosexuality*. London: Cassell, pp. 183–203.

Epstein, Debbie and Johnson, Richard (1998). *Schooling Sexualities*. Buckingham: Open University Press.

Ewing, Christine (1995). 'A gay gene? A critique of genetic research of homosexuality'. Unpublished paper, presented at the Intercampus Gay and Lesbian Seminar Group, La Trobe University, Melbourne, Australia, 5 September.

Fenton, James (1993). 'It's not in the genes, it's in the culture', *Independent*, 19 July, p. 19.

Gilman, Sander (1991). *The Jew's Body*. London: Routledge.

*Guardian* (1993). 'Science and the single man', 17 July, p. 1 (Outlook Section).

*Guardian* (1993). 'Opting for a gay child', 20 July, p. 17 (Letters to the Editor).

Habgood, John (1993). 'We are all people, not gene models', *The Times*, 24 July, p. 7.

Hall, Stuart *et al.* (1978). *Policing the Crisis: Mugging, the State, and Law and Order*. London: Macmillan.

Hawkes, Nigel (1993). 'Tampering with the bad temper gene', *The Times*, 1 July, p. 15.

Hawkes, Nigel (1993). 'Is homosexuality all in the brain?', *The Times*, 8 July, p. 15.

Hawkes, Nigel (1993). 'Gays may have genetic link', *The Times*, 16 July, p. 3.

Hawkes, Nigel (1993). ' "Gay Gene" raises screening fear', *The Times*, 17 July, p. 3.

Hope, Anthony (1993). 'Scan babies "more often left-handed" ', *Daily Mail*, 16 July, p. 26.

Hope, Jenny (1993). 'Genes that may chart course of a sex life', *Daily Mail*, 17 July, p. 20.

Hubbard, Ruth (1990). *The Politics of Women's Biology*. New Brunswick and London: Rutgers University Press.

*Independent* (1993). 'Gay genes do not exclude choice', 16 July, p. 19.

*Independent* (1993). 'A controversial chromosome', 17 July, p. 15 (Letters to the Editor).

*Independent* (1993). 'The genetic tyranny', 18 July, p. 24.

*Independent* (1993). 'Nothing new in predicting sexual orientation', 19 July, p. 17 (Letters to the Editor).

Johnson, Richard (1986). 'The story so far and further transformations?', in D. Punter (ed.), *Introduction to Contemporary Cultural Studies*. London: Longman.

Jones, Steve (1993). 'Genes, gays and a moral minefield', *Daily Mail*, 17 July, p. 8.

Jones, Steve and Van Loon, Borin (1993). *Genetics for Beginners*. Cambridge: Icon Books.

Kear, Adrian (1997). 'Eating the other: imaging the fantasy of incorporation', in Deborah Lynn Steinberg, Debbie Epstein and Richard Johnson (eds), *Border Patrols: Policing the Boundaries of Heterosexuality*. London: Cassell, pp. 253–74.

McKellen, Ian (1993). 'Through a gay viewfinder', *Guardian*, 22 July, p. 20.

Moore, Suzanne (1993). 'Kiss and don't tell', *Guardian*, 23 July, p. 15 (Tabloid Section).

Morgan, P. (1993). 'My dinosaurs scared the life out of Di says Spielberg', *Sun*, 17 July, p. 3.

Mort, Frank (1987). *Dangerous Sexualities: Medico-moral Politics in England Since 1830*. London: Routledge & Kegan Paul.

Nead, Lynn (1988). *Myths of Sexuality*. Oxford: Blackwell.

Parris, Matthew (1993). 'Genetic genies won't go back in the bottle', *The Times*, 17 July, p. 16.

Patton, Cindy (1985). *Sex and Germs: The Politics of AIDS*. Boston: South End Press.

Plummer, Ken (1995). *Telling Sexual Stories: Power, Change and Social Worlds*. London: Routledge.

Proctor, Robert N. (1988). *Racial Hygiene: Medicine under the Nazis*. Cambridge, MA: Harvard University Press.

Radford, Tim (1993). 'Your mother should know', *Guardian*, 17 July, p. 1 (Outlook Section).

Radford, Tim (1993). 'Code of conduct', *Guardian*, 21 July, p. 2 (Tabloid Section).

Redman, Peter (1997). 'Invasion of the monstrous others: heterosexual masculinities, the "AIDS Carrier" and the Horror Genre', in Deborah Lynn Steinberg, Debbie Epstein and Richard Johnson (eds), *Border Patrols: Policing the Boundaries of Heterosexuality*. London: Cassell, pp. 98–117.

Smyth, Lisa (1996). 'The making of a "moral panic": the X case in Ireland'. Unpublished paper presented for the MA course option *Feminist Media Studies*, Warwick University, Coventry, England.

Sontag, Susan (1991). *Illness as Metaphor/AIDS and Its Metaphors*. Harmondsworth: Penguin.

Stacey, Jackie (1991). 'Promoting normality: Section 28 and the regulation of sexuality', in Sarah Franklin, Celia Lury and Jackie Stacey (eds), *Off-Centre: Feminism and Cultural Studies*. London: Routledge, pp. 284–304.

Steinberg, Deborah Lynn (1991). 'Adversarial politics: the legal construction of abortion', in Sarah Franklin, Celia Lury and Jackie Stacey (eds), *Off-Centre: Feminism and Cultural Studies*. London: Routledge, pp. 175–89.

Steinberg, Deborah Lynn (1996). 'Languages of risk: genetic encryptions of the female body', *Women a Cultural Review Special Issue: 'Cultural Regimes of the Body'*, 7(3): 259–70 (Guest editor: Deborah Lynn Steinberg).

Steinberg, Deborah Lynn (1997). *Bodies in Glass: Genetics, Eugenics, Embryo Ethics*. Manchester: Manchester University Press.

Steinem, Gloria (1984). *Outrageous Acts and Everyday Rebellions*. London: Fontana.

Swain, Gill (1993). 'Men inherit gay genes from mum', *Daily Mirror*, 17 July, p. 9.

Terry, Jennifer (1997). 'The seductive power of science in the making of deviant subjectivity', in Vernon A. Rosario (ed.), *Science and Homosexualities*. New York: Routledge.

*The Times* (1993). 'Genes and the man: scientific discoveries do not resolve moral dilemmas', 17 July, p. 17.

*The Times* (1993). 'Homosexuals and a tolerant society', 20 July, p. 17 (Letters to the Editor).

Usher, Jane (1991). *Women's Madness: Misogyny or Mental Illness?* New York: Harvester Wheatsheaf.

Walkowitz, Judith R. (1980). *Prostitution and Victorian Society: Women, Class and the State*. Cambridge: Cambridge University Press.

Watney, Simon (1988). 'AIDS, "moral panic" theory and homophobia', in Peter Aggleton and Hilary Homans (eds), *Social Aspects of AIDS*. Philadelphia: Falmer Press.

Watson, Pascoe (1993). 'Mums pass gay gene to sons say doctors', *Sun*, 17 July, p. 6.

Whitfield, Martin (1993). 'My fear is having straight children', *Independent*, 17 July, p. 1.

Williams, Raymond (1977). *Marxism and Literature*. Oxford: Oxford University Press.

# Part Two

## Sexualities as Globalization and Commodification

# 6

# Sex in the World

## *R. W. Connell*

W E NORMALLY TAKE sex to be the most intimate and personal of matters, a matter of 'private life' in the strongest sense. Yet, on reflection, we must acknowledge that sex is shaped by large-scale social forces: religion, the state, mass media, markets. In this section we take this observation to its logical extreme, and reflect on the relationship between sex and world society. If it is true that sex is strongly affected by globalization, educators must understand this dimension in order to teach well.

### What is globalization?

'Globalization', like 'modernity' and 'postmodernity', tends to be discussed as a sweeping, undifferentiated process, homogenizing local cultures into a world culture – a United Colors of Benetton image of the world. Recent cultural theory is full of evocations of this process, lyrical descriptions of the cultural mixing that brings South Asian food to Los Angeles, Afro-Caribbean music to Moscow and so on.

As Said (1993) has vividly shown, this image of equal exchange in a global cultural market is far from the reality of a world where conquered people and subaltern groups struggle for meaning in the face of the violence, economic strength and arrogance of imperial powers. Any analysis of contemporary 'global culture' must be based on an understanding of the history of colonialism and neocolonialism.

Imperialism involved military conquest, creating the formal empires whose history and symbolism ('the flag on which the sun never sets') dominate our thinking about empire. But it also involved a much broader process of economic transformation and control, in which regions not directly ruled were brought under the influence of the imperial powers as markets and fields of investment. In the twentieth century, international financial markets and multinational corporations centred in the United States, Europe and Japan have become the central institutions of control.

Imperialism was also a cultural process. Widespread destruction of culture and learning in conquered societies was followed by the implantation of new institutions controlled by the colonizers: missionary churches, labour discipline in plantations and mines, westernized school systems. Though rarely obliterating local culture, these characteristic products of colonialism provided the main channels through which members of colonized societies participated in 'world culture'. In the twentieth century, commercial mass media have become the dominant means of cultural influence.

Imperialism changed the colonizers as well as the colonized. The economies of the 'advanced' capitalist countries have long been influenced by the growth of international investment and international markets. Imperialism has also had an immense impact on metropolitan culture, acknowledged since Kiernan's survey *The Lords of Human Kind* (1969).

The contemporary global order bears the marks of this history. Contrary to the speculations of theorists of globalization, genuinely 'transnational' corporations are rare; the main companies operating in global markets remain firmly based in their home countries and regions (Hirst and Thompson, 1996). The 'North' – which means, basically, the former imperial powers – remains completely dominant in the world economy, despite the emergence of newly industrializing countries such as the Asian 'tiger' economies.

## The world gender order and sexuality

Though few theories of imperialism have acknowledged it, imperial expansion and rule was a powerfully gendered process (Mies, 1986). The initial agents of conquest were almost all men, and colonial regimes proceeded to restructure gender relations among the conquered. They generally tried to draw men into production as cheap labourers and constructed servicing roles for women: the process Mies (1986) calls 'housewifization international'. The post-colonial world economy and military–political system is still strongly gender-structured (Enloe, 1990).

Conquest and settlement disrupted local gender orders as much as other structures of indigenous society. The disruption took many forms, ranging from the pulverization of indigenous communities (as in the seizure of land in south-eastern Australia), through gendered labour migration (as in Rand mining and the Natal sugar industry), to ideological assaults on local gender arrangements (as in missionary endeavours in Polynesia).

The power relations of empire meant that indigenous gender orders were usually under pressure from the colonizers, rather than the other way around. But the colonizers too might change. The racial barriers erected in late colonial societies were not only to prevent sexual pollution from below, but to forestall 'going native', a well-recognized possibility (the starting-point, for instance, of Kipling's novel *Kim*). In the metropole, images of the 'primitive' world as either an Eden of free sexuality, or an arena of animal brutality and backwardness, have been important to the sexual imagination. The real sexual encounters at the colonial frontier, and in the metropolitan societies when populations of colonized peoples entered, as slaves or immigrants, have also been important in shaping metropolitan sexualities.

For the many effects of empire to become a process of globalization requires a parallelism, and a linking, of dynamics that begins to produce an interconnected social order on a world scale. In relation to gender and sexuality, it is obvious that this process is incomplete; at best we have a half-emerged world structure. Yet a movement towards such a structure can be seen in many arenas:

*The division of labour.* On every continent there is evidence of the process of 'housewifization' named by Mies (1986). This is the restructuring of local production systems to produce the wage-worker/housewife couple, making women unpaid workers for men, and thus institutionalizing their dependence in the new market economies. The growth of informal prostitution on a large scale is an important consequence.

*Power relations.* The colonial and post-colonial world has tended to break down purdah systems of patriarchy in the name of modernization, if not of women's emancipation. At the same time, the creation of a westernized public realm has seen the growth of large-scale gendered power structures in the form of the state and corporations.

*Emotional relations.* Both religious and cultural 'missionary' activity has corroded indigenous homosexual and cross-gender practice (e.g. the Native American 'berdache' and the Chinese 'passion of the cut sleeve').

Recently developed Western models of romantic heterosexual love as the basis for marriage, and gay identity as the main alternative, have now circulated globally.

*Symbolization.* European gender and sexual imagery have been widely implanted through westernized media (e.g. Xuxa, the blonde television superstar in Brazil). In counterpoint, 'exotic' imagery has been used in the marketing of goods and services from newly industrializing countries (e.g. airline advertising from South-east Asia).

Contemporary research on sexuality in 'the West' has given much attention to the fact of change. What is so often taken as a realm of unchanging 'natural' processes turns out to be an arena of immensely complex transformations. Changes in practice are documented in both close-focus studies of personal lives (Dowsett, 1996) and broad social surveys (Laumann *et al.*, 1994). Historians trace the production of new categories of sexuality and new erotic objects, a process emphasized by Weeks (1986). Studies of fashion (Wilson, 1987) chart historical changes in the object of heterosexual desire, and show how intricate are the social processes involved. Wilson's story is particularly interesting in showing a sustained interplay between feminism and fashion, long before the era of 'lipstick lesbians' and power dressing.

The most profound changes in sexuality at present are not, however, in the rich industrialized countries. As shown in ethnographies such as Clark's (1997) study of a highland community in Papua New Guinea, the more sweeping changes are the transformations of sexual categories and practices during dependent capitalist development in poor countries. Murray's (1991) study of street traders and prostitutes in Jakarta traces this process in an urban setting. One type of prostitution in this case involves servicing the westernized sexuality of business men by lower-class women, who use this trade as a way into the modernized sector of Javanese society. But sexuality is also changing among Javanese men. As Altman's chapter notes, Javanese society traditionally provided a space for *waria*, cross-dressing men who typically had sex with straight men. This pattern is now being displaced by a new sexual category, gay men, modelled on the gay sexuality of North American cities (Oetomo, 1990).

Altman argues correctly that such cases do not involve the simple substitution of a 'Western' sexuality for a 'traditional' sexuality. Globalization involves both domination *and* negotiation. Both proceed through an enormously complex interaction between sexual regimes that are in any case diverse and divided. The result is a spectrum of sexual practices and categories, formed in contexts of cultural disruption and massive economic inequalities. The situation mapped by Sears in the Philippines is, in this regard, entirely typical of contemporary globalization.

## Vectors of change

It is important to think of globalization as a process, not just as an end point. This raises the question of the means of globalization: the institutions and processes which serve as 'vectors' for the movement of sexual practices.

Population movements are the first and most obvious. The creation of empire was the original 'elite migration', though in colonies of settlement mass migration followed. Through this process, something very close to the gender order and sexual practices of Western Europe was reassembled in North America and in Australasia. Labour migration within the colonial and post-colonial systems was a means by which practices were spread, but also a means by which they were reconstructed, as labour migration was itself a gendered process. In contexts like the mines of South Africa, a whole new regime of sexual practice was created (Moodie, 1994).

Mass communications are the favourite vector for the theorists of an emerging 'global culture'. Popular entertainment, dominated by US media (not only Hollywood but also popular music and television), circulate fictional gender images with strongly sexualized narratives. News media are also controlled from the metropole (if not directly owned, then powerfully influenced by metropolitan networks) and circulate Western definitions of authoritative masculinity, criminality, desirable femininity, etc. There are, I think, important limits to the role of global mass communications. Media research emphasizes that audiences are highly selective in the reception of media messages, and there is perhaps more recognition of the fantasy character of media than cultural studies generally allow.

More important than media, I would argue, is the export of institutions. The colonial and post-colonial world saw the installation in the periphery, on a very large scale, of a range of institutions on the North Atlantic model: armies, states, bureaucracies, corporations, capital markets, labour markets, schools, law courts, transport systems. These are gendered institutions, and have directly reconstituted masculinities and femininities in the periphery. They have not only promoted, but have directly instituted, particular sexual practices: conjugal sexuality in the patriarchal nuclear family, female prostitution servicing armies and male labour forces, etc.

This has not meant Xerox copies of European practices; rather, pressures for change which are inherent in the institutional form. Let us examine, briefly, the two key institutional forms in the global capitalist system: the state and the market.

*States*. Though we often talk of 'the state', in fact there are different kinds of states with different histories, stemming from their different positions in imperialism. The post-colonial states are often fragile and were sometimes established with difficulty, through a process that disrupted the indigenous gender order.

Some anti-colonial movements mobilized women's support and contested traditional forms of patriarchy, Chinese Communism being the best-known case (Stacey, 1983). However the establishment of a post-colonial or post-revolutionary regime often meant the reinstallation of patriarchy. The intimidation of women by Islamic-revival movements in Afghanistan, Iran and some Arab countries is a current example, where feminist attitudes amongst women are seen as evidence of the corruption of religion and culture (Tohidi, 1991).

The metropolitan states operated under different conditions, given the tremendous wealth concentrated in the imperial centres, and now in the financial centres of the global economy. This wealth allowed the rising expectation of life and the 'demographic revolution' (drastic drop in birth rate) that created the first demographic panics, and led to state intervention in sexuality to promote population growth. It also led to cultural changes that allowed the extension of citizenship to women, and the collapse of legal control by men over the sexuality of women.

But women's increased presence in the public realm has been counterbalanced by a decline of the public realm itself, and a relocation of power into market mechanisms dominated by men. The old form of state patriarchy, with masculine authority embedded in bureaucratic hierarchies, was vulnerable to challenge by liberal feminism. New forms of co-ordination through commodification of state services (privatization, corporatization, programme budgeting) and neo-liberal administrative reform agendas (Yeatman, 1990) reconstituted state power in forms less open to challenge. The 'minimal' state of the new world order may claim to get out of the citizens' way, but as the current politics of abortion, pornography and the 'drug war' show, state power can still be used for a vehement agenda of social control.

A striking feature of twentieth-century political history is the development of agencies that link territorial states without themselves having a territorial base: the International Labor Organization, the League of Nations, the United Nations and its various agencies, the World Bank, the International Monetary Fund, etc. The 'international state', as we might call this collection, is an important feature of globalization, though it is far from the former ideal of a World Government. The United Nations network was the base for the most ambitious attempt yet to develop a global educational programme on sexuality, the World Health Organization's 'Global Program on AIDS' (now an inter-agency programme, beyond the WHO).

*Markets.* Global markets are perhaps the defining feature of 'globalization', and although the degree of integration of the world economy is often overestimated, there can be no denying the scale of world trade, or the scale of global financial markets. As means for disseminating social practices, markets are certainly becoming very important.

Markets circulate goods and services, and the sexual practices associated with them. This includes the representations of sexuality in popular music, film and television, and technologies of sexuality (e.g. condoms, sex aids, pornography). It also includes generalized attitudes and forms of practice which sweep across many areas of life. Market operations, for instance, are based on a calculative egocentrism which market participants do not necessarily have to set aside when they walk out of the workplace door. It is curious and telling that one of the first cultural representations of a totally egocentric modern sexuality, Mozart's *Don Giovanni*, should highlight (in the Catalogue Aria) the international dimension of the Don's sexual conquests.

### Processes of change

Taking a long historical perspective, we can understand the globalization of sexuality as an outcome of the disruption of indigenous practices (in the metropole as well as the colonized world) and a reordering on new terms. The reordering could be done in a number of ways:

*Displacement*, where colonizers' practice was substituted for the indigenous one (example: the destruction of Polynesian sexual arrangements in

Hawaii and the substitution of missionary prudery [the origin of the '*muu-muu*'] and marriage customs);

*Subsumption*, where local practice was incorporated into a structure of the imperial world (example: the constitution of masculinity in long-distance motor transport – now recognized as an issue in HIV dissemination);

*Hybridization*, where local structures synthesized with those of imperial society (example: the figure of the 'ayah' in British India; the sexual culture of French Polynesia, immortalized by Gaugin).

These forms of change are possible not only because of a power imbalance between local and metropolitan societies, but also because of the crisis tendencies embedded *within* a system of gender relationships and sexual practices. Consider, for instance, the major recent change in the structure of sexual attachments in metropolitan countries, where lesbian and gay sexuality has been stabilized as a public alternative within the heterosexual order. This grows out of a long-standing contradiction in which the patriarchal gender order prohibits forms of emotion, attachment and pleasure which its own gender arrangements (e.g. homosocial institutions, the Oedipal family) produce. This has brought into the public sphere an alternative family form, the homosexual household.

At the same time there have been shifts in heterosexuality, notably a growing sexual independence on the part of heterosexual women, and a steeply declining expectation that heterosexual coupling will be lifelong. Markedly higher divorce rates have not eroded the conjugal family so much as restructured it; hence the large number of 'blended' families or single-parent families.

Some crisis tendencies emerge within the structure of gender relations; but endogenous change is not the only dynamic. The interplay of gender and sexuality with structures of class and ethnicity is also a source of change. Ethnicity is a precipitate of a history of community interactions, population movements, political mobilizations, all given cultural interpretation and represented in current practices – from speech to dancing to voting – in which identities are mobilized and enacted (Bottomley, 1992). Sexuality is woven into this process, indeed an ethnic group commonly imagines itself as a kinship group. As Vickers (1994, p. 174) observes in a discussion of new nationalisms, 'patriarchal sex/gender arrangements constitute the deep structure of many political conflicts by establishing identities, maintaining group cohesion and transmitting identities and values across generations'. Rhetoric of the (new) 'nation as family' locates women as mothers-of-soldiers and transmitters of the bloodline. It was not by accident that a favoured military tactic in the bitter conflict in former Yugoslavia was rape of the women of the opposing ethno-national group.

These dynamics, in turn, imply something fundamental about sexuality as a process. Sexuality is inherently of the body; for all the attention we may give to discourses, symbolism and institutions, it is absolutely necessary to remember this (Dowsett, 1996). To say this is *not* to fall back into biological essentialism. Bodies are not biological machines producing social effects mechanically. Nor are they blank pages on which cultural messages are written. Bodies are parties in social life, sharing in social agency, in generating and shaping courses of social conduct.

In sexuality, bodies are both agents and objects; the practices, thus, are body-reflexive. Such practices are not internal to the individual. Their circuits involve social relations and symbolism; they commonly encompass social institutions, even such large-scale institutions as states and markets. Through body-reflexive practices, more than individual lives are formed: a social world is formed. Sexual practice, like all other forms of practice, is constitutive of social reality.

Through body-reflexive practices, bodies are addressed by social process and drawn into history, without ceasing to be bodies. They do not turn into symbols, signs or positions in discourse. Their materiality (including material capacities to engender, to give birth, to give milk, to menstruate, to open, to penetrate, to ejaculate) is not erased. The *social* process includes childbirth and childcare, the pleasures and pains of sex, work, injury and illness.

Body-reflexive practices constitute a world that has a bodily dimension, but is not biologically determined. Not being fixed by the physical logic of the body, this practice-made world may be hostile to bodies' physical well-being. We have massive demonstrations of that in the case of sexually transmitted diseases, whose pathways are constituted by social practice though the agents (e.g. HIV) may be non-human.

The body-reflexive practice in sexuality allows sexuality to be part of large-scale social arrangements. What Hearn and Parkin (1987) call 'organization sexuality' is an ubiquitous feature of life in offices and factories. Looked at from the other direction, this dimension means the bodily effects of sexuality are constantly bound up with social structures

and the strategies groups pursue within them. In the Swedish gay community Henriksson (1995) studies, there is more unsafe sex within committed
relationships than in casual sex; so love, in his phrase, becomes an HIV/
AIDS risk factor. In much of the world, heterosexual relations are
constructed in conditions of gender inequality. Examples range from the
Jakarta prostitutes interviewed by Murray (1991) to the London teenagers
interviewed by Lees (1986). For both these groups their disempowerment
as women, and the social empowerment of men, are fundamental in the
making of sexuality.

The pattern of body-reflexive practice is what permits the commodification of sexuality, and what gives that commodification a particular
character. Sexual practice can be commodified as a service, and sexual
symbolism can enter into the commodification of an immense range of
goods and services (most often through advertising). But as Chapkis
(1997) shows, sex work, while certainly work, is not any form of work; the
body is committed in distinctive ways, and sex workers must develop
emotional techniques for handling this.

Market exchanges under capitalism do not involve the sale of the body
itself; this is the basic difference from the slave system. What is sold, rather,
is the body's capacities for practice – as in the basic labour contract, where
the capacity to work is sold (exchanged for a wage) for a specified period of
time.

The commodification of sexuality involves, thus, a specific alienation
of the body's capacities for pleasure, for giving pleasure, for self-
representation. These capacities are submitted to a logic of profit, which
means to the steering mechanisms of the market rather than to individual
or collective deliberation.

## Concluding educational note

It is not a logic of profit, but a logic of human development, which is the
basis of education. The contemporary dominance of market relations in
the new world order therefore poses specific problems for education
concerned with sexuality. The alienation of the capacities of the body, in
market exchanges, undermines the project of education itself. I think this is
probably an important reason for the acknowledged difficulty of contemporary sex education, and the ineffectiveness of many sex education
programmes – beyond the better recognized difficulties of political and
religious surveillance.

Education is rightly concerned with the consequences of action, not just with the qualities of actions in themselves; and sex education is thus concerned with the social relations constituted by sexual practice. These relations, as I have argued in an essay on the concept of 'sexual revolution' (Connell, 1997), are implicated in social structures of inequality. The pursuit of justice in sexuality is a matter of trying to reduce the levels of oppression and domination (Young, 1990) embodied in these relations. Here is one coherent goal for sexuality education.

A second is the goal of understanding. Here we must make a demand for severe realism. Many efforts at curriculum development assume children's understanding develops from the local outwards: for instance, from the family to the local community, to the nation, to the world. This sequence is tidy but it is unrealistic, given the history of imperialism, the current processes of globalization and the hybridization of cultural forms. Contemporary Australian children are almost certain to learn about the President of the United States before they learn about their local municipal council, and they are likely to hear heated discussions of the sexuality of Madonna or Michael Jackson before they are told anything significant about the sexuality of their own parents. When sexualities hybridize, what is their local pattern anyway?

Therefore sex education (and this includes sex education for adults, as in AIDS prevention programmes) cannot be content with static models of diverse indigenous sexual cultures, any more than it can rest on the assumption that there is one global pattern of sexuality. The reality is, as I suggested above, an endlessly shifting combination of domination and negotiation. This implies that sex educators need to be alert observers of contemporary society, which we certainly hope for (and try to encourage, with adequate teacher education). But it implies more strongly that the most important resource for curriculum making in sex education is the people who most intimately understand the current pattern of domination-and-negotiation because they are in it – that is to say, the students. There are good educational reasons for maximizing student participation and control in the design of sex education. In education as elsewhere, the best response to the problems created by globalization is more democracy.

100 · R. W. CONNELL


## References

Bottomley, G. (1992). *From Another Place: Migration and the Politics of Culture.* Cambridge: Cambridge University Press.

Chapkis, W. (1997). *Live Sex Acts: Women Performing Erotic Labour.* New York: Routledge.

Clark, J. (1997). 'State of desire: transformations in Huli sexuality', in L. Manderson and M. Jolly (eds), *Sites of Desire, Economies of Pleasure: Sexualities in Asia and the Pacific.* Chicago: University of Chicago Press, pp. 191–211.

Connell, R. W. (1997). 'Sexual revolution', in L. Segal (ed.), *New Sexual Agendas.* London: Macmillan.

Dowsett, G. W. (1996). *Practicing Desire: Homosexual Sex in the Era of AIDS.* Stanford: Stanford University Press.

Enloe, C. (1990). *Bananas, Beaches and Bases: Making Feminist Sense of International Politics.* Berkeley: University of California Press.

Hearn, J. and Parkin, W. (1987). *'Sex' at 'Work': The Power and Paradox of Organization Sexuality.* Brighton: Wheatsheaf.

Henriksson, B. (1995). *Risk Factor Love: Homosexuality, Sexual Interaction and HIV-Prevention.* Göteborg: Göteborgs Universitet Institutionen för Socialt Arbete.

Hirst, P. and Thompson, G. (1996). *Globalization in Question: The International Economy and the Possibilities of Governance.* Cambridge: Polity.

Kiernan, V. G. (1969). *The Lords of Human Kind: Black Man, Yellow Man and White Man in an Age of Empire.* New York: Columbia University Press.

Laumann, E. O., Gagnon, J. H., Michael, R. T. and Michaels, S. (1994). *The Social Organization of Sexuality: Sexual Practices in the United States.* Chicago: University of Chicago Press.

Lees, S. (1986). *Losing Out: Sexuality and Adolescent Girls.* London: Hutchinson.

Mies, M. (1986). *Patriarchy and Accumulation on a World Scale: Women in the International Division of Labour.* London: Zed.

Moodie, T. D. (1994). *Going for Gold: Men, Mines and Migration.* Johannesburg: Witwatersrand University Press.

Murray, A. J. (1991). *No Money, No Honey: A Study of Street Traders and Prostitutes in Jakarta.* Singapore: Oxford University Press.

Oetomo, D. (1990). 'Patterns of bisexuality in Indonesia'. Unpublished paper, Faculty of Social and Political Sciences, Universitas Airlangga.

Said, E. W. (1993). *Culture and Imperialism.* New York: Vintage.

Stacey, J. (1983). *Patriarchy and Socialist Revolution in China.* Berkeley: University of California Press.

Tohidi, N. (1991). 'Gender and Islamic fundamentalism: feminist politics in Iran', in C. T. Mohanty, A. Russo and L. Torres (eds), *Third World Women and the Politics of Feminism.* Bloomington: Indiana University Press, pp. 251–67.

Vickers, J. (1994). 'Notes toward a political theory of sex and power', in H. L. Radtke and H. J. Stam (eds), *Power/Gender: Social Relations in Theory and Practice*. London: Sage.

Weeks, J. (1986). *Sexuality*. London: Tavistock.

Wilson, E. (1987). *Adorned in Dreams: Fashion and Modernity*. Berkeley: University of California Press.

Yeatman, A. (1990). *Bureaucrats, Technocrats, Femocrats: Essays on the Contemporary Australian State*. Sydney: Allen & Unwin.

Young, I. M. (1990). *Justice and the Politics of Difference*. Princeton: Princeton University Press.

# 7

# In(ter)ventions of Male Sexualities and HIV Education: Case Studies in the Philippines

*James T. Sears*

FOR MORE THAN four centuries Spain and, later, the United States have intervened in Filipino affairs. While Catholic missionaries and Thomasite educators differ in time and appearance from HIV educators and funding agents, their roles have been essentially the same: to impart, import and impose Euro-American beliefs and infrastructures onto Filipino culture.

Examining this interplay between cultures and sexualities, I explore in(ter)ventions of Filipino male sexual identities and in(ter)ventions of HIV education. Here I argue that colonial and neocolonial interventions have dramatically changed indigenous understandings of male (homo)sexuality and that these subsequent constructions both contour and deter HIV educational efforts in the Philippines.

My fieldwork consisted of five different visits during a four-year period (1991–95), including a four-month experience as a Fulbright scholar. On the island of Luzon, which includes the metropolitan Manila area, live 10 million people; 30 per cent are destitute and another third eke out a living on about 3,000 pesos ($120) a month (Tiongon, 1994). Here, I lived in various locales ranging from the university area in Diliman to the Makati business district to the 'red light' district of Ermita.

Outside the influence of Manila, one can better appreciate the multilayered cultural complexity that defines the Philippines – an overlay of Malay, Chinese, Spanish, Indian and North American cultures. The Visayans of the central Philippines, the second geographical base for my fieldwork, is composed of seven major islands including the triangular-shaped island of Panay (12,000 square kilometres in extent) – the sixth largest of the several thousand islands forming the archipelago. Balasan is one of its northernmost municipalities. Despite resources of rice, bamboo, sugar and marble, chronic unemployment reaches 45 per cent; those who have jobs are generally underemployed. Here, I lived with an extended family.

Using indigenous ethnographic techniques such as *pagatatanong-tanong, pakikisama, pakikipagkuwentuhan, pagdalaw* and *pakikipanuluyan*, I 'hung out' in various settings ranging from family dinners, fiestas, and classrooms, interviewed persons ranging from health-care professionals and educators to sex workers and *bakla* (effeminate male homosexuals) and reviewed voluminous research reports, policy studies and related curriculum materials.

From such fieldwork, I developed a model to depict the complex interplay between culture and sexuality in the Philippines (see Figure 7.1). Here, I focus on those dimensions that directly impact in(ter)ventions and HIV education efforts.

## Education as population control

On the morning of 1 May 1898, Commodore George Dewey sailed into Manila Bay sinking most of the Spanish ships and, in the process, their colonial claim to the Philippines. Thus began a century of US colonial rule. Though perhaps less bloody than the previous three and a half centuries, American policy-makers' intent was to 'civilize and Christianize' through 'benevolent assimilation'. This marked a full-scale assault on Filipino culture.

American cultural hegemony came quickly after military conquest. Soldiers were rapidly followed by shiploads of 'Thomasite' female teachers as America, under Governor General William Howard Taft, exported herself: a public educational system; redistribution of rural estates held by the Catholic friars; construction of dams, irrigation facilities, roads, railways and ports; legal reforms; a new tax system and a renovated financial structure, duty-free trade and quotas on Philippine exports to America and the establishment of US military bases. These reforms largely retained the ruling class in positions of power and privilege while American-owned corporations acquired another foreign source for raw materials and cheap labour within a stable political milieu.

'The most effective means of subjugating a people is to capture their minds. Military victory does not necessarily signify conquest' (Constantino, 1982, p. 3). Thus, as Renato Constantino astutely observed, the US military had:

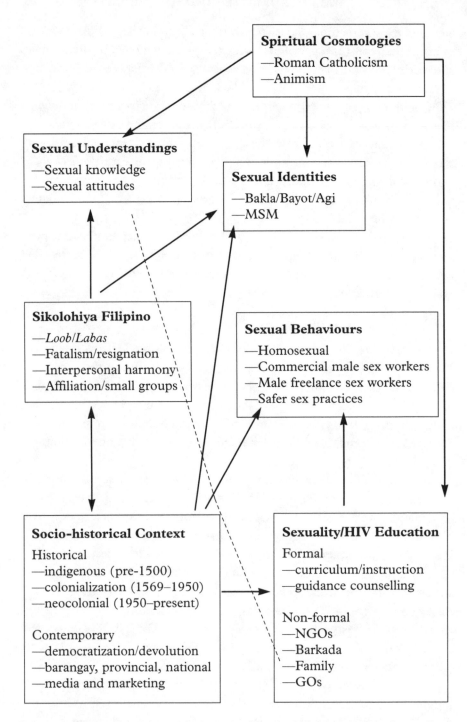

**Figure 7.1** Conceptual map of the interplay between Filipino culture and sexuality
*Source*: copyright J. Sears, 1997

to employ all means to pacify a people whose hopes for independence were being frustrated by the presence of another conqueror. The primary reason for the rapid introduction, on a large scale, of the American public school system to the Philippines was the conviction of the military leaders that no measure could so quickly promote the pacification of the islands as education ... Indigenous Filipino ideals were slowly eroded in order to remove the last vestiges of resistance. Education served to attract the people to the new masters and at the same time to dilute their nationalism which had just succeeded in overthrowing a foreign power. (Constantino, 1982, p. 5)

Tortuously, the Philippines moved from colony to commonwealth to independent state. By the late twentieth century, however, the Philippines remained a US surrogate. Presidents, ostensibly elected by Filipinos, were groomed by their American masters. Central Intelligence Agency operatives closely 'advised' a succession of presidents whose principal function was to quell domestic insurgent movements and whose principal qualification was their unquestioned loyalty to the United States (Karnow, 1989).

During the Marcos dictatorship, control of the sexual body and the body politic were synonymous as schools remained organized along the American curriculum model with English as the language of instruction. Population education, funded by Western agencies and implemented without regard to local knowledge, was literally an instrument of population control. A population education module on character education for teachers and published in the last year of the Marcos regime, for example, stated:

As young boys and girls mature, they have to learn that self-control is part of life ... What is required is character formation that will enable a man or a woman to exercise human control over what may be strong biologic forces. (Ministry of Education, Culture and Sports, 1985, p. 8)

The EDSA Revolution a year later yielded little substantive change. 'People's Power' remained leveraged by 81 families led by Filipino feudal clans with old, familiar names such as the Osmenas, Cojuangcos and Sorianos (Tiongon, 1994). 'Pop Ed', through the now influential Jaime, Cardinal Sin, was redirected toward 'quality of life'; population control, though, continued with a list of 'core messages/concepts' such as 'a small family is easier to manage' (Department of Education, Culture and Sports, 1994a). In one set of modules developed as reference material for teachers and counsellors to use with high school students the integration of religious and civil authority was complete:

> By the rules of traditional religion, law, and culture that a girl and boy must be a virgin ... There must be no sex aside from your husband and wife. These rules have been disobeyed many times ... [but] for young people who disobeyed these rules, the result is unwanted pregnancy, broken reputation ... (Philippine Center for Population, 1994b, p. 28)

Among 'psycho-sexual problems of adolescents' included in this teacher reference module was homosexuality. Again, failure to control the sexualized body was represented as a challenge to the body politic:

> Overt homosexuality may signify fear of the opposite sex or of adult responsibility. It may indicate a need to defy authority or an attempt to cope with hatred for or competitive attitudes to members of one's own sex. It may even be a flight from reality. (Philippine Center for Population and Development, 1994a, p. 40)

Although some scholars have reported a comparatively tolerant attitude toward homosexuality in the Philippines (e.g., Hart, 1968; Pomado and David, 1994; Whitam and Mathy, 1986; Whitam and Zent, 1984), more have noted the impact of Catholicism and westernization on Filipino attitudes (e.g. Acuna, 1991; Gamboa and Feenstra, 1969; Garcia, 1995; Sandoval, 1992; Singco-Holmes, 1994). Cardinal Sin, as a crusader in the 'revolution of moral values', has forcefully championed this sexual conservatism. Consequently, there has been little discussion of homosexuality in the public schools, the Department of Health HIV materials stress sexual monogamy and abstinence and non-government organizations quietly distribute condoms.

As sexuality was understood theologically and constructed dichotomously (pleasure/danger, sacred/sinful, heterosexual/homosexual) – from martial law to people power – the in(ter)ventions of sexuality and sexuality education have been Western-based. Sexuality education was conceptualized technocratically and constructed systematically under the influence of an army of curricular rationalists first appearing as Thomasite teachers, then as Filipino graduates of US universities, who uncritically embraced the techno-behaviourism of American education (e.g. Bobbitt, 1918; Taylor, 1947; Tyler, 1950).

For example, a series of 'core concepts' in health were recently translated into grade level 'learning competencies'. From the 1,699 learning competencies for elementary education, there were 51 related to population education and from the 1,431 in secondary, 188. About a quarter were to be achieved through teacher-generated materials and DECS-developed modules which included teaching procedures, pre- and post- student tests and lesson plans (Guerrero, 1995). As I detail later in this chapter, a similar approach is used in HIV/AIDS education.

## Mediation and resistance

America's legacy was its intervention in educational and political infrastructures; the Spaniards' most profound impact was their imposition of Catholicism. Here, Western concepts were mediated by indigenous secular and sacred inventions evidenced in Filipino rituals and psychology as well as health-care and sexual practices (Flores, 1968; McCoy, 1982; Tan et al., 1988; Yap, 1986). Beneath the surface features of rosaries and Latin prayers, Holy Days and civil festivities are culturally embedded beliefs and practices (Basilgo, 1994; Go, 1979; Lieban, 1960, 1967; Zialcita, 1986).

When the Catholic missionaries proselytized, for example, they appropriated *loob* (an inner essence or truth which defines a person's consciousness) to impart Western metaphysical concepts of 'self', 'will' and 'soul', employing Aristotelian dualisms such body/spirit, mind/body and I/thou (Mercado, 1975; Miranda, 1989). However, as noted Filipino scholar, Neil Garcia, observes: 'the *loob* was never successfully colonized by and converted into the "self" of Christianity' but remained 'the marker of an indigenous metaphysics . . . as the singular core of the Filipino psyche . . . a transcendental insideness' (Garcia, 1995, pp. 109–10).

This link between animism and Catholicism is not only apparent in the use of iconographic statues and religious medallions as amulets (*anting-anting*) or the appropriation of Latin prayer phrases (*oracion*), such as the Lord's Prayer, for magical spells (*pang-kontra*), but in the construction of sexualities – most notably the *babaylan* and the *bakla*.

There is no Filipino or Ilonggo term for sexual orientation (Tan,

1994c; Garcia, 1995). Unlike the westernized concept of 'homosexual' in which one's sexual orientation is defined by one's same-sex behaviour and one's gender identity socialized on the basis of external genitalia, in the Philippines, particularly the rural areas, gender identity is usually defined by what is within one's soul, not one's genetic code (Sears, 1997). In the case of the *bakla* or *agi*, persons with male bodies but female spirits, the same gendered body (*katawan*) encases the *loob*. Here, one's sexual identity is subservient to one's inner female essence (*babaeng loob*).

Unlike in the West, in Balasan, as in much of the Philippines, sexual object choice neither defines sexual orientation nor one's character. For example, two men can engage in homosexual behaviour with only one viewed as homosexual – the *agi*, who generally assumes the passive sexual role. It would, however, be as difficult for an *agi* to engage in sex with another *agi* as it is easy for a 'normal' Filipino to engage in sex (assuming the active role) with an *agi*, or to assume a long-term relationship with an *agi* while remaining happily heterosexually married. In both cases the Filipino's maleness (*loob*) is not compromised, family honour and children are insured and the tradition of the cross-dresser as an integral component of the Filipino village is continued.

Prior to the mid-sixteenth century, *babaylan* – elderly women healers and religious leaders – held a prominent role in the community alongside the secular position occupied by the upper-class *datu*. Following the Spaniards' arrival in 1569, the *datu* were compromised and enlisted as officers of the Spanish colonial administration. As a result, the *babaylan* (which now included cross-dressing men) assumed secular leadership among the peasantry, fermenting the two greatest Visayan revolts in the mid-seventeenth and late nineteenth centuries. While retaining their traditional role as a medium between the secular and the sacred, some, like the famous Visayan *bayot* (i.e. *bakla*) Buhawi, led revolts against the Spanish conquistadores, or, like Ramos, 300 years later, speared the local parish priest through the heart for condemning their rituals as devil's work (Cullamar, 1986; McCoy, 1982).

Although *babaylan* as cross-dressing shamanistic resistance fighters have long been vanquished from the Visayan hills and Filipino histories, their legacies can still be found. Orly Turingan, Jr. (1995), conducting fieldwork in remote southern Philippine tribal villages, initially noted little discussion about sexuality. After several years of fieldwork, however, he learned that one of the elders whom he assumed was a woman was, in fact, an effeminate man who lived on the town's periphery with his 'brother'.

Held in high status in the village, the location of the elder's home represents the balance between secular and profane in traditional Filipino culture.

Transformed from *babaylan* to *bakla* – from the conjunctions of *babae* (woman)/*lalake* (man) – today most Filipinos view the male homosexual with neither admiration nor affection, seeing him as weak and effeminate. A handful of urban homosexuals who seek to reclaim the *babaylan* legacy and to transform the status of the *bakla* within and outside the homosexual community find themselves at odds with those Filipino AIDS activists who, notably through non-governmental organizations, import Western sexual categories and educational models.

Professor Boy Abaya specializes in medical anthropology at the University of the Philippines. He rejects the Western-inspired, Manila-activists' proposition that a 'gay movement' must be built in the Philippines. He also has conducted extensive work on the *bakla* in Tarlac, documenting the process of 'becoming a *bakla*'. This begins first by a young man recognizing his effeminate traits but only later acknowledging his status as a *bakla* and much later embracing that status. From his experience and fieldwork, the elderly *bakla* initiates the younger into the community. Neither subscribing to a Western conception of gay identity nor a nativist position that romanticizes the *bakla* or *babaylan*, Abaya believes that the *bakla* must build on their present identities and the circumstances of a post-colonial society wherein *sihalis*, *pa man* and *Makati boys* are too often the reverential norm.

*Male (homo)sexual cultures: case studies of local knowledge*
Paradoxes and problems associated with grafting Catholicism onto animism and the imposition of Western concepts onto Eastern consciousness are apparent in the constructions of male (homo)sexuality in the Philippines – as evidenced in six case studies.

In urban areas such as Manila, there is a wide range of men who have sex with men (MSMs), but few identify themselves as gay and fewer report practising safer sex (Nierras *et al.*, 1992; Saba *et al.*, 1993; Tan, 1994b). While nearly all are aware of AIDS and most evidence an understanding of 'safer sex', the use of condoms is sporadic and they are generally improperly used. Gay-identified Filipinos – the most knowledgeable about the HIV virus – are also the most likely to engage in risky sexual behaviours – a phenomenon that is now surfacing in the United States (Turner, 1997).

This diverse group of MSMs is partly represented by several men with whom I engaged in prolonged conversations: Delta, a child *bakla* turned teen 'trendsetting' cross-dresser dating heterosexual men turned andro-gyne seeking gay men; Paul, a *pa man*, whose conception of being gay is Western-inspired; Oscar, a Marxist gay actor and activist; Eduardo, a middle-aged man with children who has yet to 'unfurl his cape' (*lalaka papaong*) yet produces Miss Gay Pageants; Leonardo, an adolescent male freelance sex worker; and Pedro, a heterosexual man who worked for a time as a call-boy.

By the age of nine, Delta considered himself *bakla*. 'I liked boys, but I played with girls.' His family supported his status of *bakla*, with his mother sometimes buying him women's clothing. 'At first I tried ladies' shoes. But, my teacher in English threatened to cut my feet off if I didn't stop!' He continued wearing women's clothes, progressing to panties, to blouses and to dresses.

Delta, who became envious of his two homosexual male cousins who are 'female' entertainers, started 'cross-dressing' when he was twelve years old. As the 'trendsetter' at his school, Delta found that 'boys started to like us more. In practical arts we were the queens of the class.' Among the dozen or so homosexual students, several were *bakla* and others were *sihalis* (bisexual) – creating sometimes vexing triangles: 'A friend of mine had a cousin – a straight guy – who had this crush on me. But, there also was this straight-acting gay who had this big crush on that cousin. Soon no one was speaking with each other.'

Walking on the streets, Delta easily passed as a female with few persons suspecting he was *bakla*:

> You wake up every day, you have to put on make-up, shave this and that, put on dresses. You don't want to let them know that you're gay, because that would blow my cover as a girl. If you are going to be a cross-dresser, you have to be sure that you think like a girl, act like a girl, and be like a girl.

Taking hormones – Delta envisioned himself transformed into a woman – not simply a man dressed as a woman or a man/woman – modelling himself as 'Linda Carter'. Dating heterosexual men, however, Delta was open about his gender, a fact that made little difference to heterosexual men who chose to view him as her. He recalls one man:

> I was walking with a friend and this guy came up to me telling me he

wanted to spend a 'short time' with me. We went to a cheap hotel where I only took off my shirt – showing my boobs. He caressed me as I lay in bed. Then, he fucked me and covered my dick with a pillow. We started seeing each other for about three weeks going to the same hotel and room.

After eight years, Delta is bored with being a 'cross-dresser'. Becoming more androgynous, 'people won't know if I am man/woman or gay/straight. Sometimes, I look like a man, sometimes a woman; sometimes I act like a man, sometimes I act as a gay.' Now preferring gay men, he believes, 'If I do it with a gay man, it will last longer than with a straight man who will be gone tomorrow.'

Noting the 'friction' between cross-dressers, *bakla*, and *sihalis*, Delta distinguished among them:

They don't want to associate with one another. When you're cross-dressing you want to be a woman, you don't want the straight-acting gays noticing you in such a way as to notice that you are also gay. To the Filipinos 'screaming fags' are those *bakla* who dress like a woman and are very open to the public. They shout; they are gay, so what? Then there are the *sihalis* – who are straight-acting – but closet queens.

Paul considers himself gay, although others like Delta would categorize him as *sihalis*. He cruises the Internet and visits the USA regularly. Although he has had sex with both women and men, he prefers men identifying himself as *pa man* (male character) whose sexual icons include Brad Pitt and Ethan Hawke.

Attending discos since he was thirteen, Paul has had his share of broken hearts and abandoned lovers, preferring sometimes the sexual pilgrimage to American bathhouses of San Jose or Chicago. An HIV-educator, Paul appreciates the lure of his attractive Hispanic features but 'protects himself', by refusing to engage in anal sex and 'wisely' choosing his sexual partners. His behaviours, though, are sometimes at odds with his professed beliefs and extant knowledge. He remembers having sex to climax with five different men one night: 'The last man I decided to do it as a favour to him since I was feeling pity. He had been following me around all night and during my 11-hour marathon of sex he had had none; so we had sex and I left with 15 minutes to spare.'

Paul does protect himself from those who might suspect he is homosexual. While one girlfriend knows of his homosexuality and some friends 'suspect', he hangs around college friends who also exhibit masculine features (*pa man*) and share stories of female conquests. Reflecting on Filipino male sexuality, Paul observes:

> Filipino men are much more likely to have sex with one another. For some as long as they are the active partner, they can justify their homosexual affairs. In fact, it's seen as being a status position for a man to have the power to force another man into the role of the woman and for that man to do sexual acts that even a proper woman wouldn't imagine doing.

For Paul being a gay man is as 'natural' as the concept of *bakla* or *babaylan* is foreign. 'Gay is universal', he declares, rejecting the notion of its McDonald's-like imposition. He reads mainly classic gay novels ranging from John Rechy's *City and the Night* to John Reid's *Best Little Boy in the World*. He also owns less popularly well-known novels such as the 1927 lesbian novel, *Dusty Answer*, Richard Amory's 1960s, pre-Stonewall gay pastoral, *Song of the Loon*, and the erotic 1970s novel *All Is Well*. Like many 'Makati-gay boys', he is fond of shopping, enjoys wearing Izod shirts and Polo briefs, and finds the music of Barbra Streisand, Donna Summers and Diana Ross emblematic of gay culture. An admirer of the Gay Handbook, he describes the universality of the gay culture in sexual encounters: the feigned aloofness of a handsome man in a New York gay bar; the confusion of one-night stands with romance; and the erotic journeys into the gay saunas of the 1990s.

Paul frequents the Blue Café, located on a fashionable street in Malate, a neighbourhood bordering Ermita. The first café to have pavement chairs and tables, it attracts mainly intellectuals and artists whose conversations fill the humid night air well into the early morning hours. By midnight a crowd of regulars are seen along the pavement tables, drinking beer and enjoying conversation. The Blue Café's gay friendliness is evident in the supportive looks from the waiters for their *bakla* customers, an occasional gay couple who hold hands amidst conversation and a few hustlers sipping coffee between tricks. Here Paul balances his intellectual cynicism with romantic beliefs, regaling others with favourite lines from Bogart or Hepburn movies or musical lyrics from *Les Misérables*.

Oscar is a student activist at a polytechnic school in Manila. Along with several other 'gay' men, he lives at the Cine Café – one of the centres for gay Filipino life in nearby Quezon City. Mixing poetry readings and political organizing with porn flicks and cruising, the café is 'a haven for those who want culture, who want fun, or who simply want to make it through the night' (Remoto, 1995, p. 162).

Oscar first came to the café in late 1993 when he and others put on its first staged play, *Karga Mano*, about a straight-acting, recently married young lawyer, Marc, who travels away with his effeminate lover, Caloy. As a *mandala*, the play 'helps us to see that our many selves – our very difference – is not a source of sorrow, but of strength. A Zen play that shows us our lives are rivers . . . (Remoto, 1995, p. 130).

Unlike Paul who is *hindi* (not) obvious, Oscar is somewhat effeminate but rejects a *bakla* identity. As a sociology major, Oscar is eager to talk about gay studies and the writings of intellectuals such as Foucault and postmodern theorists – topics that have only recently received intellectual currency thanks to a handful of public intellectuals such as Neil Garcia, Michael Tan and Boy Abaya. For Oscar, 'gay is more a social identity . . . When you say *bakla*, it means "indecisive, weak, confused". I am none of these; I am gay.' Oscar questions, though: 'How can you define a Filipino gay identity without importing ideologies from other countries?'

As we lapse into a conversation, a steady stream of young gay Filipinos enter the café paying the P100 entrance fee. While there is a kitchen, men who come here generally are looking for an evening's entertainment: talking, drinking, playing mah-jong, watching mainstream films or porn movies and – of course – sex.

Scattered around the small first floor are about eight wooden tables and chairs, with a television placed on a small stage showing cable movies. Tonight a feature by Sylvester Stallone was playing; the café also shows gay-thematic films such as *My Own Private Idaho*. Music plays in the background as photography and drawings of men with European features look down from their frames along the walls highlighted by track lighting. Only a few of the men stay for long on the first floor, preferring to round the corner and go upstairs. At the upstairs entrance there is an informational display highlighting 'safe sex behaviours', with photographs of handsome Asian men and notices about forthcoming events. (Condoms, though, are only available by asking the bartender – there is no sign.)

The mezzanine area, composed of a few Spanish-styled chairs and tables and a decorative bar, looks over the first floor. After midnight, when most men come, a few guys lean over the balcony with a drink in hand or talk quietly at a table with a friend. In one corner is a hinged door beyond which lies the café's lure. Through the door is an air-conditioned sexual carnival where the visitor is greeted by flickering erotic images – mostly of American vintage in the *Stallion* or *Blueboy* film traditions. While the benches are always crowded with Filipino watchful eyes on the screen and on the door, little sexual activity occurs here – those seeking physical contact pass through a curtain and walk up a steep blackened staircase to the third floor – where Oscar ventures on occasion. Here the sexual carnival turns into a wilderness, as all fantasies are possible and safe sex behaviour vanishes in lustful darkness.

Eduardo lives adjacent to a rice field in Balasan. Married, in his forties, he has a youthful look and boyish charm. Referring to himself as the 'third sex', Eduardo underscores the toleration that is extended for the *bakla* – or in Ilonggo, *agi*, describing his village as an 'open area' for those *agi* who have come from the hinterlands and nearby islands. Sex is readily available between friends or with a visiting *agi* at the market-place. While a young man has recently returned to his nearby village from Manila to die of AIDS, the disease is considered a plight of the cities. Not surprisingly, condoms are not often used and there are no HIV educational efforts within the community.

With daughters in college and a wife living in Manila, he prefers rural living with his male 'friend', who is a teacher, along with Joan, a former Japanese *japayuki* (transgender hostess). Together they operate 'Miss Gay Pageants' throughout the northern part of Panay, organizing about 30 each year. For a fee (an amount equal to the first place prize purse and expenses such as food, lodging and whisky), Eduardo works with local town officials, who view this as a good way to make money for their community, while the half-dozen or so contestants provide two hours of entertainment.

Each pageant, Eduardo believes, affords an opportunity to 'educate the community'. During the Question and Answer portion of the contest, he selects questions whose answers can provide insight for the local audience: 'What would you do if someone scorns you? How have you contributed to your community?' Eduardo pauses and smiles proudly: 'When we enter the community the degree of acceptance may only be 50 per cent but when we leave it is 100 per cent. After one successful contest, communities are anxious to welcome us back.'

Eduardo's use of the term 'gay', though, is not the same as mine. For example, Eduardo once asked me why I was not 'an open gay'. At first I was dumbfounded, given my activism and writing in the United States as well as my relative openness in the Philippines. However, from Eduardo's perspective I had yet to 'unfurl my cape' (*lalaka papaong*), coming out to the feminine essence of my *loob*.

Eduardo also mentors young *agi*, such as Renaldo and Alonzo, who have 'come out' long ago. In their early teens, these boys grew up in the area where the Beheya Hills descend into the Pacific Ocean. Like many Filipino children, they were told stories of the *aswang* (persons who fly in the dark with halved bodies to attack and eat the livers of sleeping children and pregnant women), *engkantada* (white lady fairies) who cast spells upon unsuspecting humans, *duendes* (dwarfs) who dwell in the mammoth acacia and lonok trees and other tales by relatives, neighbours, or friends who had seen them or whose wrath they have felt. They, too, learned early about the *agi* – persons with male bodies but female spirits.

Like Eduardo, Renaldo and Alonzo have a hard time understanding the Western categorization of 'gay' and 'straight' on the basis of sexual behaviour, or the characterization of boys showing feelings for one another as 'faggots'. They laugh. In this village, boys often express affection by dancing together, holding hands or draping their arms around one another.

At the high school these boys of 'the third sex' are accepted by most teachers, enjoy their *barkada* and seldom face problems with other students. However, both boys are sexually active yet neither is knowledgeable about HIV transmission or the proper use of condoms. And, although discussion of homosexuality or the *agi* is not part of the school curriculum, there is a marginalized acceptance among their teachers. The regional director of Population Education volunteered: 'We must accept the third sex! We must help him appreciate his own self-worth and his potential to be a *parlorista*, *manicurista* or couturier.' Of course, such sentiments are not reflective of all. For example, a former social worker in Balasan freely commented: '*Agi* here are scandalous at festivals with some wearing short dresses, drunk, smoking, heavy make-up. I do not like the *agi* ... Their behaviour is obscene.'

Leonardo is fifteen years old. He attends a Manila high school during the day where he is considered a 'good student'. He works part-time three nights a week as a 'freelance sex worker' – a job he has held since the age of twelve. Leonardo remembers his first encounter:

I was in Harrison Plaza sightseeing. A Filipino man approached me while I was watching the video and a man asked him if he wanted to buy something. I thought he just wanted to be friends. So he did. And my 'friend' asked me to see me the next day which I did. We watched a movie and then he invited me to a hotel to 'rest'. He started caressing me and I felt aroused, so I did it. I got 300 pesos.

After this first sexual experience, Leonardo returned to the plaza where he met other men willing to pay for sexual services. Averaging between one and seven 'customers' a week, Leonardo charges more for foreigners than Filipinos. His motivation, though, is generally not financial. Spending his money on clothes and books, he chooses to do it 'just for fun'.

While Leonardo tells me he has heard of AIDS and takes 'precautions', when asked to take a condom from me (he has none of his own) and describe the process of using it, he falters. Like most of the sex workers with whom I have spoken, Leonardo relies on lotion or saliva and fails to deploy the condom properly to avoid rupture.

Viewing himself as neither *sihalis* nor *bakla*, Leonardo assumes only a passive sexual role and refuses to kiss. Nevertheless, he 'enjoys the sex' – frequenting third-run cinemas. A significant amount of unsafe sexual behaviour occurs in these film theatres where most of the men indulge in oral sex and condoms are rarely used. Heterosexual self-identified men visit to be 'serviced' by the transvestites, while the freelance sex workers, such as Leonardo, ply their trade among the gay men. According to one study:

Inside the movie houses, the balcony and lounge (*itaas*) is considered safe and where sex workers hang around. The balcony is where the gay men frequent. Orgies can be done in the balcony. Most of the men use the balcony for conversations. Men in the balcony know each other and sex can be free. The orchestra (*ibaba*) is where the teenage boys (*bagets*) hang around. The orchestra allows for other moviegoers to watch when there is somebody having sex. The orchestra is where the straight men go, who prefer to be 'serviced' by the transvestites (girlie) types. Sex services in the orchestra is always charged. (Resurreccion *et al.*, 1994, p. 8)

In his ground-breaking book *Philippine Gay Culture: The Last Thirty Years*, Neil Garcia (1995) asserts that in one sense 'we are all sex workers'. Certainly, in the Philippines, where the poverty remains rampant and the influence of Catholicism is pervasive, engaging in forbidden sex for something of value is not uncommon. These forbidden but quietly sanctioned enterprises, however, are an important economic engine for a cash-starved people. However, the importance of one's *barkada* (peer group) and same-sex experiences within it, opportunities for travel, the value of living for the moment, the easy availability of drugs (most notably *shabu*, metamphetamine) and alcohol, sex tourism, sex guilt and homophobia, and a sense of fatalism and passivity coupled with animistic beliefs are also critical in understanding the burgeoning sex industry (Alvarez, 1995; Health Action Information Network, 1995).

While most male sex workers, like Leonardo, are part-time freelancers, Pedro was a full-time worker at a commercial sex establishment. Pedro also does not fit the model Filipino psyche as elaborated upon by Philippine scholars (e.g. Andres, 1987; Andres and Andres, 1987; Ligo-Ralph, 1990). In a culture generally defined as family centred, Pedro has long broken ties with his immediate family; in a culture where the *barkada* (peer group) defines choices if not selection of clothes, drinking patterns or drug use and films, Pedro resolutely stands on his own:

> I've learned that the *barkada* is only there for socializing, they're not there when you need them or you're in trouble. I've been in street fights and rather than going off and dragging my *barkada* into it, I'd just as soon fight them myself. It is my responsibility. I don't want to be responsible for what happens to others.

Pedro is known in his neighbourhood as someone who has nothing to lose and has no fear of dying. 'When someone starts the fight I lose all control. My only concern is to make sure that I don't get hurt.' On occasion Pedro has found himself in jail because of the fights by the police who often harass those in his neighbourhood. 'There is no justice for the poor', he states in a coldly distant manner.

I first met Pedro at a time when there was little awareness of HIV. He worked as a call-boy in one of the commercial male sex establishments that have long been closed by Police Chief Lim, tired of Ermita's reputation as the sex capital of Manila. In the six years since I have known Pedro his living situation has changed little: an occasional job; girlfriends whose work helps to support the couple; sneak looks at his son born out of marriage and now carefully guarded by his would-be in-laws; odd jobs around the *barangay*. What has changed, however, is his outlook on life:

There is no past, there is no future, there is only today. I accept what each day brings with dignity. You see that is all I have that is my own – my dignity, my honour, my self-respect.

Sitting around a wrought-iron patio table with a huge yellow umbrella during an afternoon summer rain shower drinking rum, Pedro, in typical Filipino manner, asks,

'Can I ask you a question?'
'Sure', I respond.
'What category am I? I have had live-in girlfriends. I have a child. But, also I have made love to men.'

Pedro has served as my interpreter for several of the freelance male sex workers I have interviewed. Without Pedro's help, finding individuals willing to talk honestly would have been as difficult for a *kano* (an American who is often viewed as a potential patron) as it is for a social service representative (who is often seen as an informant for the health department or police). During these interviews, I used a modified version of the old Kinsey scale. Rather than asking someone to label themselves as 'gay', 'bisexual' or 'straight' – categories with shifting cultural and historical meanings – I asked each young man to think about his life during the past six months and to rate himself somewhere on a seven-point scale (from completely same-sex to completely other gender) regarding with whom they socialize, whom they go to when they have joys or sorrows to share, whom they find attractive, whom they fantasize about sexually and with whom they engage in sexual intimacies. Their stories were inevitably more complex than a simple – and misleading – sexual self-characterization would have been.

'Well, you've heard me ask questions in my interviews about a person's gender preferences for different types of activities.' I pause. 'Where do you place yourself?'
    Stubbornly Pedro persists. 'Yes, I've already tried that. But, it hasn't helped.' He goes on to explain his difficulty in relating to other persons, particularly his various girlfriends. 'They don't understand me. We just can't communicate. I have no one to share my problems with, except for you. But we see one another perhaps once a year.'

'When you fantasize about sexual matters, who do you think about,' I ask, believing that he may not have really delved into these questions in sufficient depth.

'Usually it's a group encounter. Two women or one man and a woman.'

The rain has stopped and we drink another glass of rum. I persist. 'Why is it important for you to label yourself? '

'I'm not *bakla*, but neither do I feel like I'm just a heterosexual or *sihalis*. What am I?'

'Why do you have sex with the people whom you choose to have sex?'

'Because I love them. It is my way of expressing my love for them.'

Pedro has visited the Library Foundation, a private AIDS organization that is one of the focal points for the emerging 'gay movement' in Manila. The Foundation is located in a two-storey house on a neighbourhood corner: walking into the Foundation we are greeted by posters. Pedro is clearly ill at ease. One of the posters is of an Anglo with rugged features in a tank top stating, 'Yeah, I'm gay. Got a problem with that?' A multi-coloured 'gay flag' hangs over a bathroom door. On the staircase are posters with an AIDS theme; all eight are of men with European features. One reads 'Conquer AIDS' with five men elevating the gay flag in a spin-off of the famous Second World War marine photograph.

Picking up material about HIV transmission – both in English and Tagalog – we speak briefly with one of the men working at the centre. As we leave, I ask Pedro if he wishes to return with me for the night's open discussion. He hesitates and asks that he be excused 'if possible' from his interpreting duties. With nodding understanding, I agree.

The meeting was to begin at 8 p.m., but characteristically started later – around 9.30. Mixing Tagalog with English, the group of 20 or so, many of whom are veterans of the Foundation's two-day HIV workshops, are broken into pairs for conversational ice-breakers and we then move into a large discussion about 'why gays cannot relate'. Here, the discussion centres around fear, familial ties, homophobia and divisions within the community such as between the *bakla* and *pa man*, tomboys (lesbians) and gay men. At the end of an hour our discussion had moved to 'gay–gay relationships' with a wrap up by the facilitator on those 'things about being gay upon which we can agree'. These included Filipino gay men assuming 'any role and having any relationship', the need to get beyond stereotypes and 'as we transform our language, let us not take the fun out of being gay'.

Later that week, I speak with the Foundation's Director, Ted Nierras (see Nierras, 1995). Since the autumn of 1991, he explains, the Foundation has conducted HIV and safer sex efforts – averaging a two-day workshop every two months with about two dozen participants. Each workshop cohort meets six weeks later to discuss their attitudes and behaviours. These cohorts or 'batches' then interact with those from other cohorts in public sessions such as the one I had attended. He explains:

> There is a lot of misogyny in *bakla* culture; there is a lot of self-esteem issues; there's a lot of difficulty. We are trying to go beyond influencing individuals by creating groups who become a peer group.
>
> Maybe about ten in each workshop live the gay subculture of Manila. But, of those 25, one or two will actually have been in a room with these gay men talking about issues that affect their lives: talking about coming out with their families, for example. To have that experience is tremendously empowering. *Loob* becomes lighter – it is freedom; there is a sense of being unfettered.

The diversity of men who have sex with other men, though, is seldom reflected in the educational interventions which are principally targeted at gay men like Paul through groups like the Library Foundation or sex workers such as Pedro. More often, materials and instructional methods fail to take into account local knowledge.

## Educational in(ter)ventions

On the wall of a science classroom I visited at Balasan High School, adjacent to the rice field where Eduardo lives, appeared a statement of ten axioms of scientific study. Speaking to those students about HIV transmission, more than a few seem troubled with my Western explanations. Since infancy they have witnessed the power of *babaylan* and *abularios* (herbalists) in diagnosing and treating diseases – often caused by spirits or sorcery. Exasperated, I asked how many of the teenagers believed in forces unseen or unproved through scientific methods; more than half of the class raised their hands – others afterward confessed that they, too, had little faith in science but felt obliged to submit the 'right answer'.

The distance between the Ministry of Education and this rural school is as far as between science and sorcery. Although the national curriculum encourages the use of 'locally indigenous materials', no such materials had been developed. In fact, throughout the entire province, there was no formal curricular integration of materials about HIV/AIDS.

Three years earlier, in late 1992, President Fidel Ramos had signed an Executive Order creating the Philippine National AIDS Council. Within two years the government was spending P39.5 million (about 1.5 million 1995 US dollars) to implement the Council's activities (Gacad, 1995). By then, there were 587 HIV cases registered, with most occurring in the 30–39 age range and about evenly split between male and female.

Like other Asian and African countries, the primary mode of HIV transmission was unprotected sexual intercourse between men and women. Men engaging in sex with other men comprised one-quarter of reported infections (Chin, 1993; Program for Applied Technology in Health, 1994a). The AIDS Committee of the Department of Health estimated that the actual number of HIV infections in the Philippines was between 15,000 and 20,000 with a cumulative number of infections projected at over 90,000 by the year 2000 (Chin, 1993; HIV/AIDS Education Subcommittee, 1994).

During the early 1990s, the Department of Health had centred its AIDS intervention strategies on monitoring urban 'sentinel groups': female registered sex workers; freelance female sex workers; male sex workers; men who have sex with men; males with sexually transmitted diseases; and intravenous drug users. The policy objective was to reduce levels of HIV incidence and to limit seroprevalence rates in key target populations in metropolitan centres which, in turn, was anticipated to impact the periphery.

This centre-peripheral strategy was also evidenced in the role of foreign government and international health organizations' intervention in Filipino HIV education and AIDS prevention strategies. The US-funded Program for Applied Technology in Health (PATH) as well as the USAID Mission in the Philippines, for example, provided resources for prevention, surveillance and education activities, as did the Social Research and Community Intervention in HIV/AIDS offered by the Tropical Health Program of the University of Queensland. Agencies of the United Nations in the Philippines established the UN Interagency Task Force on HIV/AIDS and the World Health Organization provided assistance in the development of AIDS educational materials.

Generally, educational models, implemented by a group of non-governmental organizations (NGOs) and funded by these international agencies, have sought to develop an awareness of the disease, knowledge of its transmission and the reduction of unsafe sexual behaviour. This public health algorithm was based on Western logic, not Eastern realities.

Employing a rationalistic model that assumes linkages between awareness, knowledge and practice, most AIDS education reports from these NGOs to their funding agencies cited the number of workshops conducted, pre-post levels of knowledge and self-reported changes in behaviour (number of partners, condom use, non-penetrative sex) as evidence of their effectiveness. As these NGOs proliferated, competed and overlapped with one another, AIDS awareness was at a 'saturation point' while knowledge about prevention methods remained low, negative attitudes about those who acquired the disease were widespread and unprotected sex was still prevalent (Health Action Information Network, 1994; Program for Applied Technology in Health, 1995; ReachOut AIDS et al., 1995).

Thus, while educational interventions have fostered awareness about AIDS and condom use (Tan, 1990; 1994b), such interventions have generally been ineffective in changing behaviour (Aplasca et al., 1993; Program for Applied Technology in Health, 1995; ReachOut AIDS et al., 1995; Tiglao et al., 1991). Developed by techno-rationalists, these intervention efforts focus on information and decision-making rather than on meaning and desire.

A series of modules was also developed by the Philippine government for the use of teachers and guidance counsellors with support from the United National Population Fund under the title, 'A Guidance Program on Adolescent Development for High School Students' (Philippine Center for Population and Development, 1994a; 1994b). These modules include units on boy–girl relationships, premarital sex, adolescent pregnancy and HIV/AIDS. Emphasis is placed on facts such as primary transmittal methods and the difference between HIV and AIDS. In none of these materials is there any discussion of the phenomenon of the *bakla*, older terminology such as 'risk groups' is also used and there is an absence of any explicit figures to demonstrate the use of condoms – although anatomically correct depictions are provided. While some modification of the material has been made, much of it – including sketches, 800 numbers and references to the United States – remain.

A similar techno-rationalist approach was employed in the

development of the HIV/AIDS curriculum by the Department of Education, Culture and Sports (DECS) – the central Filipino educational
ministry. The DECS technical committee on school AIDS education was
established in 1988 to develop AIDS education into the existing school
curricula. That year, an Asian Area survey found the Philippines were
highest in the number of respondents (two-thirds) who believed 'it is
people's own fault that they get AIDS' (Tan, 1994b, p. 17), and only a year
before the Department had issued a health bulletin noting the mode of
transmission and preventive measures (DECS, 1987).

The HIV/AIDS curricula were two years in review and development.
The prototype materials were produced in conjunction with the School
Health and Nutrition Center and the World Health Organization. In this
developmental process, entry points were identified in the curriculum,
competencies for AIDS materials formulated, prototype materials tested
and evaluation measures constructed. Many of these instructional materials were borrowed directly from the United States or modified slightly with
an emphasis on rational decision-making, self-discipline and moral injunctions. As the HIV virus spread, during the next six years DECS was
'continuously pre-testing the integration of AIDS into the school curricula'
(HIV/AIDS Education Subcommittee, 1994). Bureaucratic inertia,
technocratic-mindedness and sexual conservatism typified such governmental efforts.

One of the goals for this 'school based AIDS education project', was 'to
develop matured and responsible studentry imbued with desirable health
values which can assist them in making rational decisions' (Trinidad,
1994, p. 55). Among the module's core messages, developed in 1994, was
the 'spiritual/moral dimension of human sexuality ... stages of heterosexual development appropriate to grade level' (Department of Education,
Culture and Sports, 1994a, p. 97).

In equally linear fashion, an input–output model, replete with organizational diagrams and designated job responsibilities, was employed. Core
messages were laid out in a formulaic and generalized manner (Department of Education, Culture and Sports, 1994b). For example, message 4.3
stated, 'Individuals can make rational decisions and apply these to protect
themselves from HIV infection.' Message 4.5 specifies, 'The formation of
good habits, correct attitudes, values, and behaviour towards sex and
sexuality will help prevent HIV/AIDS infection.' This was followed by
'Love, respect, close ties and faith in God should prevail in the family'
(4.5.1) and 'Self-discipline is a virtue that one should observe' (4.5.2).

The consensus among knowledgeable AIDS workers is that DECS places too much emphasis on the physiological aspects of AIDS and HIV transmission (e.g. white/red blood cells) and on 'scaring people' about AIDS and too little consideration for desire and meaning. Thus, while one of the few experimental studies of the impact of HIV education efforts among high school students concluded that most were fearful of AIDS, researchers found that 'some students who may have read or heard about HIV/AIDS have only recalled the terms but may not have recalled or understood their real meanings' (Pomado and David, 1994, p. 38). Another study using a random sampling of high school students participating in a school-based AIDS education module found similar high levels of knowledge without condom use among those sexually active (Aplasca *et al.*, 1993).

Not surprisingly, the Director of the Program for Applied Technology in Health, like others I interviewed, eventually concluded that 'little can be done within the formal educational system', choosing to direct their efforts at the NGOs. These findings echo Tan's (1994b) weariness that such programmes which 'prescribe "value change" and "value formation" programs ... may prove unproductive considering that there is very little work done on Filipinos' interpretations of sex and sexuality and their ways of rationalizing sexual behavior' (p. 18).

Generally, local knowledge and emotion not scientific knowledge and rationality dictated the sexual behaviours of those Filipinos with whom I spoke. The voluminous 'core concepts' and 'learning competencies' coupled to moral admonitions and fear tactics fail to intersect the 'cartographies of desire' (Manalansan, 1993) evidenced in the stories of Delta, Leonardo, Pedro, Eduardo, Paul and Oscar. Here the mismatch between the educational map and the sexual terrain is most evident. My findings parallel those of other researchers.

While most see themselves 'at risk', some simply are 'not bothered because AIDS is a "scientific cause and effect"' or express sentiments such as 'AIDS is to see is to believe. Only God knows what will happen' (Resurreccion *et al.*, 1994, pp. 6–7). Although aware of risk reduction measures, most of my respondents, like nearly one-half in a study of college-educated gay men, believed that 'risk of infection could be reduced by having regular check-ups, washing genitals before and after sex, taking vitamins, medicines, and antibiotics, and practicing withdrawal' (Reach-Out *et al.*, 1995). Another common perception, validated by my interview data, is 'that one needs to take a rest after a rigorous activity, especially after sex, before washing or taking a bath, or else the person develops arthritis or "pasma" ' (Resurreccion *et al.*, 1994, p. 3); this is viewed as a greater concern than contracting the HIV virus.

Generally, the informational-based approach adopted by NGOs as well as by government educational agencies may not 'always be appropriate for less rationally driven individuals'. The major funding agency for many of these groups, Program for Applied Technology in Health (1995), further observes that emotional-based approaches 'may be more effective for changing behavior or risk-takers ... [however] these have yet to be developed and tested in the Philippines' (p. 19).

## Sexual in(ter)ventions

Despite educational interventions and the subsequent high level of HIV awareness and knowledge, there is widespread unprotected casual sex among men in the Philippines – across all age groups, social classes, occupations and sexual identities. Educational interventions generally have failed to take into account sexual inventions of Filipinos. Although a few NGOs have begun culturally to calibrate their efforts, gay activism has become a powerful sexual intervention.

While some commercial male sex workers work at one of the handful of 'gay' clubs, in contrast to the female sex industry, most male sex workers work 'freelance' in the various film theatres, malls and streets of Metro Manila where condom use is sharply lower than those working in commercial establishments (Bennett *et al.*, 1995; Health Action Information Network, 1992a, 1992b; Tan, 1990). The absence of legal requirements for registration and testing – NGOs generally target commercial sex establishments – coupled with the fact that most male sex workers are part-time freelancers, like Leonardo, and few identify themselves as gay with many concerned about becoming *bakla* defines a population ill-served by conventional AIDS education interventions (Health Action Information Network, 1992a, 1992b).

In the first HIV sentinel surveillance round in the Metro Manila and Cebu areas (Dayrit *et al.*, 1993), 93 per cent of men in high 'risk groups' having sex with men reported they never used condoms. For male sex workers, there is a notable problem in negotiating with clients regarding condom use and the client's appearance (i.e. ill-looking, *bakla* or foreigner) often dictates its occasional use (Health Action Information Network, 1995; Ramiro and Ramos, 1993; ReachOut *et al.*, 1995). Further rationalistic interventions, such as safe sex workshops or certification of HIV negative status, have little positive impact on youthful Filipinos when providing the 'right' answer (not challenging authority) and animistic beliefs (not scientific schooling) predominates:

> Even after HIV workshops, many sex workers continue to think of looking for signs and symptoms for 'AIDS' in the partner as a risk-reduction measure, even if in post-workshop questionnaires they say they agree that one can still look healthy with HIV . . . sex workers carry their certificates almost as if it had protective value [*anting-anting*]. Many sex workers do not see that the certificate – if it has any value at all – 'protects' the client and not him, except in a magical way. (Health Action Information Network, 1995, p. 17)

Another group of men who have sex with men are *sihalis*. Interestingly, analyses of data from HIV workshops revealed that three-quarters of those who identify themselves as bisexual – like Paul – had engaged in exclusively homosexual behaviour during the past year (Tan, 1993, 1994a). Further, among both workshop and bathhouse samples – half of whom identified themselves as bisexual – most had tried anal sex, with a majority doing this without the use of the condom (Fleras, 1995a; ReachOut et al., 1995; Tan, 1994a). Nevertheless, 'only about a third of them thought that AIDS was a very real threat for people like them' (ReachOut et al., 1995, p. 1).

There are, too, men who engage in unsafe sex, such as Delta and Pedro, who have multiple or shifting sexual identities and who 'will take the risk and have sex with another man to whom they are attracted' (Resurreccion et al., 1994, p. 2) despite decision-making abilities and HIV knowledge. Such inventions of sexual identities and behaviours have been largely ignored in HIV education efforts.

Reporting their 'findings remain markedly constant' throughout the early and mid-1990s, another AIDS educational group, the Library Foundation (n.d., 1993, 1995) found fair to high levels of HIV knowledge among college-educated gay men, like Oscar, with about one-half of those reporting anal sex not using a condom (Tan, 1993). Nevertheless, few were willing to be tested for the HIV virus and 'attitudes with respect to issues which provide a context for safer sex, such as sexuality, promiscuity, and even testing, remain unfavorable . . . ' (Library Foundation, 1995). Even those men reporting condom usage often use non-water-based lubricants such as lotion, saliva and hair glow or fail to put the condom on properly (Health Action Information Network, 1994; Tan, 1994a). In one study, less than 2 per cent of gay men reported using water-based lubricants (Tan, 1994a). Most, though, are bothered by condom smell (during oral sex), lack of sensation or simply become too involved in the moment to use such protection (Resurreccion *et al.*, 1994).

Among the 50 or so NGOs nationwide who are members of an HIV network, only a few have sought directly to relate their intervention efforts to these diverse MSM communities, partly represented by the men portrayed in this chapter. ReachOut, an AIDS education foundation founded by a group of concerned artists, writers, doctors and other professionals, quickly discovered that reading materials had 'minimal impact because the men do not keep the materials, using the materials as fans . . . ' (Resurreccion *et al.*, 1994, p. 9). ReachOut, therefore, produced fans (few of the third-run theatres are air-conditioned) with safer sex messages and instructions (Fleras, 1995b). Similarly, the Health Action Information Network (1992a) concluded that workshop pedagogical methods had to be grounded in 'sex workers own culture. This includes indigenous medical beliefs such as hot-cold inter-action (e.g., using a condom or interfermoral sexual intercourse aggravates the "hot" state of a penis after sexual intercourse, making the person more vulnerable to pasma).'

Some AIDS educators have chosen another strategy. Whether one is gay, *bakla*, *sihalis* or a sex worker, homophobia is one common denominator (Tan, 1994a). Disempowerment, linked to deep-seated and widespread homophobia, has motivated some to adopt Western-style conceptual and organizational models for gay activism.

The Library Foundation is a 'gay men's community-based organization' which works for 'the empowerment of individual Filipino gay men', believing that 'the Filipino gay male community is central to the prevention of HIV transmission among all Filipino men who have sex with men'. The Foundation's Mission Statement goes on to cite its membership in the International Lesbian and Gay Association and the Global Alliance of Lesbian and Gay Asians as evidence of its efforts to encourage 'international and local solidarity'. Its Director, Ted Nierras (1995) observes:

We are in a very conservative culture that is overlaid by evangelical Catholicism which makes it very difficult about being gay. This is a tolerant culture only in that society will tolerate a *bakla* who lives traditionally like a *bakla*. In an urban setting that becomes very difficult if not impossible. You are going to get a lot of different identities which society will not necessarily tolerate – unless we organize.

*Bakla* is certainly more indigenous than gay. One of Neil's [Garcia] projects is to reclaim the category of *bakla*. At the same time, that should not imply that there is a cabal of westernized gay men in Manila who want to replace it. There is no plot; we simply utilize the categories we have.

We need to remember that these categories are not necessarily more Western than Eastern. Contextualized within a particular historical development, they did not exist in the West until about a century ago. These developments are now happening worldwide. Though we may appropriate Western forms, the (con)text is different.

Historicized as *babaylan*, vilified as *bakla*, ghettoized as *parloristas* or *manicuristas*, commercialized as sex workers and colonized as *sihalis* and *pa man*, 'our history spans hundreds, even thousands, of years; our geography is global and postcolonial; our genders . . . multiple and shifting' (Nierras, 1994, p. 198).

However, among the diverse group of Filipino men who have sex with men, those who self-identify as 'gay', in the Western sense, are a minority. As Nierras argues, 'The number of gay men who are apolitical far outnumber those who have a sense for what the community can be. What we want to avoid is that *pa man* is the only group that is working toward gay goals.'

The paradox of building a westernized gay movement on the back of the HIV pandemic in a culture transfixed by animism, baptized by Catholicism, transformed by colonialism and fractured sexually has not been lost within gay intellectual circles. Michael Tan (1994c) observed:

It is not surprising that in the incipient gay movement in the Philippines, group discussions continue to run into intellectual culs-de-sac because of the attempts to use these Western binary sets (gay vs. straight) . . . It is vital that a distinction be made between our situation and that of the industrialized West, where a sharper boundary divides religious and secular explanations. In transitional societies like our own, there are no such boundaries. (Tan, 1994c, p. 209)

More lyrically, Neil Garcia writes:

Between a misreading of the West from the point of view of its colony and a misreading of the colony from the point of view of the West, it is the latter that lends itself more effortlessly to producing injustice and oppression insofar as knowledge itself generally becomes officialized ... The gays [of the Philippines] of today are precisely situated at these crossroads ... The gay script is at once singular and plural in themes, the same way that our history is at once minoritized and universal, *bakla* and homosexual, feminine and masculine, funny and sad, overt and covert, inside and outside in social significance and in relation to ourselves. Finally, it is we who have fashioned, from the fibers and filaments of our dreams and loves, the soft and smooth fabric of brilliant sundry pink, green, and yellow, all colors that can ever be made to approximate the beauty which is our veritable source, for the future's one grand unfurling of lives let to fly unchallenged in the breeze. (Garcia, 1995, p. 226)

Addressing these shifting and unfurling identities in a culture without traditional Western boundaries is the greatest challenge facing the HIV educators; marginalizing these cultures by importing or imposing our sex/gender-ordered meanings is the gravest danger.

We can no longer afford to assume falsely that sexual concepts are universal (Morris, 1994; Vance, 1991); we must recognize its inventions and the problematics of our interventions – economic as well as cultural (Altman, 1996). This involves, as Simon Watney (1989) observed astutely nearly a decade ago:

a commitment to the fullest possible understanding of the ways in which the psychic reality of all aspects of human sexuality are always organized symbolically in excess of both biological needs and the demands of many cultural and political roles that sexuality is currently used to naturalize and legitimate.

Without addressing the indigenous and colonized inventions of sexuality (with its incumbent homophobia), the mixture of animism with Catholicism and the neocolonial relationships between the colonizer and the colonized, HIV intervention efforts in the Philippines will continue to be fashioned by 'fibers and filaments of our dreams and loves'.

# References

Acuna, J. (1991). 'Survey data on religion and morality', *Social Weather Bulletin*, **91** (22 November).

Altman, D. (1996). 'Rupture or continuity: the internationalization of gay identities', *Social Text*, **48**(14): 77–94.

Alvarez, R. (1995). *Narrative Report on the In-depth Interview among Male Commercial Sex Workers (MCWs) in Selected Bars in Metropolitan Manila*. Quezon City: Institute for Social Studies and Action.

Andres, T. (1987). *Understanding Filipino Values on Sex*. Manila: Our Lady of Manaoag Publishers.

Andres, T. and Andres, P. (1987). *Understanding the Filipino*. Manila: New Day.

Aplasca, M. *et al.* (1993). 'A model AIDS education program for high school students in the Philippines'. Paper presented at the 1993 International AIDS Conference, 6–11 June.

Balquiedra, M. (1994). *Remedios Foundation First Quarterly Progress Report*, 2 October. Manila: Program for Applied Technology in Health.

Balquiedra, M. (1995a). *Remedios Foundation Second Quarterly Progress Report*, 1 January. Manila: Program for Applied Technology in Health.

Balquiedra, M. (1995b). *Remedios Foundation Third Quarterly Progress Report*, 2 April. Manila: Program for Applied Technology in Health.

Basilgo, E. (1994). 'Faith healing in metro Cebu: proposed guidelines for an inculturated religious education'. Unpublished doctoral dissertation, University of San Carlos, Cebu.

Bennett *et al.* (1995). *Mid-term Evaluation of the AIDS Surveillance and Education Project*. Manila: US Agency for International Development.

Bobbitt, F. (1918). *The Curriculum*. New York: Arno Press.

Chin, J. (1993). *Consultant Report on HIV/AIDS Surveillance Strategies and Estimation and Projection of HIV/AIDS in the Philippines*. Manila: Program for Applied Technology in Health.

Constantino, R. (1982). *The Miseducation of the Filipino*. Quezon City: Foundation for Nationalist Studies.

Cullamar, E. (1986). *Babaylanism in Negros*. Manila: New Day.

Dayrit, M., White, M. and Badoy, T. (1993). *Results of the First HIV Surveillance Round*. Manila: Program for Applied Technology in Health.

Department of Education, Culture and Sports (1987, 28 April). *Information Campaign on Acquired Immune Deficiency Syndrome*. DECS Bulletin No. 2. Quezon City: DECS.

Department of Education, Culture and Sports (1994a). *A List of Core Messages/Concepts in Population Education for Elementary Level as Determined by Experts*. Quezon City: DECS.

Department of Education, Culture and Sports (1994b). Workshop on the revision of instructional materials for AIDS education. 30 May–11 June. Imus, Cavite: Philippines.

deVera, M. (1982). 'Pakikipagkuwentuhan' [Storytelling], in R. Pe-Pua (ed.), *Filipino Psychology*. Quezon City: Philippine Psychology Research and Training House, pp. 187–93.

Enriquez, V. (1977). 'Filipino psychology in the third world', *Philippine Journal of Psychology*, **10**(1): 3–18.

Enriquez, V. (1979). 'Towards cross-culture knowledge through cross-indigenous methods and perspective', *Philippine Journal of Psychology*, **12**(1): 9–15.

Fleras, J. (1995a). ReachOut AIDS Education Foundation. *First Quarterly Report*. Manila: Program for Applied Technology in Health.

Fleras, J. (1995b). ReachOut AIDS Education Foundation. *Second Quarterly Report*. Manila: Program for Applied Technology in Health.

Flores, F. (1968). 'A study of the superstitious beliefs and practices of Cebuano parents concerning pregnancy and childbirth'. Unpublished master's thesis. Cebu, Philippines: University of San Carlos.

Gacad, E. (1995). *The Philippine National AIDS–STD Prevention and Control Program*. Manila: Department of Health.

Gamboa, V. and Feenstra, H. (1969). 'Deviant stereotypes: call girls, male homosexuals and lesbians', *Philippine Sociological Review*, **17**(3/4): 136–48.

Garcia, N. (1995). *Philippine Gay Culture: The Last Thirty Years*. Quezon City: University of Philippines Press.

Go, F. (1979). 'Mothers, maids and the creatures of the night: the persistence of Philippine folk religion', *Philippine Quarterly of Culture and Society*, **7**: 179–203.

Guerrero, C. (6 June 1995). Interview with James T. Sears. Department of Education, Culture, and Sports, Manila.

Hart, D. (1968). 'Homosexuality and transvestism in the Philippines', *Behavior Science*, **3**: 211–48.

Health Action Information Network (1992a). *Final Report: HIV/AIDS Prevention Project for Male Sex Workers in Metro Manila*. Quezon City: HAIN.

Health Action Information Network (1992b). *Final Report: HIV/AIDS Prevention Project: Medical and Nursing Students in Metro Manila*. Quezon City: HAIN.

Health Action Information Network (1994). 'Social and behavioral aspects of HIV/AIDS in the Philippines', *Remedios Newsletter*, **2**(9): 1–2, 8.

Health Action Information Network (1995). *Qualitative Data Overview Report: Male Sex Workers in Metro Manila*. Quezon City: HAIN.

HIV/AIDS Education Subcommittee and Program for Appropriate Technology in Health (1994). *ASEP Education Strategy. Part I*. Submitted to the Department of Health, Republic of the Philippines and the US Agency for International Development. Manila: Program for Applied Technology in Health.

Library Foundation (1993). *Research Report for TOT and HIV 1–7*. Manila: Program for Applied Technology in Health.

Library Foundation (1995). *HIV Workshops 24–27, Preliminary KAP Profile*. Manila: Program for Applied Technology in Health.

Library Foundation (n.d.). *Initiating and Sustaining Safe Sexual Behavior among Filipino Men Who Have Sex with Men*. Manila: Program for Applied Technology in Health.

Lieban, R. (1960). 'Sorcery, illness, and social control in a Philippine municipality', *Southwestern Journal of Anthropology*, **16**(2): 251–60.

Lieban, R. (1967). *Cebuano Sorcery*. Berkeley: University of California Press.

Ligo-Ralph, V. (1990). 'Some theses concerning the Filipino value system', *Philippine Quarterly of Culture & Society*, **18**: 149–61.

McCoy, A. (1982). 'Baylan: animist religion and Philippine peasant ideology', *Philippine Quarterly of Culture and Society*, **10**: 141–94.

Manalansan, M. (1993). '(Re)locating the gay Filipino: resistance, postcolonialism, and identity', *Journal of Homosexuality*, **26**(2/3): 53–72.

Mataragnon, R. (1977). 'A conceptual and psychological analysis of "sumpong"', *Philippine Journal of Psychology*, **10**(1): 45–54.

Mataragnon, R. (1979). 'The case for an indigenous psychology', *Philippine Journal of Psychology*, **12**(1): 3–8.

Mercado, L. (1975). *Elements of Filipino Theology*. Tacloban City: Divine Word Publications.

Ministry of Education, Culture and Sports (1985). *Human Sexuality and Reproduction, IX Module*. Manila: Author.

Miranda, D. (1989). *Loob: The Filipino Within*. Manila: Divine Word Publications.

Morris, R. (1994). 'Three sexes and four sexualities: redressing the discourses on gender and sexuality in contemporary Thailand', *positions*, **2**.

Nery, L. (1979a). 'Pakikisama as a method: a study of a subculture', *Philippine Journal of Psychology*, **12**(1): 27–32.

Nery, L. (1979b). 'The covert subculture of male homosexual prostitutes in Metro-Manila', *Philippine Journal of Psychology*, **12**(1): 27–34.

Nierras, E. (1994). 'This risky business of desire: theoretical notes for and against Filipino gay male identity politics', in J. Garcia and D. Remoto (eds), *Ladlad: An Anthology of Philippine Gay Writing*. Manila: Anvil, pp. 196–201.

Nierras, T. (1995). Interview with James T. Sears, 9 June, Manila.

Nierras, T., Austero, B., Santos, J. and de Real, A. (1992). 'HIV/AIDS and the Filipino gay male community'. Paper presented at the International Conference on AIDS, 19–24 July.

Pe-Pua, R. (ed.) (1982). *Filipino Psychology: Theory, Method and Application*. Quezon City: Philippine Psychology Research and Training House.

Pe-Pua, R. (1989). 'Pagtatanong-Tanong: a cross-cultural research method', *International Journal of Intercultural Relations*, **13**(2): 147–63.

Philippine Center for Population and Development (1994a). *A Guidance Program on Adolescent Development for High School Students: Module 2 for Fourth Year Students*. Manila: PCPD.

Philippine Center for Population and Development (1994b). *A Guidance Program on Adolescent Development for High School Students: Module 2 for Third Year Students*. Manila: PCPD.

Pomado, N. and David, F. (1994). *Awareness, Knowledge and Attitudes of Practices on HIV/AIDS among Junior and Senior High School Students in Iloilo City: A Baseline Study*. Iloilo City: Buas Damlag Foundation.

Program for Applied Technology in Health (1994). ASEP Consultative Workshop, 7 February 1994. Santa Cruz, Manila: PATH.

Program for Applied Technology in Health (1995). *First Annual Report*, 1 January–31 December 1994. Submitted to the Department of Health, Republic of the Philippines and the US Agency for International Development. Manila: PATH.

Ramiro, L. and Ramos, M. (1993). 'Risk-taking behavior in relation to AIDS among child sex workers'. Paper presented at the International Conference on AIDS, 6–11 June.

ReachOut AIDS Education Foundation, Institute for Social Studies and Action, Health Action Information Network and Children's Lab. (1995). *Qualitative Data Relevant to Aids Prevention Gathered from Sex Workers in the Metro Manila Area of the Philippines*. Manila: Program for Applied Technology in Health.

Remedios Foundation (1993). *Remedios AIDS Hotline*, 1993 profile. Manila: Remedios Foundation.

Remoto, D. (1995). *Seduction and Solitude*. Manila: Anvil.

Resurreccion, P., Castro, J. and Fleras, J. (1994). *A Qualitative Study on Drugs and Substance Use, Sex Practices, HIV/AIDS: Knowledge of Men Who Have Sex with Men Cruising Metro Manila Moviehouses and Establishment-based Female Sex Workers in Pasay City*. Manila: ReachOut AIDS Education Foundation.

Saba, S. *et al.* (1993). 'Accessing and educating men who have sex with men'. Paper presented at the International Conference on AIDS, 6–11 June.

Sandoval, G. (1992). 'Filipino attitudes toward sexual relations', *Social Weather Stations*, **92**(13–14): 1–11.

Santiago, C. and Enriquez, R. (1976). *Tungo Sa Makapilipinong Pananaliksik*. Sikolohiyang Pilipino, **4**: 4–10.

Sears, J. T. (1997). 'Centering culture: teaching for critical sexual literacy using the sexual diversity wheel', *Journal of Moral Education*, **26**(3): 273–83.

Singco-Holmes, M. (1994). *A Different Love: Being Gay in the Philippines*. Manila: Anvil.

Tan, M. (1990). *Synthesis of an AIDS KAP (Knowledge, Attitudes and Practices) Survey among Sentinel Groups in Metro Manila*. Report prepared for the AIDSCOM project and the Department of Health. Manila.

Tan, M. (1993). *An Analysis of the Data from the Library Foundation's Workshop Surveys*. Quezon City: Health Action Information Network.

Tan, M. (1994a). *The Impact of HIV Prevention Workshops for Filipino Men Who Have Sex with Men (MSM) in Metro Manila: Pre- and Post-Workshop Questionnaire Results*. Manila: Library Foundation.

Tan, M. (1994b). *A Review of Social and Behavioral Studies Related to HIV/AIDS in the Philippines*. Manila: Health Action Information Network.

Tan, M. (1994c). 'Sickness and sin: medical and religious stigmatization of homosexuality in the Philippines', in J. Garcia and D. Remoto (eds), *Ladlad: An Anthology of Philippine Gay Writing*. Manila: Anvil, pp. 202–19.

Tan, M., Querubin, M. and Rillorta, T. (1988). 'The integration of traditional medicine among community-based health programmes in the Philippines', *Journal of Tropical Pediatrics*, 34 (April): 71–5.

Taylor, F. (1947). *The Principles of Scientific Management*. New York: Norton.

Tiglao *et al.* (1991). *Psycho-Social Determinants of Risk-Taking and Preventative Behavior Related to HIV–AIDS*. Manila: Program for Applied Technology in Health.

Tiongon, J. (1994). 'A proposal to cooperativize the government hospitals', *COOP*, 1(1).

Trinidad, A. (1994). 'School AIDS education program and DECS thrust'. Paper presented at the Workshop on the Revision of Instructional Materials for AIDS Education, 30 May–11 June. Imus, Cavite: Philippines.

Turingan, O. (1995). Personal communication with James T. Sears.

Turner, D. (1997). *Risky Sex? Gay Men and HIV Prevention*. New York: Columbia University Press.

Tyler, R. (1950). *Basic Principles of Curriculum and Instruction*. Chicago: University of Chicago Press.

Vance, C. (1991). 'Anthropology rediscovers sexuality', *Social Science and Medicine*, 33(8): 875–84.

Watney, S. (1989). *Policing Desire: Pornography, AIDS and the Media*. Minneapolis: University of Minnesota Press (2nd edn.).

Whitam, F. (1990). 'Philippines', in W. Dynes, E. Johansson and W. Percy (eds), *Encyclopedia of Homosexuality*. New York: Garland, pp. 979–82.

Whitam, F. and Mathy, R. (1986). *Male Homosexuality in Four Societies*. New York: Praeger.

Whitam, F. and Zent, M. (1984). 'A cross-cultural assessment of early cross-gender behavior and familial factors in male homosexuality', *Archives of Sexual Behavior*, 13(5): 427–39.

Yap, J. (1986). 'Philippine ethnoculture and human sexuality', *Journal of Social Work and Human Sexuality*, 4(3): 121–34.

Zialcita, F. (1986). 'Popular interpretations of the passion of Christ', *Philippine Sociological Review*, 34(1–4).

# 8

# The Internationalization of Gay and Lesbian Identities

## *Dennis Altman*[1]

M OST PEOPLE OUTSIDE the rich enclaves of the First World live in a
constant state of negotiation between 'modernity' and 'tradition',
seeking to make sense in everyday life of a vast confusion of images,
precepts, values and beliefs while struggling to survive. In a paradoxical
way 'modern' and 'postmodern' can be used here interchangeably, for they
both represent the rapid reshaping of yet more extensive areas of life and
economy in previously 'underdeveloped' parts of the world to fit the needs
of Western/capitalist dominance. This trend is increasingly referred to as
'globalization'; there is a vast literature defining that word, which, as
Roland Robertson points out, 'refers both to the compression of the world
and the intensification of consciousness of the world as a whole' (Robertson, 1992, p. 8).

Nowhere is this development more common than in the structures of
sex and gender which shape so much of everyday experience. It has
become fashionable to point to the emergence of 'the global gay', the
apparent internationalization of a certain form of social and cultural
identity based upon homosexuality (*Economist*, 1996). He – sometimes,
though less often, she – is conceptualized in terms largely derived from
recent American fashion and intellectual style: young, upwardly mobile,
sexually adventurous, with an 'in your face' attitude to traditional restrictions and a liking for both activism and fashion. Glimpses of young men in
baseball caps and Reeboks on the streets of Budapest or São Paulo;
'lipstick lesbians' flirting on portable telephones in Bangkok or demonstrating in the streets of Tokyo: such images – none of them fictitious – are
part of the construction of a new category, or more accurately the expansion and recuperation of an existing Western category which can be seen as
part of the rapid 'globalization' of lifestyle and identity politics.

Note: 'Western' here is taken to mean North America, Western
Europe and Australasia. There are, of course, differences between, say,

Italian and American constructions of 'modern' homosexuality, but for the purposes of this chapter they are not very important. 'Modern' homosexuality is characterized by its ability to draw on cultural influences from a number of sources, and its development across borders is assisted by very considerable travel and international networks of friends and lovers. I have discussed the particular relationship between Australian and emerging Asian gay movements elsewhere (Altman, 1997).

There is evidence of this new gay world particularly in South/East Asia, in South/Central America and in Eastern Europe. Because both discursive and institutional influences are required for globalization to occur this development takes place in both the material and the cultural realm; one of the common problems of postmodern discussions of globalization is that it concentrates too much on imagery to the exclusion of how such images are translated into practice.

Thus the most obvious indicator is the development of commercial space, that is entertainment venues/restaurants/shops which cater to a distinctly homosexual clientele. Both Western and non-Western experience would suggest that such space is very important in providing opportunities for gay men and lesbians to meet and develop social and political ties (Bell and Valentine, 1995). Other significant indicators are the development of a specific gay/lesbian press, almost always dependent on both a commercial world (for advertising revenue) and enough political freedom to escape censorship. There are examples of such publishing from Mexico, Brazil and Hungary; in 1993 Hong Kong got its first 'gay' magazine – *Contacts Magazine*. Most significantly the past decade has seen the emergence of specifically gay/lesbian political groups in many non-Western countries.

Gay organizing has something of a history in South/Central America, with origins in the 1970s in Brazil, Mexico and the southern cone, which were then crudely – and cruelly – repressed by the rise of military regimes (Adam, 1987, pp. 142–3; Lumsden, 1991; MacRae, 1992; Trevisan, 1988). But such organizing has sped up worldwide in the 1990s, especially in eastern Europe and Asia. This is reflected in a growing number of groups – albeit usually very small – from non-Western countries associated with the International Gay and Lesbian Association (ILGA) which by 1997 could claim member organizations in over 70 countries.

In a number of cases the growth of gay organizing has been closely related to the development of global strategies against AIDS. This works in both directions: gay communities were central in the early stages of community-based responses to AIDS in a surprising variety of countries, while the requirements for intervention in sexual behaviour, and the sometimes grudging recognition that 'men who have sex with men' were a group particularly vulnerable to infection by HIV, opened up space and *de facto* government support for mobilization around homosexuality (Altman, 1994; MacKenna, 1996). There are examples of such mobilization in countries as disparate as Morocco and Vietnam; recently the recognition of HIV/AIDS as a problem has allowed the emergence of homosexual groups in the Central Asian republics of Kazakstan and Kyrgysztan (Naz Foundation, 1997).

Do these developments suggest a change equivalent to the creation of powerful communities with economic, social and political clout as in North America, Australasia and northern Europe? Is there, in other words, a universal gay identity linked to modernity? This is not to argue for a trans-historic or essentialist position but rather to question the extent to which the forces of globalization (both economic and cultural) can be said to produce a common consciousness and identity based on homosexuality. Shifting understandings of homosexuality result from changes in both the material and the cultural realm; one of the common problems of post-modern discussions of globalization is that it concentrates too much on imagery to the exclusion of how such images are translated into practice.

Against all the examples of contemporary change and apparent homogenization we need to remember Rosalind Morris's warning that:

> We know that the apparatus of power is different in every society and that the discourses of sex and gender differ from context to context. Yet a considerable body of critical theory persists in a mode of historical analysis – the emphatically linear genealogy – that derives from the West's specific experience of modernity. (Morris, 1994, p. 39)

To avoid slipping into this 'linear genealogy' we need to understand sexuality as involving the complex and varied ways in which biological possibilities are shaped by social, economic, political and cultural structures. There is a simultaneous creation/solidification of identities and their dissolution: we do not know yet if identities based on sexuality will be as strong as those based on race/religion. The idea of 'gay/lesbian' as a sociological category is only about a hundred years old, and its survival even in Western 'developed' countries cannot be taken for granted (Lofstrom, 1997).

To find the right balance between 'tradition' and 'modernity' means recognizing that these terms themselves are vague, problematic and politically contested; appeals to 'traditional moral values' in many African and Pacific countries means appealing to imported Christian ideals which were central to the colonial destruction of existing social structures. There is a constant danger of romanticizing 'primitive' homosexuality, seen very clearly in the popular anthropology of Tobias Schneebaum who writes (and presumably believes):

> It was in Asmat [West Irian], however, that I felt for the first time part of a universal clan, for Asmat culture in some regions not only allowed for sexual relationships between men but demanded that no male be without his male companion, no matter how many wives he had or how many women he might be sleeping with. (Schneebaum, 1988, p. 433)

Equally a romanticized view of the apparent 'tolerance' of homoeroticism in many non-Western cultures disguises the reality of persecution, discrimination and violence, sometimes in unfamiliar forms. Firsthand accounts make it clear that homosexuality is far from being universally accepted – or even tolerated – in such apparent 'paradises' as Morocco, the Philippines, Thailand or Brazil:

> Lurking behind the Brazilians' pride of their flamboyant drag queens, their recent adulation of a transvestite chosen as a model of Brazilian beauty, their acceptance of gays and lesbians as leaders of the country's most widely practiced religion and the constitutional protection of homosexuality, lies a different truth. Gay men, lesbians and transvestites face widespread discrimination, oppression and extreme violence ... (Steakley, 1994)

## What constitutes a 'modern' gay identity?

The very idea of a homosexual/heterosexual divide is modern. George Chauncey argues that it only became dominant in the United States in the mid-twentieth century:

> The most striking difference between the dominant sexual culture of the early twentieth century and that of our own era is the degree to

which the earlier culture permitted men to engage in sexual relations with other men, often on a regular basis, without requiring them to regard themselves – or be regarded by others – as gay ... Many men ... neither understood nor organised their sexual practices along a hetero-homosexual axis. (Chauncey, 1994, p. 65)

Chauncey's formulation rings true for most societies, many of which are far more relaxed about homosexual behaviour, at least among men, than was pre-gay liberation United States or Western Europe. Of Java, for example, Ben Anderson argues that 'male homosexuality at least was an unproblem-atic, everyday part of a highly varied Javanese sexual culture' (Anderson, 1990, p. 278), and similar comments are often made of Bali. North African men are often claimed to regard sex with 'boys' as totally 'natural' (Schmitt and Sofer, 1992).

The only possible generalization may be that there exists a far greater variety of understandings of sex/gender arrangements than is recognized in official discourses. Moreover attempts to use Western terminology – 'gay people'; 'men who have sex with men', 'bisexuals' – often blocks us from understanding the rather different ways in which people understand their own sexual experiences and feelings (e.g. Jenkins, 1996). Reporting a discussion among 'gay and lesbian' Asians at a recent International AIDS Conference Shivananda Khan argued that:

There were strong cultural frameworks of 'third gender' which have had a long history and many within such groups have played socio-political-religious roles in their societies. To transpose western understandings (and subsequently HIV/AIDS prevention programs) is to destroy these social constructions and recreate them in a western mould. Discussion revolved around moving away from gender dimorphic structures that arose from the West and talk about Alternate Genders, in other words more than two genders ... Similarly we should be talking about lesbian identities and gay identities, should be discussing homosexualities instead of homosexuality, communities instead of community. (Khan, 1994, pp. 7–8)

In most 'traditional' Asian and Pacific societies there were complex variations across gender and sex lines, with 'transgender' people (Indo-nesian *waria*, Madagascan *sekatra*, Filipino *bayot*, Polynesian *fa'fafine*, etc.) characterized by both transvestite and homosexual behaviour. As

Herdt says: 'Sexual orientation and identity are not the keys to con-
ceptualizing a third sex and gender across time and space' (Herdt, 1994,
p. 47). In many societies there is confusion around the terms – for example
the *hijras* of India, who were literally castrated, are sometimes considered
as equivalent to homosexuals even though the reality is more complex
(Khan, 1996; Nanda, 1986). Different people use terms such as *bayot* or
*waria* in different ways, depending on whether the emphasis is on gender –
these are men who wish in some way to be women – or on sexuality – these
are men attracted to other men. There are fewer such terms for women,
although this does not mean the absence of women who contested orthodox sexual and gender roles. Certainly their existence is far less well known
and described outside their own societies.

'Modern' forms of homosexuality often exist side by side with older
'traditional' ones, and the boundaries can appear either blurred or distinct
depending on one's vantage point. Thus some 'modern' homosexuals in
non-Western countries will seek to establish historical continuities with
pre-colonial formations, while others will be more interested in distancing
themselves, psychologically and analytically, from 'old-fashioned' forms of
homosexuality, especially those which seem based on cross-gender lines.
In Indonesia, for example, local men who identify as 'gay' will both sharply
distinguish themselves from *banci* or *waria* (terms which include effeminate men and, occasionally, 'masculine' women) (Oetomo and Esmond,
1990) but in other contexts identify with them. The title of the Indonesian
lesbian/gay journal *Gaya Nusantara*, which literally means 'Indonesian
style', captures this ambivalence nicely with its echoes of both 'traditional'
and 'modern' concepts of nation and sexuality. It is often assumed that
homosexuals are defined in most 'traditional' societies as a third sex, but
that too is too schematic to be universally useful.

That one can have a sense of oneself as 'homosexual' without rejecting
conventional assumptions about masculinity or femininity (as in 'macho'
gay or 'lipstick lesbian' styles) might well seem one of the distinguishing
features of 'modern' homosexuality. 'Modern' homosexualities are characterized by a differentiation between sexual and gender transgression, an
emphasis on emotional as much as sexual relationships and the development of public homosexual worlds. In parts of the 'developing world' a
small elite see themselves as interconnected with a global network, via
groups such as the International Lesbian and Gay Association and an
international commercial scene in which they participate. Others (often
from similar class positions) are more critical, sometimes employing

critiques which are themselves imported via Western conceptualizations of post-colonial and subaltern analysis.

There are a series of interconnected problems here: as 'modern' concepts of homosexuality are dispersed through the world they in turn displace both traditional and earlier imported constructs, leading a number of gay/lesbian groups to claim some sort of continuity with pre-colonial traditions. There is a clear political reward for such claims: they provide an easy rebuttal to the official voices who decry homosexuality as a result of Western influence, thus ignoring the rich homoerotic traditions of their own history. At the same time the claim for historical continuity tends to underestimate the extent to which contemporary images and discourses are shaping general understandings of sexuality. The depictions of homosexuality in American television shows are more widely available than the imagery of traditional poetry.

It seems clear that some form of gay and lesbian identity will become more common across the world. It is also possible that many people in developing countries, whatever their exposure to Western media imagery and consumer affluence, will not adopt Western sexual identities, or that terms like 'gay', 'lesbian' or even 'queer' will be taken up and changed much as are English words in naming the gay bars of Patpong and Shinjuku. This is reminiscent of warnings that 'even' in the West many men-who-have-sex-with-men but do not identify as gay may not be 'closeted' (imperfect) homosexuals but may be consciously rejecting a particular identity. Yet many non-Western homosexuals are attracted to a Western model, which they seek, consciously or not, to impose on their own movements. They are aided by discourses of human rights and the more specific language of AIDS/HIV, which has created its own surveillance of homosexual practices – and further internationalized the language of gay identity.

## Globalization and sexual identities

The images and rhetoric of a newly assertive gay identity spread rapidly from the United States and other Western countries after 1969, at least in part a result of the ongoing dominance of the First World. Filipino writer Vicente Groyon III reflects all the contradictions and ambivalences at play when he writes:

> You are reading the latest copy of *Interview*, one of the trendy fashion-slash-lifestyle monthlies that tell you what to wear, what to talk about

and how to live. You are under the impression that you belong to the world the magazine describes, and not in this tropical, underdeveloped, unstable country. You dream of escaping to this world full of perfect people, with perfect faces and perfect lives and perfect clothes and perfect bodies. (Groyon, 1994, p. 111)

Clearly the ever-expanding impact of (post)modern capitalism is redrawing 'traditional' sex/gender orders to match the ideology and consciousness imposed by huge changes in the world economy. The impact of economic growth, of consumerism, of urbanization, of social mobility, of large-scale population movements, of increasing telecommunications, all place great strains on existing familial and 'personal' relations, and on the very conceptions of self with which people make sense of these arrangements. Discussion about the changes demanded by capitalism tend to fluctuate between nostalgia and celebration; what one person sees as an increase in personal liberty another may well read as the destruction of valuable traditions.

In a sense 'globalization' is 'capitalist imperialism' writ large, and many of its features continue and perpetuate the erosion of custom, of existing kinship and village/communities and of once private space in the interests of an expanding market dominated by the firms of the First World. What was once accomplished by gunships and conquest is now achieved via shopping malls and cable television. Both economic and cultural forces are changing sexual regimes and the relationships between the sex/gender order and other economic and cultural structures. What is less clear is how such changes enter into the psyche. Are the luxurious saunas of Bangkok or the emerging gym cultures of Buenos Aires affecting deeply held values, or are they merely superficial shifts in style?

What is significant about the contemporary globalization of capitalism is the growth of affluence in many countries, and the corresponding greater freedom for individual choice this makes possible. Affluence, education, awareness of other possibilities are all prerequisites for the adoption of new forms of identity, and the increasing spread of these conditions will increase the extent to which gay identities develop beyond their base in liberal Western societies. (They are not, however, sufficient prerequisites, as authoritarian governments in both the Middle East and East Asia have made clear.) In turn the development of such identities may well swamp existing homosexual/third sex cultures, as has been claimed for Indonesia, Mexico and India.

The reality in most parts of the world remains that described eloquently by Roger Lancaster:

> For the working-class youth who meets men in the cracked hull of the ruined Managua Cathedral, for the 'Zocolo' boy in Oaxaca who plays techno-pop cassettes on his boom-box, for the undocumented worker in rural North Carolina who cruises parks in a pick-up truck, the emergent ways of being are neither fully local nor fully global; they neither reproduce 'traditional' identities nor do they import altogether 'Northern' ones. Perhaps it would be better to say that these identities flicker across transitional spaces and scurry along nomadic routes; they take up temporary homes at the interstices of world systems. (Lancaster, 1997, p. 7)

Globalization in the form of increasing travel and communication between countries adds to the pressure to adapt to hegemonic cultural forms; while tourism plays a very uneven role in the construction of new forms of homosexuality, it has clearly been crucial in areas such as the Caribbean, North Africa and parts of Asia such as Sri Lanka and Bali (Aldrich, 1993; Altman, 1995). Moreover travel works both ways, which is to say that the increasing number of people from 'Third World' countries going to the West becomes another factor in cultural transmission. Thus South-east Asian gay men and lesbians speak increasingly of visiting San Francisco, or going to Sydney for Gay and Lesbian Mardi Gras.

The crucial question is how 'new' forms of sexual identity interact with 'traditional' scripts of sex/gender order. Peter Jackson has argued eloquently for a continuum:

> while gayness in Thailand has drawn selectively on Western models, it has emerged from a Thai cultural foundation as the result of efforts by Thai homosexual men to resolve tensions within the structure of masculinity in their society. Given this, the proposition that gayness in Thailand is a 'Western borrowing' is misplaced and overlooks the internal structuring of Thai masculinity, from which Thai gay male identity has emerged as a largely continuous development. (Jackson, 1997a, p. 167)

In rather different ways such reservations would apply to a range of

societies which appear to have taken over Western definitions and identities.

The forces of global economic and cultural interdependence means
that homosexuality is increasingly interrogated and brought under examination. This also means that some people will benefit from imposing a
Western analytic model to explain sexuality; often they will be 'Third
Worlders' with a personal or professional investment in 'modernity'.
Traditionalists will respond either by denial (often because of Western-
derived moralities) or by seeking to build a nationalist version of
homosexuality, with romantic claims to a pre-colonial heritage which is
seen as differentiating them from Western homosexuals. In my own
conversations with homosexuals in Asia there is an ongoing ambivalence
around the extent to which they are constituting themselves as part of a
global identity. As Eduardo Nierras puts it: 'When we say to straight
people, or, more rarely, to Western gay people, "We are like you" we must
remember to add, "only different"'(Nierras, 1994, p. 199).

Peter Drucker has made the interesting point that:

> While European or North American influences may at times have
> facilitated the emergence of Third World gay–lesbian communities,
> the process of capitalist development inside Third World countries has
> been at least as important. If anything, Third World dependence on
> imperialist economies has helped to delay development of the material
> basis for Third World gay–lesbian communities. (Drucker, 1996,
> p. 77)

While I am not sure that he is right, what is clear is that the interconnected
(though not synonymous) processes of political democratization and capitalist expansion in the past decade are central to the spread of gay/lesbian
movements. Nowhere is this more obvious than in Eastern Europe; and,
not surprisingly, the greatest resistance comes in those countries –
Romania, Serbia, Albania – where the end of Communism has been most
troubled (Davidovich, 1996). As late as 1996 the Romanian Parliament
voted to retain criminal sanctions against homosexual behaviour – for both
women and men – and to criminalize membership of gay organizations. In
the Czech Republic and Hungary, on the other hand, already existing
movements have been able to expand and become far more visible (Miller,
1992, pp. 308–20).

In Russia, China and other Communist and ex-Communist societies, official attitudes towards homosexuality tend to reflect a simple-minded view that it is a symptom of bourgeois decadence: lack of information and discussion about sexuality is a common theme in writings about the former Soviet Empire (Gessen, 1996; Tuller, 1996). In Zimbabwe there has been considerable debate over whether homosexuality is acceptable, following the much publicized banning of the Zimbabwe Gay and Lesbian Association from participating at a book fair in 1995 and attacks by President Mugabe on homosexuals as 'pigs' and 'perverts' (Peck, 1996; Clark, 1996, pp. 231–6). Most available 'grand narratives', whether based on religion or science, can be drawn upon to denounce what is often seen as 'Western decadence', whether by Marxists in Vietnam and Cuba, Muslims in Algeria and Iran or the free market rationalists of Singapore. Whatever their other disagreements, all can agree that the assertion of homosexual identity is an unacceptable part of modernization.

One might note that, unlike the religious tradition of condemnation of homosexuality (itself less clear-cut than is often assumed: see Boswell, 1980), it is slightly surprising that official Marxist regimes adopted this position. The element in Marxism which saw itself as scientific and modernizing could have been expected to oppose 'traditional' condemnations of unorthodox sexuality, and this indeed was the case in the early years of the Soviet Union. The development of a rigid condemnation of homosexuality seems related to the specifics of Stalinism and then became linked to the peculiar puritanism of contemporary Communist movements. In certain countries and places – e.g. Cuba before Castro and the Philippines under Marcos – a certain sort of flamboyant homosexuality was connected with the ruling elite or with rich foreign tourists, and therefore lent itself to revolutionary denunciation.

There is a larger issue here. Historically acceptance of homosexuality – indeed, the existence of what Drucker rather inelegantly calls 'reciprocal gay-lesbian sexuality' – is undoubtedly related to certain economic and political developments. Whether it is true, as a tradition of gay leftists have argued, that authoritarian regimes of all ideological hues will repress and suppress homosexual identities is not altogether clear, but in practice it is likely to be the case that only where there is political space and a certain degree of affluence will homosexual identities and communities emerge. It is perhaps not surprising that in the post-apartheid constitution of South Africa that country became the first to extend constitutional rights to cover homosexuality.

## Sexual identities and pedagogy

If we understand globalization to include those forces which lead to changes in the ways by which people understand the world and themselves, then the creation of 'global' gay and lesbian identities and communities becomes yet another example of globalization as a set of both discursive and institutional practices. This can be viewed either as emancipatory (implicit in the language of groups such as ILGA) or as destructive of traditional cultures (even if in practice there are few such cultures left unscathed).

This clearly has considerable implications for sexual pedagogies. It is probably not surprising that the official discourses around homosexuality in much of the world reflect an outdated and largely condemnatory view, often linking homosexuality with child abuse and prostitution. In the last few years there has been something of an international hysteria around pederasty, symbolized by the hugely reported allegations against Michael Jackson. Whatever the reasons fuelling these concerns they too have become globalized, through government attempts to regulate images on the Internet and to make sex with minors in overseas countries a legal offence. (For an example of the linking of the Internet with 'the child sex trade' see Sancton, 1996. Compare Califia, 1994.) In such cases there seems to be a response to the uncertainties and anxieties provoked by changes in social and technological relationships. Globalization can act both to disperse homosexual assertion – and homophobic reactions thereto.

A fascinating example of the conflict around understandings of homo-sexuality occurred recently in Thailand, usually regarded as a very sexually tolerant society. At the end of 1996 the controlling body of all Thai teachers' colleges declared that it would bar homosexuals from enrolling in any of its colleges. There was some opposition to the ban from human rights groups within Thailand, as well as the lesbian group Anjaree, and at the time of writing it seems likely that the ban will be reversed. Comment-ing on this incident Peter Jackson wrote:

No Thai gay movement in the western sense exists. This may be because anti-queer sanctions in Thai society are so diffuse – unwritten cultural attitudes rather than legal statutes or religious edicts – that they cannot be overturned by western-style activism. The Rajabhat Institute ban on 'sexually deviant' students is one of the few occasions in Thai history when these diffuse anti-queer attitudes have been codified, and perhaps the explicitness of the ban will provide a focus for opposition that will spur the emergence of gay/lesbian activism. (Jackson, 1997b)

Whether this is right or not – and Jackson also suggests it is equally likely that the issue will be resolved quietly and without claims of victory – it is not accidental that the issue was one which revolved around education. Even in countries which do not share Christian/Islamic/Communist strictures about homosexuality it appears that there is particular sensitivity around contact with students.

A better understanding of history, and the complex ways in which cultures have intermixed and influenced each other, might help improve the larger understanding of sexuality and remove some of the worst sorts of homophobic prejudices. If people learnt how far 'traditional values' are often manufactured out of previous imperialist ideologies, and had a better understanding of the range of human constructions of gender and sexuality, perhaps they would find diversity less threatening.

## Acknowledgements

I am grateful to the Australian Research Council for support, and to a number of people whose ideas have helped me shape this chapter, among them Ben Anderson, Shivananda Khan, Peter Jackson, Laurence Leong, Alison Murray, Dede Oetomo, Richard Parker, Robert Reynolds, Anthony Smith, Michael Tan and John Treat.

## Note

1. Some of this chapter appeared in a somewhat different form in *Social Text*, **48** (14):3, Autumn 1996, pp. 77–94.

## References

Adam, B. (1987). *The Rise of a Gay and Lesbian Movement*. Boston: Twayne.

Aldrich, R. (1993). *The Seduction of the Mediterranean*. London: Routledge.

Altman, D. (1994). *Power and Community: Organisational and Cultural Responses to AIDS*. London: Taylor & Francis.

Altman, D. (1995). 'Encounters with the new world of "gay Asia"', in S. Perera (ed.), *Identities, Ethnicities, Nationalities: Asian and Pacific Inscriptions.* Melbourne: Meridian Press.

Altman, D. (1997). *Defying Gravity.* Sydney: Allen & Unwin.

Anderson, B. (1990). *Language and Power.* Ithaca: Cornell University Press.

Bell, D. and Valentine, G. (eds) (1995). *Mapping Desire: Geographies of Sexualities.* London: Routledge.

Boswell, J. (1980). *Christianity, Social Tolerance and Homosexuality.* Chicago: University of Chicago Press.

Califia, P. (1994). *Public Sex: The Culture of Radical Sex.* Pittsburgh: Cleis.

Chauncey, G. (1994). *Gay New York.* New York: Basic Books.

Clark, B. (1996). 'Zimbabwe', in R. Rosenbloom (ed.), *Unspoken Rules: Sexual Orientation and Women's Human Rights.* London: Cassell.

Davidovich, B. (1996). *Serbian Diaries.* London: GMP.

Drucker, P. (1996). ' "In the Tropics there is no sin": sexuality and gay–lesbian movements in the Third World', *New Left Review,* **218**, July–August.

*Economist* (1996). 'It's normal to be queer', 6 January 1996, pp. 82–4.

Gessen, M. (1996). 'Russia', in R. Rosenbloom (ed.), *Unspoken Rules: Sexual Orientation and Women's Human Rights.* London: Cassell.

Groyon, V. (1994). 'Boys who like boys', in N. Garcia and D. Remoto (eds), *Ladlad: An Anthology of Philippine Gay Writing.* Manila: Anvil.

Herdt, G. (1994). *Third Sex, Third Gender.* New York: Zone Books.

Jackson, P. (1997a). 'Kathoey > < Gay > < Man', in L. Manderson and M. Jolley (eds), *Sites of Desire/Economies of Pleasure.* Chicago: University of Chicago Press.

Jackson, P. (1997b). 'Gay Bangkok: beyond the bars and the boys', *Outrage* (Melbourne), June.

Jenkins, C. (1996). 'The homosexual context of heterosexual practice in Papua New Guinea', in P. Aggleton (ed.), *Bisexualities and AIDS.* London: Taylor & Francis.

Khan, S. (1994), in *Quarterly Review.* The Naz Project London, July–September.

Khan, S. (1996). 'Under the blanket: bisexualities and AIDS in India', in P. Aggleton (ed.), *Bisexualities and AIDS.* London: Taylor & Francis.

Lancaster, R. (1997). 'Sexual positions: caveats and second thoughts on "categories"', *The Americas,* 53(1): 1–16.

Lofstrom, J. (1997). 'The birth of the queen/the modern homosexual: historical explanations revisited', *Sociological Review,* February: 24–41.

Lumsden, I. (1991). *Society and the State in Mexico.* Toronto: Canadian Gay Archives/Mexico City: Solediciones.

McKenna, N. (1996). *On the Margins.* London: Panos Institute.

MacRae, E. (1992). 'Homosexual identities in transitional Brazilian politics', in

E. Escobar (ed.), *The Making of Social Movements in Latin America*. Boulder, CO: Westview.

Miller, N. (1992). *Out in the World*. London: Random House.

Morris, R. (1994). 'Three sexes and four sexualities: redressing the discourses on gender and sexuality in contemporary Thailand', *positions*, **2**(1).

Nanda, S. (1986). 'The hijras of India: cultural and individual dimensions of an institutionalized Third Gender role', in E. Blackwood (ed.), *The Many Faces of Homosexuality*. New York: Harrington Park Press.

Naz Foundation and UNAIDS (1997). 'Sexualities, sexual behaviours and sexual health'. Report of Consultation on HIV/AIDS Prevention for the Central Asian Republics.

Nierras, E. (1994). 'This risky business of desire: theoretical notes for and against Filipino gay male identity politics', in N. Garcia and D. Remoto (eds), *Ladlad: An Anthology of Philippine Gay Writing*. Manila: Anvil.

Oetomo, D. and Esmond, B. (1990). 'Homosexuality in Indonesia'. English version of a paper published in Indonesian (private communication).

Peck, J. (1996). 'The queer rights struggle in Zimbabwe', *Wisconsin Light*, 6–19 June.

Robertson, R. (1992). *Globalization*. London: Sage.

Sancton, T. (1996). 'Preying on the young', *Time Magazine*, 2 September.

Schneebaum, T. (1988). *Where the Spirits Dwell*. New York: Grove.

Schmitt, A. and Sofer, J. (1992). *Sexuality and Eroticism among Males in Moslem Societies*. New York: Harrington Park Press.

Steakley, S. (1994). 'Brazil can be tough and deadly for gays', *Bay Windows* (Boston), 16 June.

Trevisan, J. (1988). *Perverts in Paradise*. London: GMP.

Tuller, D. (1996). *Cracks in the Iron Closet*. London: Faber.

# Part Three

## Sexualities as Identities

# 9

# Sexing the Globe

*Michelle Fine and Corrine Bertram*

WITH THE GLOBAL bleeding of multinational capitalism, another late twentieth-century iteration of colonialism, we witness the transnational search for the global villain – the character who threatens state/nationhood, rebounding economies, international peace and family life as each of these mythic institutions bears witness to its own crumble. Perhaps the optimal villain would be found in the global movement of bodies, the assault on men, women and children called 'aliens', 'illegals', sometimes for polite company called 'immigrants'. And yet, in the chapters of this book we watch another more insidious, yet intimately linked, assault, an ideological and material assault on the minds, souls, freedoms and bodies of those who dare to be sexual, that is, to sex the globe in the face of, in resistance to, with a flaunting rejection of patriarchal racist heterosexuality. And, for those young women and men who dare to be the carriers of *this* virus, a price will be exacted. You will be exported – or not allowed to leave the country. Silenced – or on display. Invisible – or hyper-visible. Tortured by us – or, better yet, by your own people. Either way, your body, your sexing, your mind, your identities and your politics will be a site for ideological and material warfare.

As you will read, the details in each state/region/country vary – swagger, if you will – to fit the 'stubborn particulars' (Cherry, 1995) of history, the Church, the colours of colonialism, the 'hard and fast' rules of the local patriarchy. But in each state through which we will travel – England, Australia, Ireland or South Africa – you will see, hear and feel the embodied pains of state-sponsored surveillance on the bodies of men and women who dare – to be gay or lesbian and teach (see Crowley, this volume); to agitate for queer rights within racially marginalized communities (see Holmes; Deacon, Morrell and Prinsloo, this volume), to seek an abortion in a country in which the state and the Church have long had an 'illegitimate' affair (see Smyth, this volume). You will witness the interpolations of 'purity' in state formations rife with the bodies of women, racially oppressed minorities and those who are queer. The state as subject positions itself in alignment with (that is, on, against and in co-dependence with) the deviant, the villain, the virus. And, thus, we see we have successfully queered the body politic (Honeychurch, 1996).

Across these essays shimmer a set of theoretical and political stories about identity that we lift up here – not because we choose to posit a universal homophobia or homosexuality, not because we seek to flatten the differences within and across nation states, not because we elect to collapse the axes of gender, race, ethnicity, class or sexuality under an umbrella of state-supported heterosexism or sexism. Only that we do seek to connect, theoretically and on the ground, that which has been severed in ideology but remains parasitic in praxis, as Dennis Altman (1997) would argue; we seek to recouple a global move to create local roach motels for those residents who dare to sex against or despite the state. We seek, further, to reveal how schools are at once implicated in the surveillance and assault and are obligated in the transformative possibilities for radical social change.

While the search for a gay gene, brain or biology continues (see Hegarty, 1997; LeVay, 1991; LeVay and Hammer, 1994; Ordover, 1996), some non-Westerners and critical scholars have continued the spirit of these questions of origin – racial, cultural and sexual purity/stasis – by blaming Westerners for the creation of 'new' queer and feminist identities around the globe. No doubt the effects of the spread of global capitalism have had their effects on sexualities, but to say that the relationship is simple and unidirectional is to ignore scholarship that has documented sexualities and feminisms across the globe (see Altman, 1997; Almaguer, 1993; Espín, 1996; Herdt and Stoller, 1990, for a few examples). The present essays move beyond the limits of origins to the complications of lived experience in these localities.

Holmes's first section in his chapter on the intersection of Aboriginal and gay identities begins with the phrase 'It's everybody's business', which appeared on a banner at a recent Sydney Gay and Lesbian Mardi Gras. Although we think Holmes and the banner meant that everyone should be concerned and aware of gay and lesbian identities and discrimination, these words offer a playful and disturbing alternative interpretation concerning the commodification of identities under capitalism. Many writers have begun to theorize this relationship in the West (including Field, 1995; Clark, 1993) and Altman (1997) has begun comparable work in

Asia. While we recognize the state's role in the shunning of queers, the marginalization of those who dare to challenge, we are left, none the less, with unanswered questions about the role of the state in constructing, shaping, bifurcating sexualities, in creating the very categories of difference we love and that we hate (Altman, 1997; Kitzinger, 1987).

Our first political story, then, concerns the global search for embodied states of danger, what Leslie Roman (1996) would call 'moral spectacles', bodies onto which local, national and international anxieties are displaced while the unproblematized notions of state identity, the family, economic prosperity and whiteness shiver. As counter-hegemonic winds and movements whistle by, the search for the moral spectacle grows more desperate and more pathetic. Contradictions in the voice of state fracture the official ideology. While conservative governments presume to want to reduce the size and influence of the state, you will read about the overstretched arm of the state blocking pregnant girls and women in Ireland seeking abortions (see Smyth, this volume) and interfering with queer curriculum initiatives across the globe. At the same time, in the United States and elsewhere, as these texts testify, even when gay discrimination is against the law, we can witness an active passivity, a refusal to intervene against racialized, gendered and homophobic violence (see Deacon, Morrell and Prinsloo, this volume). At these moments, the states go limp, as if deferring to the bullies of the Right, enabling, encouraging, if not inviting the persecution of those who dare.

Our second political story addresses the nasty webbing of patriarchy, state identities, racism and the heterosexual mandate. Gayle Rubin (1984), Mik Billig (1994), Dennis Altman (1997) and Valerie Polakow (1993) have written far more eloquently than we about affairs within this 'ménage à quatre' (4) (trois plus one). And yet, in these essays we witness the scars – economic, political, psychological and social – engraved on the bodies of those elected to be the poster children of this nasty webbing. Contradictions understood, multiple consciousness granted, resistance acknowledged, nothing coherent about the state taken for granted, these essays nevertheless begin a conversation about the internalized grief and desire saturating all of our bodies.

Third, these chapters pry open a slowly widening circle of scholarship on what we consider knowledges, that which our bodies know that our minds may or may not, will or will not, queer knowledges among them. One can turn to the work of Honeychurch (1996) to hear how the body should, does and could affect questions of social science methods.

Sean Massey (1997) writes on the embodied knowledge of gay men-as-boys, whose desires – shunned, terrifying and delicious – offer a kind of sexual agency to children otherwise surrounded by a rejecting sexualized world. Sarah Carney's (1998) work on young girl skaters provides images of the power and strength, not only pathology, carried in the bodies of girls. Rosemarie Roberts (1997) speaks of the body as an archive of resistance, a museum of refusal wrought through historic oppression, manifest in dance, ritual, and performance. And yet we know so little from social science or educational research of the personal and cultural knowledges stored in, carved on, performed through the body. We do know that schools fear much and allow so little of the body to 'contaminate' the official knowledges of school life. Yet, while the testosterone-flooded hallways echo with shouts of 'faggot' and the snapping of bras, the official script presumes no sexing here. But, like any good geography of shifting institutions and moving bodies, these essays and related works suggest that these knowledges of bodies are leaking and can be sited well beyond the bathroom cubicles.

Each of us – Michelle and Corrine – has also intentionally inserted the body into our college classrooms, sometimes ambivalently when students presume an intimate knowledge of instructors who 'come out' about their sexualities or simply (maybe not so easily) by teaching courses surveying the psychologies of women, communities of colour, gay men, lesbians, bisexuals, the transgendered and the poor. Some of our students resist and reproduce their privilege by asking questions like, 'what makes you gay?' or 'what do lesbians do in bed?' without imagining similar questions posed to straight selves. The bodies of students within these classrooms often pose conflicting demands. Conflicts are relatively easy to resolve when one body is marginalized and another is not, but what if both bodies have legitimate claims for safety? How does one balance the needs of queer students to voice their experiences and sexualities, and the needs of students who have experienced sexual violence that makes the open airing of sexuality painful? These questions trouble the most thoughtful teachers.

Fourth, in these essays we confront yet another political challenge. That dominant ideologies sit neatly atop, make love with and depend upon the perversions of heterosexism has long been spoken. Well known but far less often said are the deeply embedded beliefs, boiling at the core of some historically marginalized communities to expel the queer – often, not always; we know many exceptions, of course. Oliva Espín (1996) has written of Latina immigrant lesbians, for whom the task of constructing and securing ethnic identities – always in contestation, always under scrutiny from outside and from within and yet always, for women, embroidered with loyalty oaths that insist on pink, [hetero]sexual, with boys and often for babies – demands the display of heterosexuality which Latina lesbians are unwilling to perform. Recognizing that lesbian communities in the United States into which many of these women have arrived suffer their own perversions of racism and classism, this play between cultures demands a brilliant brokering, an exhausting juggle, a thrilling kaleidoscopic consciousness from lesbians who have the fortune, the burden, the opportunity, the strength to connect across communities. One might conclude this border-crossing work is simply aerobic, good for the soul, the mind and the body. One might also conclude that this work is exhausting, confusing. No doubt it is work (see Moraga and Anzaldúa, 1981; Anzaldúa, 1987).

Our fifth question provoked by the essays surrounds the notion of the public intellectual, the outraged queer or queer advocate, the teacher, researcher, organizer and activist who dares to speak with, against, for and despite. In the classroom, the stakes may be high but the need irresistible. The task at hand may be to understand the 'common sense' of one's culture, one's globe and then to interrupt brutally. Transform maybe. Act up definitely.

But we, too, end up with questions – should activist educators and researchers try to do the border work, translating from contemporary racist, patriarchal and homophobic 'common sense' into a more progressive conception of human rights and communities of difference? Or should we be doing research which slices through to the pain of social oppression and even the damage produced? If so, how can we make sure that this work does not backfire into a reproduction of social stereotypes, only used to reinforce structures and castles of discrimination and oppression? Finally, do we do work that simply and outrageously changes the subject, that credits not at all the perversions of dominant ideologies, that moves instead into the joys, struggles, plastic subjectivities, the camp of queer lives with a refusal to educate in conversation with homophobic 'common sense'?

The sixth question swirls around spaces – public, private, segregated or infused with 'differences' – spaces, none the less, in which historically marginalized youth and adults can reclaim identities; embrace taboo relations and queer public stares; critique hegemony and turn it on its head. We ask, globally and locally, where are these spaces for gay, lesbian and bisexual youth? Where are the corners in which class, race, language, gender, sexuality and (dis)abilities can be reclaimed, reconstituted and taken back? We ask this not because we are nostalgic (although Michelle at least is) for counter-hegemonic sofas in which politics could be discussed, unravelled, taken to the streets. But we ask this because we struggle to find (and delight when we do) those spaces from which the next generation of political work emerges (Fine *et al.*, 1998).

In recent work on urban young adults in the United States, Michelle and Lois Weis, with our students, including Corrine, have stumbled into such spaces. Despite much despair in the narratives of working-class and poor women and men at the turn of the century, these women and men are not simply depressed, despairing and isolated with no glimmer of hope. Much else is happening in late-twentieth-century America. These young men and women are 'homesteading' – finding unsuspected places within their geographic locations, their public institutions and their spiritual lives to sculpt real and imaginary spaces for peace, solace, communion, personal and collective identity work.

These spaces offer recuperation and 'home', often a 'home' away from 'home', one that is often safer and more nurturing than the one they come from or the one in which they currently live. These 'new homes' are not just a set of geographical/spacial arrangements, but theoretical, analytical and spatial displacements – a crack, a fissure in an organization. Individual dreams, collective work and critical thoughts are stolen, smuggled in and reimagined. Not rigidly bound by walls/fences, these spaces are often corralled by a series of fictional borders where community intrusion and state surveillance are not permitted. These are spaces where trite social stereotypes are precariously contested. Young women and men, in the constant confrontation with harsh humiliating public representations of their race, ethnicity, class, gender and sexuality, use these spaces to break down public images for scrutiny and invent new ones.

Political scientist Nancy Fraser (1993) argues that it is advantageous for 'marginals' to create what she calls 'counterpublics' where they may oppose stereotypes and assert novel interpretations of their own shifting identities, interests and needs. She theorizes that these spaces are formed, ironically, out of the very exclusionary practices of the public sphere. We, too, have found that in the midst of disengagement by the public sector and relocation of private sector jobs 'down south', or more likely overseas, it is into these newly constructed 'free spaces', as Sara Evans and Harry Boyte

(1992) would call them, that poor and working-class men and women have fled from sites of historical pain and struggle, and reconsituted new identities.

Engaged daily in the sweat and labour of being poor, men and women across racial and ethnic groups, across sexualities and politics, are finding small spaces in which they can make life meaningful, maintain or resist a spiritual life, try to sustain a sense of self in spite of state policies that are made in their name and strip them of their dignity. Borrowing from Evans and Boyte:

> Free spaces are public spaces in the community . . . in which people are able to learn a new self-respect, a deeper and more assertive group identity, public skills, and values of cooperation and civic virtue . . . settings between private lives and large-scale institutions . . . with a relatively open and participatory character. This definition seeks to identify a category of political space that is useful in understanding the origins and sustaining bases of democratic social movements. Free spaces are 'schools for democracy' owned by participants themselves . . . (Evans and Boyte, 1992, p. ix)

These 'free spaces' are rarely studied by social scientists. Typically we enter people's lives and communities and ask *them* the questions that titillate *us*. As Keith and Pile (1993) argue, by asking questions of arbitrary closure, social scientists fail to see the world as it unfolds and is reshaped by community members across 'spatialities' and time. Floating as a rich underground to community life, these spaces are vibrant, alive, fundamentally self-created and often deeply contradictory. They may be transitory, healing and mobilizing. They may be segregated spaces or contexts in which individuals cross borders of race, ethnicity, gender and sexuality, to find a small corner in which to breathe in peace. These spaces may be geographic (Hall, 1997; Hayden, 1995; Rivlin, 1987), or they may be spiritual, diasporic, temporary or long-lasting. They may be defined by geography, walls, beliefs, terror, delights, escapes and/or demography. Spaces are, for us, broadly conceived. We realize further that no space is 'free' of the larger hegemonic and oppressive structural arrangements within which it sits. As Foucault (1997) argues in 'Panopticism', 'Inspection functions ceaselessly. The gaze is alert everywhere.' And yet from our informants we hear that in contrast to the toxic rains through which their gendered, raced, ethnic, classed and sexual lives are daily assaulted, these spaces are indeed safe. 'Free' for a moment. Not necessarily lasting, but a breath of fresh air.

By examining many different kinds of urban spaces, through what Keith and Pile call 'spatiality', we hope to understand how these spaces operate to enable members to explore their many identities and also rethink, review and rework these identities as fluid and mobile. That is:

> In relational terms, we want to move away from a position of privileging positionality and towards one acknowledging spatiality. Such a move takes us towards an understanding of identities as always contingent and incomplete processes rather than determined outcomes and of epistemologies as situated and ambivalent rather than abstract and universal. It is an acknowledgment of difference that gives no concessions to relativism. The ethical and political agenda can remain structured by social justice, but it is a justice that radically contextualizes the various forms of oppression to find the ground on which progressive action can be taken ... The effort is to re-vision radical subjectivity and communities of resistance through 'simultaneously real and imagined geographies' ... In order to empower alliances between marginalized people, a different sense of space needs to be invoked – no longer static and passive, no longer devoid of politics. (Keith and Pile, 1993, pp. 34, 36)

We are interested in remapping the globe, through a lens of sexualities, flagging some sites as sites of explicit political resistance as Evans and Boyte describe, and others are more nearly recuperative spaces (Oldenburg, 1989). That is, places for breathing, relaxing, sitting on a couch without the constant arrows of stereotype and social hatred. Inspired by the words of Patricia Williams we search for

> A public place to speak, and speak again ... Who knows? Something, everything, a space to counter this repetitive motion sickness by which we are driven, liked doomed sheep leaping in a sleepless dream, nowhere but over and over the same unmoving ground. (Williams, 1991, p. 8)

The good news is that scholars, activists and educators, and those of us who think of ourselves as all three, across the globe are outing our lives, our bodies, our scholarship and our outrage, and that schools and communities can be viewed, at once, binocularly, as sites of oppressive surveillance, humiliation and scrutiny, patrolling the borders of racism, patriarchy and heterosexism, and as free(ish) spaces in which incredibly productive, democratic and radical relations for social transformation are being ignited. These essays would suggest that the task before us is enormous, and the moment is now (or yesterday).

## References

Almaguer, T. (1993). 'Chicano men: a cartography of homosexual identity and behavior', in H. Abelove, M. A. Barale and D. M. Halperin (eds), *The Lesbian and Gay Studies Reader*. New York: Routledge, pp. 255–73.

Altman, D. (1997). 'Global gaze/global gays', *GLQ: A Journal of Lesbian and Gay Studies*, 3: 417–36.

Anzaldúa, G. (1987). *Borderlands/La Frontera: The New Mestiza*. San Francisco: Aunt Lute Books.

Billig, M. (1994). 'Repopulating the depopulated pages of social psychology', *Theory and Psychology*, 4(3): 307–35.

Carney, S. (1998, March). 'The language of girls' bodies: out of pathology comes possibility'. Paper presented at the Ethnography in Education Research Forum at the University of Pennsylvania, Philadelphia.

Cherry, F. (1995). *The 'Stubborn Particulars' of Social Psychology: Essays on the Research Process*. London: Routledge.

Clark, D. (1993). 'Commodity lesbianism', in H. Abelove, M. A. Barale and D. M. Halperin (eds), *The Lesbian and Gay Studies Reader*. New York: Routledge, pp. 186–201.

Espín, O. (1996). ' "Race", racism, and sexuality in the life narratives of immigrant women', in S. Wilkinson (ed.), *Feminist Social Psychologies: International Perspectives*. Buckingham: Open University Press, pp. 87–103.

Evans, S. M. and Boyte, H. C. (eds) (1992). *Free Spaces: The Sources of Economic Change in America*. Chicago: University of Chicago Press.

Field, N. (1995). *Over the Rainbow: Money, Class, and Homophobia*. East Haven, CT: Pluto Press.

Fine, M., Weis, L., Centrie, C. and Roberts, R. A. (1998). 'Educating beyond the borders of schooling'. Unpublished manuscript, City University of New York, Graduate School and University Center, New York.

Foucault, M. (1997). 'Panopticism' (extract), in *Rethinking Architecture: A Reader in Cultural Theory*. London: Routledge, pp. 356–67.

Fraser, N. (1993). 'Rethinking the public sphere: a contribution to the critique of actually existing America', in B. Robbins (ed.), *The Phantom Public Sphere*. Minneapolis: University of Minnesota Press.

Hall, S. (1997). 'Subjects in history: making diasporic identities', in W. Lubiano (ed.), *The House That Race Built: Black Americans, U.S. Terrain*. New York: Pantheon, pp. 289–99.

Hayden, D. (1995). *The Power of Place: Urban Landscapes as Public History*. Cambridge, MA: MIT Press.

Hegarty, P. (1997). 'Materializing the hypothalamus: a performative account of the "gay brain"', *Feminism and Psychology*, 7(3): 355–72.

Herdt, G. and Stoller, R. J. (1990). *Intimate Communications*. New York: Columbia University.

Honeychurch, K. G. (1996). 'Researching dissident subjectivities: queering the grounds of theory and practice', *Harvard Educational Review*, **66**(2): 339–55.

Keith, M. and Pile, S. (eds) (1993). *Place and the Politics of Identity*. London: Routledge.

Kitzinger, C. (1987). *The Social Construction of Lesbianism*. London: Sage.

LeVay, S. (1991). 'A difference in hypothalmic structure between heterosexual and homosexual men', *Science*, **253**: 1034–7.

LeVay, S. and Hammer, D. H. (1994). 'Evidence for a biological influence in male homosexuality', *Scientific American*, **270**: 44–9.

Massey, S. G. (1997). 'The potential of gayness: meaning making in the lives of gay men'. Unpublished master's thesis, Graduate School and University Center of the City University of New York, NY.

Moraga, C. and Anzaldúa, G. (eds) (1981). *This Bridge Called My Back: Writings by Radical Women of Color*. Watertown, MA: Persephone Press.

Oldenburg, R. (1989). *The Great Good Place: Cafés, Coffee Shops, Community Centers, Beauty Parlors, General Stores, Bars, Hangouts and How They Get You through the Day*. New York: Paragon House.

Ordover, N. (1996). 'Eugenics, the gay gene, and the science of backlash', *Socialist Review*, **26**(1 and 2): 125–44.

Polakow, V. (1993). *Lives on the Edge: Single Mothers and Their Children in the Other America*. Chicago: University of Chicago Press.

Rivlin, L. G. (1987). 'The neighborhood, personal identity, and group affliations', in I. Altman and A. Wandersman (eds), *Neighborhood and Community Environments*. New York: Plenum, pp. 1–34.

Roberts, R. (1997). 'Stones, metal, and water: sustaining community through conflict and difference – the Orisha community in New York City'. Unpublished manuscript, Graduate School and University Center of the City University of New York, NY.

Roman, L. G. (1996). 'Spectacle in the dark: youth as transgression, display, and repression', *Educational Theory*, **46**(1): 1–22.

Rubin, G. S. (1984). 'Thinking sex: notes for a radical theory of the politics of sexuality', in C. S. Vance (ed.), *Pleasure and Danger: Exploring Female Sexuality*. New York: Routledge and Kegan Paul, pp. 267–319.

Williams, P. J. (1991). *The Alchemy of Race and Rights*. Cambridge, MA: Harvard University Press.

# 10

# Discipline and Homophobia in South African Schools: The Limits of Legislated Transformation

*Roger Deacon, Robert Morrell and Jeanne Prinsloo*

## Introduction

Education, like most other features of South African society, is undergoing rapid and large-scale transformation. It is five years since the first election based on a universal franchise brought a Government of National Unity to power, along with a new, egalitarian, Constitution and Bill of Rights. Dominated by the discourse of the liberation movement and emphasizing democracy, equity, human rights and nation-building, conscious attempts to transform South African education have been embarked upon. The legislative flagship of this process was the South African Schools Act passed in 1996. Despite the law being on the statute books, however, much remains the same within the schools themselves, where old styles of school governance and pedagogy remain intact. The persistence and power of these patriarchal forms of authority, rooted both in colonialism and in indigenous politics and taken further under racial capitalism, have produced complex and contradictory situations which are basically in conflict with government policy and law. Drawing upon a small survey of largely Zulu-speaking African teachers, this chapter examines the disciplinary production of gendered subjects in relation to South African education with specific reference to the impact of two significant features of recent legislation: the prohibition of corporal punishment in schools, and the prohibition of discrimination on grounds of sexual orientation.

It will be argued that the egalitarian democratic discourse, which has recently become hegemonic at the level of the state and which is being expressed through these laws, exists uneasily with historically older and much more widespread patriarchal discourses. The laws of the land, it appears, are far in advance of the people in whose name they were passed. This suggests that transformation is a long-term process which cannot simply be legislated into existence, and may be threatened by ongoing everyday practices of corporal punishment and homophobia. It thus remains to be seen whether the hegemonic discourse will be translated into local contexts and so overcome subordinate or unacknowledged discourses rooted in older traditions and power structures, or whether the local (and now illegitimate) discourses will themselves exert a counter-effect, forcing a reversal in the democratic direction and content of state discourse and law. This raises important questions about the status of such hegemonic discourses or 'master narratives', and about the adequacy of conventional top-down explanations of social and educational transformation which ignore the role of local disciplinary mechanisms in producing a complex range of gender identities in schools and the wider society.

## Education, patriarchy and gender identities

South African schools, both black and white, have been renowned for their authoritarianism (Holdstock, 1990). Christian National Education, an apartheid education policy for both black and white children, was a profoundly conservative approach which conceived of the teacher as an active and authoritative transmitter of absolute truth and divinely ordained values. Pupils were seen as passive, docile and obedient, in a context characterized by socially sanctioned inequalities, and autocratic and often technicist directives. Information was pre-selected by experts and disseminated uncritically in support of a social engineering project phrased in terms of the 'general interest'. This system admitted few alternatives and was dominated by strict discipline (Deacon, 1996, p. 228; Enslin, 1984; Grundlingh, 1990/1; Moodie, 1975). Some of the impetus for apartheid education policy came from the political imperative to solve 'the youth problem', associated with crime and delinquency and seen as politically dangerous. In the late 1940s, the size of the African urban youth population suddenly swelled as a result of the relaxation of pass laws during the Second World War. At the same time, but only partly as a consequence of this, the mission schools which provided the bulk of schooling for Africans[1] experienced a spate of rebellions (Hyslop, 1987a). The existing education system manifestly could not deal with this situation and so the state moved in to provide compulsory education for African children (Hyslop, 1987b).

This top-down view of the establishment of an authoritarian education system, however, overlooks the importance of structures of discipline and authority within the family and in social relations. South African society in general, and traditional African society in particular, is overwhelmingly patriarchal in nature. Men occupied, and still occupy, positions of authority, and until very recently, women of all races largely occupied subordinate and frequently menial positions. Relationships between men and women and adults and children, while occasionally reciprocal (Hunter, 1979, pp. 25–8), are predominantly hierarchical and, historically, challenges to adult authority and responses to such challenges have been violent (Carton, 1993; Campbell, 1992; Prins, 1980, pp. 94–5). The Bantustan policies implemented during the 1950s 'froze' social relations in the rural areas and ensured that patriarchal authority and the subordination of women were entrenched. A consequence of this is that, even today, there are large parts of South Africa where traditional social practices continue. Institutions (such as circumcision lodges) and procedures (such as stick fighting) which ritualize and formalize the superior status of the male adult (Ntsebeza, 1993) are sustained by the continuing power of chiefs (virtually all of whom are men). These patriarchal social relations are also buttressed by widespread homophobic practices, to the extent that gay people are often objects of derision and liable to unprovoked physical assault, where their existence is admitted at all. Amongst Africans, for example, homosexuality is branded as 'un-African' and blamed on colonialism, whereas in white society, the obsession with competitive and physically demanding sport is coupled to strident homophobia visible in a generalized locker-room social atmosphere.

The existence of corporal punishment and homophobia in both black and white schools was and is largely consistent with patriarchal social and domestic practice. Viewed from this perspective, apartheid education was as much a product of unequal everyday relations of power between men and women, adults and children and heterosexuals and homosexuals as it was a product of racial capitalism. This was apparent in the localized nature of African opposition to Bantu Education in 1955: the numbers of African children going to school during the period of the boycotts actually rose (Hyslop, 1993, p. 406), and a major reason for this was the widespread view amongst Africans that ill discipline amongst pupils was a problem that needed to be dealt with (Kros, 1990/1, pp. 33–4). During the same period, women were identified as ideal teachers, partly because they could be paid lower wages but also because of stereotypes relating to their supposedly inherent nurturing qualities: 'a woman is by nature so much better fitted for handling young children', claimed H. F. Verwoerd, Minister of Bantu Education (Truscott, 1994, p. 42).[2] All teachers were expected to maintain sober Christian home and family lives in which even a hint of non-heterosexual liaisons would not only be scandalous but occupationally ruinous for the individual concerned. A bottom-up view of apartheid education thus sheds additional light on the prevalence – indeed, the taken-for-granted status – of practices of corporal punishment and homophobia.

There can be no doubt that the changes wrought by colonialism and apartheid deeply affected African social structures, none more so than the family. On the one hand, migrant labour and the increase in the permanently urbanized African population has fragmented the extended family, at least as a socially functioning unit. Nuclear and, latterly, single-parent and mostly female-headed families, have become the norm. On the other hand, the family has ceased to have much reality for the thousands of orphaned, abused or runaway children who roam the streets of South Africa's cities. The steady erosion of the agricultural base of the African 'homelands' was largely responsible for these debilitating effects upon family structures. A significant effect of this changing context was the emergence of an antisocial and violent culture of machismo amongst African youth, whose cultural appropriation of the cinematic style of American gangs and gangsters (Glaser, 1992; Fenwick, 1996) provided the backdrop for the emergence of the youth as a factor in anti-apartheid politics after 1976.

It was the revolt in the 1970s of these highly assertive and politically confident 'young lions' that not only rocked the state, but also prompted the formation of the discourse of People's Education. This drew upon a wider international progressive discourse around education (Freire, 1978) but responded to specifically South African concerns. It was committed to enlightening pupils, teachers, parents and workers about the oppressive structures of apartheid and to preparing them for organized, collective, active and critical participation in a future non-racial democracy (Mashamba, 1990; Mkatshwa, 1986). People's Education was in part a response to fears that the widespread boycotts of schools would lead to a situation of ungovernability that would undermine not only the legitimacy and authority of the state but also that of the family, the liberation movements and education itself. It thus signified an attempt by parents, teachers, leaders, and adults in general to re-establish their authority over the youthful 'shock troops of the revolution' (Deacon, 1996, pp. 234–5).

While People's Education offered legitimacy to the call of COSAS (Congress of South African Students) for an end to corporal punishment and sexual harassment and for students to be given a say in school governance, it also contributed to the demobilization of the youth. While it helped to dissipate the anarchic impetus, it was unable to enlist the youth in a disciplined crusade. This disciplinary reaction must also be held as a partial explanation for the subsequent degeneration of their campaigns. Invariably violent and initially targeting the security forces and political opponents such as Inkatha, the campaigns degenerated into factionalism and eventually to car-hijacking and 'jackrolling' (or organized rape) (Mokwena, 1991). The context of apartheid education, the breakdown of family structures within a patriarchal society and the politics of the liberation struggle thus created a specifically macho gender identity amongst urbanized African youth which stressed violence as a mark of being a man and accepted violence as a way of resolving problems (Freund, 1996, pp. 190–3).

Clearly, patriarchal social structures do not merely produce varying styles of manhood, but concomitantly construct feminine gender identities. In the countryside, African girls were initiated into a domestic economy where respect and labour were interwoven with the idea that women were dependent. Indeed, this was encoded within customary law and until very recently African women were defined as minors and prevented from owning land or opening bank accounts in their own right.[3] Despite these legal and customary impediments, the place of women in the countryside had its strengths. This can be seen, for example, in the power of the Inkatha Women's Brigade (Hassim, 1990) and the continuing support for such customs as the monitoring of virginity by older Zulu women (Ndlovu et al., 1994). The breakdown of the extended family and the weakening of kinship ties has multiplied female-headed households (Budlender, 1991, p. 5). This trend is allied to increases in the rate and levels of female employment,[4] even though, in macro terms, women continue to constitute a substantial minority in the formal labour market. Being economically and conjugally independent has also given women greater responsibility for discipline (Vogelman, 1990, p. 124) which continues to be exercised corporally, while the absence of a parent or parents due to pressures of work has produced the phenomenon of 'the uncontrollable child' (Burman and Fuchs, 1986, p. 134). In short, increasing economic opportunities and political space for African women in the last decade have been accompanied by greater demands on their physical and emotional resources and most resort to disciplinarian methods of child rearing, or look to schools to do so on their behalf (Jones, 1993, p. 194).

The paradox of the entrenchment of strict disciplinary regimes coincidental with the elaboration of a libertarian human rights discourse is also reflected in the realm of the politics of sexuality. Internationally, the challenge to compulsory heterosexuality has been extended to schools (Epstein, 1994; Mac an Ghaill, 1994). Dissident discourses around sexuality have also emerged. In the last decade there has been a rise in the visibility and vocality of the gay movement in South Africa. Gay pride marches occur annually in certain major cities where the Gay and Lesbian Alliance has active branches, and gay activists have been successful in influencing policy-makers to enshrine their rights in law. While it may be argued that the extension of formal equality to gays in a largely homophobic culture is likely to result in 'a dispersion of sexualities, a strengthening of their disparate forms, [and] a multiple implantation of "perversions"' (Foucault, 1981, p. 37), schools are among several major social institutions which have barely registered these changes in society.

Homophobia and discrimination against gays have been and remain unquestioned features of African and white schooling. The heavy emphasis on competitive sport in elite, formerly exclusively white, schools is frequently associated with homophobia. In a recent newspaper report on a secondary school in northern KwaZulu-Natal, gay African pupils were told by teachers that 'they could not teach us because we were the spirits of the devil and because they were Christians' (*Saturday Paper*, 12 April 1997). The extreme homophobic remarks of Winnie Mandela, then head of the ANC Women's League, endorse and capitalize on a persistent prejudice towards lesbians and gay men (Holmes, 1994). Permissive and tolerant attitudes toward homosexuality did exist historically in enclaves such as Durban's Mkhumbane township in the 1950s where homosexuals were acknowledged members of the community (Louw, 1995), but gay-bashing or at least prejudice towards gays is common in African society today (Gevisser and Cameron, 1994, pp. 69–73).

It is against this background of changing patriarchal social structures, the imposition and transformation of authoritarian political structures and social and political violence, that it is possible to explain both the development of a human rights culture which underpins new legislation and the continued flourishing, in many schools, of corporal punishment and homophobia, despite the penalties and strictures against both. The gap between law and social practices will now be explored via the views of a select group of teachers.

## On the edges of the law: teachers' responses to transformation

Fifty-three teachers studying a part-time postgraduate BEd course in gender and education at the University of Natal, Durban, filled out a questionnaire in April 1997. The teachers ranged in age from 23 to 46, but most were under 35 years old. Over three-quarters of the teachers were African, and virtually all of these spoke Zulu as a home language. Two-thirds of the teachers were women. Half of them taught in primary schools and of these 72 per cent were women. As pupils, most of the teachers had attended co-educational schools, and nearly three-quarters of them had grown up with their biological parents although 10 per cent had grown up with single mothers and 6 per cent with single fathers.

The questionnaire sought the opinion of the teachers on issues of discipline, gender and sexuality in schools. It was abundantly clear that the everyday, 'on the ground' discourse amongst teachers is strongly patriarchal. Although it differs between men and women, there is a broad consensus on the issues under discussion (punishment, gender and sexuality) and, more generally, around the roles men should fulfil. The views below, articulated by men in the sample, were not contradicted by women in the sample. While they expressed some desire that men grant them more independence and take more responsibility for domestic chores, there was an acknowledgement that adult men are public actors, family heads and, if need be, warriors.

> [A]s a boy ... I had to look after my father's cattle, goats and to run errands and be brave under difficult circumstances. In my culture a boy may not cry under all circumstance and that is the beginning of manhood.

> The most import [sic] duty of a man is to look after his family together with his wife so that gives the man the higher status on his family.

Almost all respondents reported that corporal punishment had been a major feature of their own early childhoods and that, once they were in school, the pattern continued. Few found the practice egregious. During their childhood, a range of disciplinary strategies had been used, though beating was the most frequent. Both girls and boys were beaten, though boys were beaten more severely and more frequently. This pattern was accentuated at school, where corporal punishment tapered off for girls (particularly as they got older) while boys continued to be routinely beaten. One male student (from a rural area) reported that:

> corporal punishment was applied to both boys and girls for coming late to school, for failing class tests and for making noise in class. We really felt that the punishment we received was fair and appropriate ... Girls were whipped for making noise in the class and boys punished for smoking ... our principal used to punish soccer players when we were beaten by other schools' soccer teams. We enjoyed this sort of punishment and it encouraged us to play with the intention to win the game. This applied to both boys' teams and girls' teams.

Later the same respondent reported that, as principal of a primary school, he

> applied the method that was used by my primary principal to whip the footballers and netballers when they had lost the game. Through this spirit I have two boys who are my products and are playing for professional teams and they are very proud of me. Corporal punishment did not make my students to hate me but instead they love and honour me.

In the home, respondents' mothers bore a large share of responsibility for discipline, often primarily so in the case of female respondents. Not surprisingly, therefore, having as children frequently been beaten themselves, the women respondents reported frequently resorting to corporal punishment in their classrooms. Their views and practices conform to national trends. A 1996 national survey of 1000 women over 18 years old found that 75 per cent supported the return of the cane (*Sunday Times*, 2 December 1996). These findings raise additional questions about female gender identities. While the connection between males receiving and giving corporal punishment supports the view documented in other contexts that men should be tough, it is significant to find such large support amongst women for corporal punishment. This contrasts strongly with findings in countries such as Britain, where women teachers have the reputation of opposing corporal punishment.

There are two levels of explanation for this kind of 'hard femininity' encountered in our survey. On one hand, it could be understood as a result of the familiarity with receiving and giving corporal punishment that tends to normalize it, to make it 'common sense'. This explanation is validated by recourse to a moral understanding of such action (that it is good when motivated by caring) and the belief that it is functional within the school context. The acceptance of corporal punishment and a willingness to use it in the classroom is not uncomplicated. In our survey, 15 per cent of female respondents said that, as pupils, they hated being beaten at school, 18 per cent stated that it made them angry and 10 per cent found the experience very bad or terrible. Twenty per cent accepted it, apparently believing that they deserved to be beaten and that its effect was salutary. Most female respondents said that they preferred other punishments such as detention, periods of silence, gardening or extra school work. Only 12 per cent of them as compared to 28 per cent of male respondents preferred beating to other forms of punishment. In spite of this, they indicated broad support for corporal punishment. As an institutional practice it has become normalized by its repetition.

At another level, however, the willingness to endorse corporal punishment can be explained in terms of the difficulty of maintaining discipline in class. Many teachers feel that there are few alternatives to beating. This is compounded by the rise in youth frustration with schooling and growing scepticism about government's capacity to deliver jobs and a better life. Teachers are resented as authority figures and held accountable for the shortcomings of the education system. This has resulted in physical attacks on teachers which have on occasion led to death. Many teachers live in fear.

Teacher attitudes are part of a broad social counter-movement in the country which is challenging the human rights ethos of government and legislation. On a range of fronts, 'progressive' laws are being challenged. Calls are being made to reinstate the death sentence, castrate rapists and tighten up on bail. In an atmosphere of mass hysteria, plans to build underground prisons in old mine shafts have been seriously debated. Street justice – the killing of 'criminals' by the public – has also become common. Hence, the dominant, state-sponsored master narrative is in danger of being overturned or discredited. At the very least it has to acknowledge the existence of turbulent and vociferous counter-narratives.

Support by women teachers for corporal punishment does not necessarily negate the idea that men have the major responsibility for discipline.
Even though women can be as firmly disciplinarian as men, they often
accept or live in a position of dependency. 'Female[s] enjoy the fruits of
being cared for by males', wrote one female respondent. This notion of
chivalry contrasts a strong awareness of inequality and even, to some
extent, of inverted superiority: the reality of being in paid labour as well as
carrying out traditional domestic duties makes a woman tougher – 'a girl
never rest[s]' – and furthermore allows for a degree of questioning and
disrupting of patriarchal relations:

> My mother answered 'do not tell me about boys, they cannot wash
> dishes and clean the house'. I then realised because of my sex I am the
> one to do much work at home ...

> The way I was brought up also made me feel that a woman is not given
> a chance in life like man. My father is depended [sic] on my mother
> (financially) but my mother is treated like a minor by my father and the
> family. This according to our tradition is accepted as man must be
> masters of everything even if they don't do their job.

The gender identity of women is uneven and contradictory. At the other
end of the spectrum, for example, women respondents spoke of a new-
found independence:

> I am proud of being a woman at my age of 33. Well in the olden days
> one could fill [sic] threaten if you are a woman because man were using
> extra power to us treating woman as a slave. So now being a woman I
> fill [sic] I could do whatever I can, nobody is restricting me.

> Through all this I have learned to depend on myself. I do not believe in
> failure. I do not believe I have to beg someone for his/her property. I
> believe in working hard for all that I have in life. I take life as an
> adventure ...

The widespread acceptance, by teachers and pupils alike, of corporal
punishment in schools flies in the face of the demands of the People's
Education movement in the 1980s and runs counter to the South African
Schools Act of 1996 which explicitly prohibits the practice. A similar
paradox exists in teacher attitudes about sexual orientation. Responses to

our survey indicated some tolerance of gays but the majority of responses suggest homophobia. Asked how they would respond to same-sex sexual overtures, a third of the male respondents said that they would get angry, threaten or assault the offender. Half said that they would ignore the overture and only one member of the sample was willing to talk to the person. The response of women differed, but in degree only. Nearly half said that they would ignore such overtures, while over a third said that they would get angry or threaten such a person. Less than 20 per cent said that they would talk to the person. Verbal discussion concerning the issue demonstrated that 'talking to the person' would involve reference to the Bible and an attempt to draw the person from his or her evil ways. As was to be expected, respondents testified to the existence in schools of a homophobic lexicon including words such as 'moffie', 'sitabane'[5] and 'fag'. When asked what they thought of boys or men holding hands,[6] half of the respondents disapproved, justifying their responses by suggesting that such a practice was 'not manly', that such men were 'acting like females' or that it was 'strange' and 'unnatural'. The homophobia referred to above must also be located within a gendered world-view that is captured in the teachers' responses to questions about what made them feel manly or womanly. While the most popular responses for both men and women related to academic or sporting successes, men also emphasized hard physical work and having a girlfriend, which contrasted with women's preferences for being an active church member or wearing stylish clothes.

These responses by mostly African and middle-class teachers suggests that, while there are unquestionably variations in terms of race and class, there is a vast gap between the policy documents and government legislation over the past three years and the actual world of the classroom. The government projects a human rights discourse which is profoundly bound up both with international liberal conceptions and the local rhetoric of the 1980s, encapsulated in People's Education. In short, the hegemonic discourse or master narrative bears the residue of the anti-apartheid struggle (particularly that of the youth). This discourse has largely been sanitized of its revolutionary rhetoric but has retained an anti-authoritarian ethos. However, it has as yet had little impact upon a schooling system which is still deeply scarred by generational, class and racial violence, and which is still attempting to come to terms with the campaigns of ungovernability in the 1980s and from the subsequent rise in student power within the mass democratic movement.

It can be argued that a power vacuum exists in schools at a time when the domestic institution of the family can no longer provide a firm foundation for social cohesion and generational hierarchies of respect. Teachers are deprived by the new Schools Act of that two-edged sword: the right physically to punish pupils. While it gave them authority in the school, at the same time it laid them open to student resentment and worked against the possibility of creating participatory learning experiences. But in the absence of adequate mechanisms for monitoring the many changes which have been decreed over the past few years, teachers have continued, illegally, to resort to corporal punishment. The (re)production of (heterosexual) gender identities by local disciplinary practices shows the limits of state-driven transformation.

The dissonance between the legislating discourse and everyday practice has dangerous implications for both transformation and identity. The teachers in our survey express views which suggest that the harsh realities of schooling show little sign of changing. Their own identities are far removed from the heroically progressive, critical and empowering conception of teachers implicit in official government discourse. They appear to be either unaware of the contradiction between their everyday practices and wider educational transformation, or unable to reconcile it. While teachers are in danger of being forced to relinquish their cherished power, the government risks having its credibility undermined if the gap between law and practice remains as large as it is.

The support of female teachers for corporal punishment and the absence of a campaign for sexual liberation may ironically both reinforce and threaten patriarchy. On the one hand, such support is dangerous for women to the extent that their acquiescence to the use of physical violence could be turned against them and used to legitimize rape and battery. On the other hand, and more significantly perhaps, women's stronger position in the workplace and consequent challenge to men's capacity to be breadwinners (Lemon, 1995) is underpinning this more bellicose and non-compliant version of womanhood or 'hard femininity'. The amazing durability of Winnie Mandela, erstwhile wife of the President, testifies to the development of this hybrid female identity. Despite adverse press and public rebuffs, she swept to power as president of the ANC Women's League. She represents an emergent 'hard femininity' in South Africa, assertive, independent, standing aside for neither man nor woman, ready to endorse violence against the state or against children (Gilbey, 1993) and to take a public stand against homosexuality.[7] 'Hard femininity' may thus collaborate with the attempts of male educators to entrench a culture of authority in schools and at the same time directly challenge the authority of male teachers. In these terms it seems fairly certain that female teachers, with their supposedly nurturing qualities, are unlikely alone to enact the new state creed of sexual tolerance and non-corporal punishment in schools.

## Conclusion

This chapter has argued that, at the moment when the South African state is being democratized, important sections of 'the people' have clung to familiar regimes of understanding and discipline. This is one possible reading of our analysis. By starting from specific, local instances and descriptions of educational practices, we have attempted to show how these are not the effects of state legislation but, on the contrary, have thus far been only superficially conditioned by the latter. Rather, the disciplinary effects of local practices of patriarchy, such as corporal punishment and homophobia, are at present far more constitutive of gendered subjectivities than the human rights discourse of the state. This calls into question the characterization of the latter as a 'master narrative' within these contexts. Yet it would also not be appropriate to shift this label to local practices, which not only are constantly mutating and being contested but give rise to new and hybrid identities (for women and gays, in particular, but also men and youth) which do not cohere easily with conventional classifications. The intensification and transformation of gender identities on the educational terrain is a complex and contradictory process which often takes place at a distance from the loci where power is commonly said to reside and places in stark relief the limits of legislated transformation.

## Acknowledgement

Our thanks to Richard Devey for assisting with the statistical analysis.

## Notes

1.  We follow the convention of using the term African to refer to indigenous black South Africans, in contrast to the term black, which would include those South Africans who were designated Indian or Coloured under apartheid's curious linguistic and social categories.

2. The term 'Bantu' was adopted by the previous regime to refer to indigenous African people and put into effect by the Bantu Authorities Act which was promulgated in 1952. It replaced the term native as racial categorization.

3. Under apartheid, African women were governed by a different set of laws from all other women in South Africa. Whereas women other than African were able to engage in independent legal contracts, African women were unable to escape the status of minor. Although falling under more lenient laws, Indian women who ascribed to Islam were also affected *de facto* by religious laws which diminished their status. Significant changes to the legal status of women in South Africa is inscribed in the current constitution, but subsidiary clauses that also respect religious and cultural practices arguably dilute this.

4. Demographic and political changes have also affected women: there are now, for example, a number of women cabinet ministers and a high proportion (25 per cent) of parliamentary members are female.

5. 'Isithabane' refers to a man who displays 'feminine' characteristics – the person so described may or may not be homosexual – but it is used to describe homosexuals as well – which is probably why a lot of African gay men who are 'masculine' do not call themselves gay. It is a derogatory term, but has to an extent been appropriated by the 'gay-homosexual black men'. Our thanks to Ronald Louw for this definition.

6. This question was included to call forth a common practice of hand-holding among African men as fraternal rather than sexual. It is difficult to explain this response. It is possible that the respondents were conscious of the research context and of the possibility of misinterpretation by non-African research-ers.

7. It is not the intention of the authors to pose these as opposing and exclusive gendered positions, but complexities that inscribe contradictory and varied subjects. Personal histories, too, are complex. Ironically, as explanation for her political tenacity Winnie Mandela offered the historical detail of herself as having grown up stick fighting and beating the boys at it (*Sunday Independent*, 8 June 1997, p. 17).

# References

Budlender, D. (1991). *Women and the Economy*. Cape Town: CASE.

Burman, S. and Fuchs, R. (1986). 'When families split: custody on divorce', in S. Burman and P. Reynolds (eds), *Growing up in a Divided Society*. Evanston: Northwestern University Press.

Campbell, C. (1992). 'Learning to kill: masculinity, the family and violence in Natal', *Journal of Southern African Studies*, **18**(3): 614–28.

Carton, B. (1993). 'Taxing loyal ties: Bambatha's followers and the destruction of family in Natal and Zululand, 1890–1910'. African Studies Seminar. Durban: University of Natal.

de Villiers, E. (1990). *Walking the Tightrope: Recollections of a Schoolteacher in Soweto*. Johannesburg: Jonathan Ball.

Deacon, R. (1996). 'Discourses of discipline in South Africa: rethinking critical pedagogies in postmodernity', *Discourse*, 17(2): 227–42.

Enslin, P. (1984). 'The role of fundamental pedagogics in the formulation of educational policy in South Africa', in P. Kallaway (ed.), *Apartheid and Education*. Johannesburg: Ravan.

Epstein, D. (ed.) (1994). *Challenging Lesbian and Gay Inequalities in Education*. Buckingham: Open University Press.

Fenwick, M. (1996). ' "Tough guy eh?": the gangster-figure in *Drum*', *Journal of Southern African Studies*, 22(4): 617–32.

Foucault, M. (1981). *The History of Sexuality: An Introduction*. Harmondsworth: Penguin.

Freire, P. (1978). *The Pedagogy of the Oppressed*. Harmondsworth: Penguin.

Freund, B. (1996). 'The violence in Natal', in R. Morrell (ed.), *Political Economy and Identities in KwaZulu-Natal: Historical and Social Perspectives*. Durban: Indicator Press.

Gevisser, M. and Cameron, E. (eds) (1994). *Defiant Desire: Gay and Lesbian Lives in South Africa*. Johannesburg: Ravan.

Gilbey, E. (1993). *The Lady*. London: Jonathan Cape.

Glaser, C. (1988/9). 'Students, Tsotsis and the Congress Youth League: youth organisation on the Rand in the 1940s and 1950s', *Perspectives in Education*, 10(2): 1–15.

Glaser, D. (1992). ' "The Mark of Zorro": sexuality and gender relations in the Tsotsi sub-culture on the Witwatersrand, 1940–1960', *African Studies*, 51(1): 47–67.

Grundlingh, A. (1990/1). 'Politics, principles and problems of a profession: Afrikaner historians and their discipline, *c.*1920–*c.*1965', *Perspectives in Education*, 12(1): 1–19.

Hassim, S. (1990). 'Black women in political organisations: a case study of the Inkatha Women's Brigade, 1976 to the present'. MA thesis, University of Natal, Durban.

Holdstock, T. L. (1990). 'Violence in schools: discipline', in B. McKendrick and W. Hoffman (eds), *People and Violence in South Africa*. Cape Town: Oxford University Press.

Holmes, R. (1994). 'White rapists make Coloureds (and homosexuals): the Winnie Mandela trial and the politics of race and sexuality', in M. Gevisser and E. Cameron (eds), *Defiant Desire: Gay and Lesbian Lives in South Africa*. Johannesburg: Ravan.

Hunter, M. (1979). *Reaction to Conquest*. Cape Town: David Philip.

Hyslop, J. (1987a). 'Food, authority and politics: student riots in South African schools 1945–76', *Africa Perspective*, 1(3/4): 3–41.

Hyslop, J. (1987b). 'The concepts of reproduction and resistance in the sociology of education: the case of the transition from "Missionary" to "Bantu" education 1940–1955', *Perspectives in Education*, 9(2): 3–24.

Hyslop, J. (1993). ' "Destruction coming in": Bantu education as response to social crisis', in P. Bonner, P. Delius and D. Posel (eds), *Apartheid's Genesis 1935–1962*. Johannesburg: Ravan/Wits University Press.

Jones, S. (1993). *Assaulting Childhood: Children's Experiences of Migrancy and Hostel Life in South Africa*. Johannesburg: Witwatersrand University Press.

Kros, C. (1990/1). ' "Deep Rumblings": Z. K. Matthews and African education before 1955', *Perspectives in Education*, 12(1): 21–41.

Lemon, J. (1995). 'Masculinity in crisis?', *Agenda*, 24.

Louw, R. (1995). 'The emergence of a black gay identity in Durban'. Paper presented at the First South African Colloquium on Gay and Lesbian Studies, University of Cape Town, 19–21 October.

Mac an Ghaill, M. (1994). *The Making of Men: Masculinities, Sexualities and Schooling*. Buckingham: Open University Press.

McLean, H. and Ngcobo, L. (1994). ' "Abangibhamayo bathi ngimnandi" (Those who fuck me say I'm tasty): gay sexuality in Reef Township', in M. Gevisser and E. Cameron (eds), *Defiant Desire: Gay and Lesbian Lives in South Africa*. Johannesburg: Ravan.

Mashamba, G. (1990). *A Conceptual Critique of the People's Education Discourse*. Johannesburg: Education Policy Unit, University of the Witwatersrand.

Mkatshwa, S. (1986). Keynote Address to the First National Consultative Conference, in *Proceedings of the First National Consultative Conference*. Johannesburg: University of the Witwatersrand.

Mokwena, S. (1991). 'The era of the jackrollers: contextualising the rise of youth gangs in Soweto'. Paper presented at the Project for the Study of Violence Seminar, University of the Witwatersrand.

Moodie, D. (1975). *The Rise of Afrikanerdom: Power, Apartheid and the Afrikaner Civil Religion*. Berkeley: University of California Press.

Ndlovu, J., Seery, U. and Mshengu, T. (1994). *Our Past, Our Pride*. Durban: Natal Worker History Project.

Newell, P. (ed.) (1972). *A Last Resort? Corporal Punishment in Schools*. Harmondsworth: Penguin.

Ntsebeza, L. (1993). 'Youth in urban African townships, 1945–1992: a case study of the East London Townships'. Unpublished MA thesis. University of Natal, Durban.

Prins, G. (1980). *The Hidden Hippopotamus: Reappraisal in African History: The Early Colonial Experience in Western Zambia.* Cambridge: Cambridge University Press.

Stiebel, V. (1968). *A South African Childhood.* London: André Deutsch.

Truscott, K. (1994). *Gender in Education.* Johannesburg: University of the Witwatersrand/NECC.

Vogelman, L. (1990). *The Sexual Face of Violence. Rapists on Rape.* Johannesburg: Ravan.

Wolpe, A. M. (1988). *Within School Walls: The Role of Discipline, Sexuality and the Curriculum.* London: Routledge.

# 11

# Race, Sexuality and Education: What Does It Mean to Be Aboriginal and Gay in Education in Australia?

*John Holmes*

### 'It's everybody's business'

'It's everybody's business' – so the banner read on the first float of the Sydney Gay and Lesbian Mardi Gras on 2 March 1996. It soon was everybody's business that this Mardi Gras paraded in front of half a million people, that it was viewed across Australia and the world via 46 television crews and that it has never had government financial support yet has become the country's second largest tourist attraction, injecting multi-millions of dollars into the economy each year.[1] It is now everybody's business that it is about gay, lesbian, bisexual and transgendered people, our families and friends. The parade was led once again by lesbian and gay Aboriginal and Torres Strait Islander women and men, Australia's 'original gays',[2] carrying, dancing around, marching behind the banner emblazoned with 'It's everybody's business'.

This chapter references gay Aboriginal men within the Mardi Gras contingent, for it is the words, and the layers of play on words, of the opening float of the Mardi Gras which are suggestive reminders of the frequent claims that being gay is often not regarded as part of the domain of Aboriginal men's business. The banner suggests that being gay is not an accepted aspect of broader traditional Aboriginal business, and demands a place for gayness in the business of all aspects of our communities.

The problem of visibility and coming out for Aboriginal gays is in many ways similar to coming out for all gays. There is, however, a series of contextual and historical overlays that make this complex. As a small, extremely marginalized and oppressed group, Aboriginal and Torres Strait Islander peoples have had to argue along universal appeals for recognition of existence, rights and oppressions. The shape of the struggle has occurred inside a particular politics. To be anything other than traditional, including gender roles, is to be disloyal, suspect, even non-Aboriginal. Aboriginal identity, recognizable to non-Aboriginal Australians, has been very constrained – appealing to traditionalism. Thus being gay, and coming out, is a vexed and complex site of struggle.

## The impact on education

The impact on education is profound. Addressing issues of Aboriginal gayness means challenging reductive framings of Aboriginality without co-opting the struggles named from within. It means supporting Aboriginal gay men across the site of the struggle. It means doing work on racism in the gay community. These are challenges for educators at all levels of schooling and in all aspects of adult education. These are challenges that must be met by teacher educators.

### There is a silence around gay Aboriginal men

There is a silence around gay Aboriginal men in the studies of Aboriginal peoples in education. There is a paucity of written material from Australia on the intersecting area of race and sexuality. There is little written by or about gay Aboriginal men. There is a silence in the biographical, fictive and pictorial literature around gay Aboriginal men and schooling. Perhaps Australia's closest response to the North American race and sexuality literature is Dino Hodge's *Did You Meet Any Malagas?* (1993). This homosexual history of Australia's tropical capital is a collection of interviews with gay men, including gay Aboriginal men, in the Northern Territory or the 'Top End' of Australia.

The tensions and contradictions come through the voices of men who are exploring sexuality within a framework of Aboriginal communities. It is intersubjectivity, identities and identity construction in general that informs and is of concern. The connectiveness of the available literature, anecdotes of lived experiences of gay Aboriginal men and we the educators provide the challenge.[3]

Gay Aboriginal men, men who self-identify as gay or homosexual, often do not publicly disclose a gay sexual orientation because of anticipated disapproval, derision or exclusion from Aboriginal communities. Communities often oppose gay men forming relationships within, or across, varying Aboriginal communities and clans. There are strong anti-homosexual attitudes resulting in the stigmatization of Aboriginal men who publicly disclose their homosexuality. There is physical abuse within gay Aboriginal relationships which is even more likely to be ignored than it is in heterosexual relationships, for although physical abuse is not uncommon, it is not talked about, it is not dealt with.[4] The issue is avoided rather than confronted.

There is a range of drug abuses which Aboriginal support groups see as escape mechanisms from the active denial of family and community. Such stigma, opposition, ignorance and denial have been a mitigating factor against a gay culture in Aboriginal communities in Australia, and it is only recently that gay Aboriginal men feel the strength and freedom to form public support and social groups, groups which are concerned with everything from HIV/AIDS, housing, money, politics, the press and Mardi Gras to drag.[5]

Aboriginal gays may resort to affiliation with the non-Aboriginal gay community to pursue social and sexual opportunities with other gay men, but are frequently dissuaded because of experiences of racism and prejudice in gay bars and restaurants. When forming interracial relationships, gay Aboriginal men confront racism from both the Aboriginal and the non-Aboriginal communities. The partners in the middle experience considerable negative pressure from all sides.

Faced with varying anti-gay attitudes in Aboriginal communities, anti-Aboriginal attitudes in gay communities and racist attitudes from all, Aboriginal gay men experience a conflict between an Aboriginal identity and sexual orientation. I suggest that the various education systems in Australia have little understanding of these conflicts.

To be Aboriginal and gay means being in a minority status in all communities in Australia – the Aboriginal, the gay and the mainstream non-Aboriginal heterosexual communities. It can result in being ostracized because of sexuality by an Aboriginal community, ignored due to race by a gay community and criticized as a result of an interracial relationship by both. One might well wonder about the silence around gay Aboriginal men.

## 'Play it, but don't say it'[6] – Aboriginal communities, families and homophobia

It is important then to analyse, to have an understanding of, the areas of perceived tradition, constructed communities and redefined families. Specifically, in the issue of Aboriginal communities and families and how the communities react to gay male members, there is to be found a range of reactions from oppression and conflict, through to tacit acceptance and in a few cases open approval. The literature supports the verbalized stories that being gay is not readily acceptable in Aboriginal communities.

E. J. Milera, a gay Ngarrindjeri-Kaurna man, knows that being gay often results in oppression and conflict, and 'when you're being shunned or disowned by your own community it really hurts. You do have people in your own community that support you ... but I think it's basically ignorance, and people just really don't understand' (Aldrich, 1993, p. 48). And Patrick, a leader in the Aboriginal gay community in Adelaide, South Australia, says there is 'certainly lots of denial in the Aboriginal community that gay Aboriginal people exist' (Patrick, 1994, p. 36). In Sydney, Luke Close agrees that 'being gay in an Aboriginal community is the same as being black in a white community. You are not accepted and in some cases forced to leave' (Close, 1992, p. 23). And in the Northern Territory, Lance's cousins come out into a shocked community. He sees that:

> The Island is now crawling with queens. I have five cousins who are gay over at Bathurst Island. And the whole island is outraged. All these gay people coming out of their closets over at Bathurst. It's a real shock, horror. And I'm thinking one day I'll go there and explain to the families: 'They're not lepers; they're quite human, they're normal people.' (Hodge, 1993, p. 80)

Homophobia is not too severe a term to apply.

> Within my own peer group, or family group, or extended family, there is certainly very strong traits of homophobia or discrimination. I mean I prefer to use the word discrimination because that's, I suppose that's the word that we've used for a long time. Our community discriminates against us. (Patrick, 1994, pp. 15–16)

The resulting effect is that many young men feel forced to leave, 'to escape the persecution by their families' (Patrick, 1994, p. 36) and head for the anonymity of the larger urban centres and capital cities. The divisive and counter-productive nature of homophobia causes frustration and anger amongst some gay Aboriginal men, who see their communities losing valuable support in economic, social, educative and familial areas.

For Aboriginal people to blame others, outsiders, for the homosexuality of their men does not hold any weight with gay Aboriginal men. The whole exercise of blame is seen as not only irrelevant to living contemporary lives, but intrinsically wrong. The construction of history that holds the view that homosexuality is a white man's disease is not acceptable to Rea Saunders, Jim Wafer, Gary Lee and Maureen Fletcher who discuss the issue in their paper 'Demythologising the White Man's Disease'. As Rea says in the transcribed discussions that make up this paper, 'I get that all the time, "it's a White man's disease" . . . As far as I know, homosexuality has existed here for a long time, it's not a White man's disease – it's probably the only thing we didn't catch off the White man!' (Aldrich, 1993, p. 9). Placing the blame at the feet of non-Aboriginal men holds no credence for gay Aboriginal men who either do not know where Aboriginal cultures stood on the issue of same-sex relations prior to European invasion, or do not care.

The fundamentalism of much of the early Western religious teachings in Australia in many ways remains unchanged in modern Christianity, and the enforced 'civilizing' that occurred throughout contact history has resulted in complexities of beliefs and intolerances. As John Newfong said in the television production *Double Trouble*:[7]

> The imposition of the Judeo-Christian ethic has brought in a lot of homophobia, but one needn't be a church-goer to pick this up – it's now societal conditioning. A lot of urban Aboriginal people, however radical and however bellicosely Black they may be, in fact have adopted White, working-class values, towards sexuality, and those White, working-class values, in this country, are Catholic. (quoted in Aldrich, 1993, p. 12)

The influences of Judeo-Christian religion, and of gender roles in traditional Aboriginal culture, are powerful mitigators against acceptance of Aboriginal men who are gay. Many changes occurred in the name of Christianity and colonization, and these changes were invariably intended to alter traditional values and behaviours. Enforced institutionalization, and massive social and cultural changes, had a long-lasting effect on all aspects of Aboriginal societies. However, while some allocate cause and blame on outside forces, Aboriginal gay men are far more concerned with acceptance, and with getting on with living in as non-homophobic an environment as possible. In this manner there is allegiance with gay politics in general, where a rationalist and functionalist view is anathema, for it is also apparent that members of Aboriginal communities sometimes tacitly tolerate homosexual members without publicly approving – 'play it, but don't say it' (Ann Allen Shockley in Gomez and Smith, 1990, p. 33), keeping gayness a family secret. And some families treat their son's sexuality, and his partner's, as quite an ordinary part of the diversity of the family structure – 'he's family and that's it'[8] – adding further multifaceted dimensions to the complex lives of gay Aboriginal men.

## 'Why aren't you with a black man?'[9] – racism in interracial relationships

As Lance says during an interview, friendships between Aboriginal and non-Aboriginal gay men are often confounded by problematizing any venturing from the group of Aboriginal 'sisters'. He believes as a group his sisters become quite overprotective, and get annoyed when he, or anyone else, moves to form a relationship with a non-Aboriginal man. 'I suppose they put us into a set of how we're queens, coloured girls, we've got to stay together' (Lance in Hodge, 1993, p. 85). Patrick is proud to concede that, in general:

> Black men love each other, they do. Heterosexual black men love each other. But, so do gay men, gay black men, they love each other. They also respect one another, and they also work quite well together, and they have loving relationships whether they be sexual or friendship. (Patrick, 1994, p. 26)

But for Patrick, being involved with a non-Aboriginal gay man is very problematic, for Aboriginal communities do not talk about sexuality, nor about perceived racist reactions to gay men's interracial relationships. For Patrick his relationship is not at odds with his own self-perception, self-identification or self-love as an Aboriginal man, but 'even Aboriginal gay men are quite racist – "Why am I with a white man? Why aren't I with a black man?" And my answer is that I basically fell in love with this guy' (Patrick, 1994, p. 36). Aside from the racism directed at him by Aboriginal men, his lover's family does not accept their own son's homosexuality, and seemingly place the 'blame' on Patrick. He is attacked from all sides.

When sexuality and race are linked in the form of a gay relationship between an Aboriginal man and a non-Aboriginal man there is much tension. The question 'Why aren't you with a black man?' (Patrick, 1994, p. 30) raises the issue of interracial relationships, which is one of the most private, yet recurring, topics of discussion amongst gay Aboriginal men. The tension for Aboriginal men comes from families blaming homosexuality on the other partner, from general homophobia in the family and community and the racism overlaying it all. Sometimes these antagonistic pressures come from both sides of the relationship, and gay Aboriginal men tend to find that the only support is in particularized gay communities. Such constructed communities are formed and used to satisfy needs that family or the Aboriginal community could not. There is debate within such gay communities regarding the politics of interracial and intraracial relationships, with opinions being as diverse as the members. The overriding consideration by gay Aboriginal men is that those who cause the antagonism towards Aboriginal men in interracial relationships should address their own fears and prejudices.

## 'There are a lot of racist gay whites around':[10] racism in the gay community

An examination of gay Aboriginal experiences in the mainstream gay communities finds that the manifestations of racial discrimination are numerous, both covert and blatant, with verbal anecdotes and literature providing graphic illustrations. To paraphrase Wendy Dunn/Holland (Aldrich, 1994, p. 47), it is sort of scary when people within the gay community in Australia, whom you presume understand homophobia, can turn around and dump on a person who is Aboriginal and gay. Some gay people do not stop to think how they have been affected by mainstream society. It is one thing to be oppressed by non-gay people, it is another when gay people are oppressing each other.

There is often an invisibility of gay Aboriginal men within the gay culture, and the responsibility for this is sometimes laid at the doors and bars of gay venues, while the mainstream and the gay press often ignore gay Aboriginal perspectives. Stereotyping by gay men of Aboriginal gays is coarse and derogatory, and there is the feeling by gay Aboriginal men of being sexually used by non-Aboriginal gay men. There develops in older men a sense of a loss of youth in the struggle to grow up in the various unaccepting communities. Involvement in the gay community may increase the likelihood of Aboriginal gay men experiencing racism.

The most visible form of discrimination in the gay community is at the bars which are our most popular and public meeting places. Getting into a bar may be the first problem for Aboriginal men, who could experience subtle means of being deterred in order to keep the 'white gay fellars' happy. Gurra, a Larrakia Aboriginal, refers to the little, seemingly unobvious, yet quite significant things that occur when he goes into a gay bar in Darwin in the Northern Territory. From the looks – 'It's the scrunching of the nose and it's like they've just eaten something rotten, the way their mouth is twisted' – to the insults – 'What's that black cunt doing here?' (Hodge, 1993, p. 69). Although Gurra does not say that all gays are racist, he knows that 'there are a lot of racist gay whites around', and he blames it on 'the attitudes that they've obviously picked up from parents, or whatever, about black people' (Hodge, 1993, p. 70). He considers that one of the effects of such behaviour is that Aboriginal gays in Darwin have their own jargon, humour and stereotypes about white gays. The amount of energy to sustain a presence in some gay venues is too demanding, and unnecessary, so that a most empowering effect has been to encourage Aboriginal gay men to form social groups and societies separate from non-Aboriginal gay groups – then 'we just ignore them' (Hodge, 1993, p. 70).

Gary Lee recognized racism coming from the gay community from his teenage years, but was surprised to hear the same sort of racist remarks directed towards him in a gay bar in Sydney as he was used to hearing directed against women in heterosexual encounters in the Northern Territory. 'As a put-down, the term "Black Velvet" quickly acquired its current derogatory status, and in the Sydney bar I was surprised to hear it in a gay environment. Just another level of racism, I thought' (Aldrich, 1993, p. 18). He knows that in many instances white gay men are critical of society's marginalizations of gays and Aboriginal people, yet in practice live out the racist attitudes of parents and the wider society which marginalize gay Aboriginals.

## Some positive changes

Although he still experiences racism in the general gay community, Patrick now finds that the gay scene in Adelaide is itself more diverse than it was twenty years ago, and that Aboriginal gay men like himself have made a niche within that scene as well as forming their own gay social structures. One of the reasons for the positive recognition of Aboriginal men within the gay community has come about as a result of the AIDS pandemic, and Patrick argues that the co-operative fight against AIDS, and the changing face of the old main players on the gay scene, work towards fewer racist overtones in attitudes and behaviour. 'AIDS has certainly changed the community. It's made it a more caring community, and that's the sad thing about it – why couldn't it happen before?' (Patrick, 1994, p. 21). He knows that he and his friends are able to go into bars or into any gay social group and be accepted. Most of the time. He also believes that the Adelaide Mardi Gras Collective's float and dance team in the 1994 Mardi Gras were indicative of the local community's ability to recognize where it had come from, and acknowledge where it could be going – namely, from private closeted dinner parties to visibly being 'out' in Sydney; there was even footage of the float edited into the film *The Sum of Us*.[11] 'That goes to prove that Adelaide is coming of age' (Patrick, 1994, p. 22).

During interviews Patrick notes another aspect of change. He perceives that whereas the mainstream press ranges from blatant racism in local regional newspapers to more covert commentary in city papers, the gay press is different. 'I think the gay press has certainly been very clever in the way that they've portrayed Aboriginal people. There seems to be a pro-Aboriginal image' (Patrick, 1994, p. 35). An example of the way both the gay press and the daily papers are currently dealing with issues of race and sexuality is that of the murder of an Aboriginal man in Veale Gardens, Adelaide, in May 1993. *Adelaide Gay Times*, the *Advertiser* and the *Sunday Mail* liaised with the family and the community, 'and took it on as quite a strong battle to find out who the guy's murderers were' (Patrick, 1994, p. 35).[12] But who spoke about the murder? What did they speak about, and what did they omit? How was the Aboriginal community represented, and what did its members say? The mainstream press during that time, namely the daily morning newspaper, focused on a response from gay white males about gay bashings and on an article from the Aboriginal relatives of the murdered man. What was the story, and who told it? What was omitted, by whom and why? The newspaper clippings of the period in May 1993 are informative. Different family groups of the deceased had their responses fully reported, and these were varied and quite different, publicly indicating great divergence in the Aboriginal community's acceptance of the man's sexuality. The newspaper reporters desensationalized, rather than trivialized, the murder. There was a quick and public involvement of the gay community, in this case the white gay community. With regard to the reporting of another murder at about the same time, there 'did not seem to be anything derogatory' about the way the press presented the murder of an Aboriginal girl in Gouger Street, Adelaide. Aboriginal gay men helped with that particular investigation but were not part of the interviewing or reporting scenario; however, the local press managed 'very straightforward reporting' (Patrick, 1994, p. 35).

In both instances, however, there was no particular reporting from or by gay Aboriginal men. The spokespersons and those photographed were the non-Aboriginal men of the mainstream gay community in Adelaide. There was no comment from any member of the gay Aboriginal community, and there certainly has never been a feature of Aboriginal men in articles concerning homosexuality in these newspapers. Although the gay press is accommodating of difference, why are there no voices from minorities within the community? Why are not Aboriginal men speaking or being seen? The same questions could be asked of the AIDS Council, Gay Counselling Services or Gayline – all run by middle-class white males.

The Safe Sex Summer Campaign of 1993 attempted to be more inclusive, and a few gay Aboriginal men made an effort to be portrayed in a positive image within the gay community, but felt they were required to go 'along for interviews to have photos taken to put some Aboriginal faces in the posters' (Patrick, 1994, p. 30). In essence gay Aboriginal men had to justify to the Campaign organizers why they should be included in the pictorial representation of gay men. The result was, as Patrick recalled, 'the usual stereotypical beautiful young white gay male. And I thought, "Well, oh fuck you" ' (Patrick, 1994, p. 30). Gay Aboriginal men see that this is consistent with the way sections of the gay community react, even when there is a desire to be more inclusive.

Gay Aboriginal men make allowances for a mainstream and gay press which does not derogate gay Aboriginal men, yet are not at ease with the pictorial representations of gay Aboriginal men. However, I question both the cause and the acceptance of this silent exclusion. Why are there no representations of and by gay Aboriginal men? Why is this tolerated by those very people who are excluded? Why is it tolerated by non-Aboriginals who are not excluded yet do not condone? Perhaps it is the guilt of exclusion by silence. Perhaps the gay community should take on board Jackie Goldsby's comment that 'an analysis of race, along with a commitment to eradicate racism, must remain on the forefront of gay theory and political activism' (Goldsby, 1990, p. 15).

Gay Aboriginal men understand that racism pervades all levels and all areas of the gay community. Some non-Aboriginal gay men still persist in portraying Aboriginal men in stereotypic fashion. There remains the objectification of gay Aboriginal men and the racially inspired name-calling. Although there are perceptible changes on the mainstream gay scene, many gay Aboriginal men seem to prefer to form their own social groups, conduct their own functions and ignore the gay press. Many gay Aboriginal men are a major part of the mainstream gay community – in the AIDS prevention and support groups, in the bar and night club scene and in the general support groups for gay men. Yet there is discrimination by the gay community on the basis of Aboriginality.

## Conclusion

To be Aboriginal and gay means complex, hybrid lives, lived in multiple ways. It means dealing with Aboriginal and non-Aboriginal homophobia, traditionalism and loyalties to communities. It means racism in multiple forms – Aboriginal, non-Aboriginal, gay and non-gay, and it means racism in interracial roles.

Despite being Aboriginal and gay meaning an almost total silence in the oral and written stories 'it's certainly going to be time shortly when we're going to get Aboriginal gay people in this country starting to write about who they are, and where they come from, and talk about it in a contemporary issue, rather than the historic issue' (Patrick, 1994, p. 38). For gay communities it means doing work on racism. For education communities it means addressing homophobia and racism and it means supporting gay Aboriginal men in speaking and writing about lived experiences in education. Racism and homophobia are invidiously configured oppressions and must be challenged on multiple fronts. The intersections, competitions and collisions of multiple subjectivities must be analysed to avoid reductionist tendencies, encourage a notion of difference and diversity and enable new forms of dialogue. For as children, young Aboriginal gays are invisible in the adult world, as men invisible in the male-dominated world, as Aboriginal invisible in the gay world (Epstein, 1994, p. 35), and gay Aboriginal students are almost totally invisible in all levels of the education world.

'We're here, we're queer' expresses our energy in all our differences, our struggle and celebrations. As Aboriginal gay activist Patrick often says:

I suppose Aboriginal gay men now, and certainly me, we're saying to the community that we want recognition, we want to be recognised, we don't want to hide in the closets any more . . . We're out. We're coming out, and there's nothing you can do about it. (Patrick, 1994, p. 16)

As we again celebrate a Mardi Gras behind an Aboriginal banner asserting that 'It's everybody's business', and while there are gay Aboriginal men and women for whom communities insist that it is nobody's business, it is time for all educators to make it our business.

## Notes

1.  The entire Mardi Gras parade was replayed on ABC TV, 6 March 1996, and highlighted on SBS TV, 20 March on its *Indigenous Cultural Affairs Magazine*.
2.  *Double Trouble* (1991) – TV documentary produced by Diane Hamer and directed by Tony Ayers; a Big and Little Production for Channel Four (UK) and SBS (Australia); copyright Channel Four.
3.  John Holmes (1995). 'Race and sexuality: What does it mean to be Aboriginal and gay?', draws together the literature about gay Aboriginal men. The coupling of Aboriginal and gay is an uncommon linkage in the literature, and often regarded as two 'unsuitable' (Sparkes, 1993, p. 1) aspects of the Australian character.
4.  Physical abuse within relationships, especially gay relationships, is problematic. While not being acknowledged it is not going to be dealt with, and hence another example of 'nobody's business'.
5.  In South Australia gay Aboriginal issues are a priority of the Health Commission and the AIDS Council, and although Aboriginal men are in a minority on the gay social scene, there is an emergence and strengthening of attitude and resolve. In 1997 the President of the AIDS Council is a positive gay Aboriginal man.
6.  Ann Allen Shockley in Gomez and Smith (1990), p. 33.
7.  *Double Trouble* (1991).
8.  Grandmother's comment in a short play on Australian SBS Television, 20 March 1996, on its *Indigenous Cultural Affairs Magazine*.
9.  Patrick (1994), p. 30.
10. Gurra in Hodge (1993), p. 70.
11. The film *The Sum of Us* contained footage of the Gay and Lesbian Mardi Gras Parade in Sydney in 1994. One scene in the film showed the Adelaide Mardi Gras Collective's entry 'Guess Who's Coming to Dinner'. The Collective's

float portrayed contrasting images of the Adelaide dinner scene – formal above the dinner table, and outrageously informal below, while the dance team continuously sensualized the idea through movement and costume for the length of the Parade.

12. There was coverage in the South Australian newspapers – David Pemberthy and Bill Power wrote, with accompanying photographs, in the *Advertiser*, the daily newspaper; Shane Maguire's article appeared with photographs in the *Sunday Mail*, a weekly tabloid; *Adelaide Gay Times*, the fortnightly gay publication, had front-page reporting.

## References

Aldrich, Robert (1993). *Gay Perspectives II: More Essays in Australian Gay Culture.* University of Sydney: Department of Economic History with the Australian Centre for Gay and Lesbian Research.

Close, Luke (1992, April). 'Gay, Aboriginal and proud', *National AIDS Bulletin*, 7 (3).

Epstein, Debbie (ed.) (1994). *Challenging Lesbian and Gay Inequalities in Education.* Buckingham: Open University Press.

Goldsby, Jackie (1990). 'What it means to be coloured me', *Out/look*, Summer.

Gomez, Jewelle and Smith, Barbara (1990). 'Taking the home out of homophobia: black lesbians look in their own backyards', *Out/look*, Spring.

Hodge, Dino (1993). *Did You Meet Any Malagas? A Homosexual History of Australia's Tropical Capital.* Nightcliff, Northern Territory: Little Gem.

Holmes, John A. (1995). 'Race and sexuality: What does it mean to be Aboriginal and gay?' Unpublished master's thesis, University of South Australia.

Maguire, Shane (1993). 'A night of evil in the garden', *Advertiser*, 16 May, pp. 4–5.

Patrick (1994). Interviews conducted by John Holmes with pseudonym Patrick, transcribed and stored in accordance with protocol of Human Research Ethic Committee of University of South Australia: 51 pages, 18,000 words. Unpublished raw data.

Pemberthy, David (1993). 'Police, gays join force in hunt for killer', *Advertiser*, 13 May, p. 3.

Pemberthy, David (1993). 'Park vigils for leads to murder', *Advertiser*, 14 May, p. 5.

Power, Bill (1993). 'Man killed in parklands – murder warning to gays', *Advertiser*, 12 May, p. 1.

Power, Bill (1993). 'Behaviour of slain man out of character, says relative', *Advertiser*, 17 May, p. 13.

194 • JOHN HOLMES

Sparkes, Andrew C. (1993). *Identity Management Strategies in Shifting Contexts: A Life History Analysis of a Lesbian Physical Educator.* Manuscript submitted for publication.

# 12

# Abortion and Family Values: The X Case, Sexuality and 'Irishness'

*Lisa Smyth*

## Prologue

In 1992, the Irish High Court issued an injunction to prevent a 14-year-old rape victim from travelling to Britain for an abortion. The X case, as it is known, prompted national and international outrage, and came to occupy central political space in Ireland. It underlined how abortion involves a particular interrelation between the state, the nation and women. A considerable feminist resistance movement, both in Ireland and abroad, gained popularity, not least due to a wave of intense media interest in what was referred to in the *Irish Independent* as the 'child rape' case. The issue of rape, and child rape in particular, became a key point in effecting a shift in popular opinion and state policy on abortion.

## Introduction

This paper will consider the pedagogical effects of the newspaper coverage of the X case. I will argue that this case illustrates the ways that sexual identities and gendered citizens are reproduced, in terms of post-colonial discourses of national identity.[1] The case highlighted the gendered nature of 'belonging' to a nation state, through a 'sexual contract' where citizenship is mediated by positioning in the family (Pateman, 1988), an institution which is constitutionally defined as the 'primary unit' of society.

I am primarily concerned with how hegemonic discourses, which construct the nation through gender, sexuality and the nuclear family, were both contested and reproduced within and through the media.[2] This chapter will look at newspaper coverage of the initial High Court injunction preventing X and her parents from travelling abroad to obtain an abortion, concentrating on the high point of media attention following the injunction, namely the week of 17–22 February 1992, in the three national dailies of the period, the *Irish Times*, *Irish Independent* and *Irish Press*. To provide a context for this discussion, I will briefly outline the historical formation of contemporary national identity in Ireland, and the more immediate background to the X case.

## Abortion, gender and national identity: historical formations

Irish national identity has been constituted not only through a history of colonialism and partition, but also through patriarchal social reformation in the aftermath of the Great Famine of the 1840s. The social structure changed dramatically after the famine, as land became essential to status and power.[3] A social code of sexual puritanism, tightly policed by an increasingly authoritarian patriarchy, was established (Hynes, 1978). This was reinforced by an Augustinian belief system stressing the subordination of women, which was reinforced through the post-famine Catholic 'devotional revolution' (Larkin, 1976). By the 1930s, religion had become the central characteristic of Irish nationalism, and the political and cultural hegemony of the Church was cemented (Keogh, 1988, p. 105). The 1937 Constitution explicitly made women responsible for both the reproduction of the population and the transmission of national identity through the practice of mothering. Women's lives were, in principle, to be restricted to the domestic sphere, in order to secure a 'common good'.[4]

Puritanical and patriarchal forces maintained and strengthened their hegemony in 1983, when the position of women in Ireland was further damaged as the people accepted the 'pro-life' amendment to the Constitution:

> The state acknowledges the right to life of the unborn and, with due regard to the equal right to life of the mother, guarantees in its laws to respect, and, as far as practicable, by its laws to defend and vindicate that right. (Article 40.3.3)

This was the culmination of a three-year crusade by the Pro-Life Amendment Campaign (PLAC), an association of lay Catholic groups established in the aftermath of the Pope's visit to Ireland in 1979.[5] The success of the movement was due not least to the powerful persuasive force of its title as 'pro-life', implying as it does that its opponents are 'anti-life', or 'pro-death'. This opposition has never been accepted by the pro-choice movement, although many feminists are uncomfortable with the 'pro-choice' label, since the right to choose cannot compete with the right to life in terms of winning public sympathy and support (McNeil *et al.*, 1991, p. 215).

PLAC, it has been argued, chose to campaign around the abortion issue precisely because of their perception of popular consensus on main-taining its illegality (Girvin, 1986). They used nationalist arguments that defined all outside influence as contamination, leading inevitably to the fragmentation and collapse of the nation. PLAC framed their arguments in terms of the need to maintain the purity of the nation for the future of its children (see Hesketh, 1990; O'Reilly, 1992). Changing conceptions of a woman's role were emerging, and Randall (1986) has argued that it was precisely these changes that spurred conservatives to initiate the 'pro-life' amendment campaign, in an attempt to shore up their hegemonic position, through constructing a discourse around abortion tightly linked with national identity and continuity.

## Newspaper coverage of the X case, 1992

The 1992 abortion debate was also framed in terms of national identity.[6] Three key pedagogical narratives in particular emerged. Firstly, 'child rape' became the focus for constructing/instructing who are the 'real' or 'innocent' (as opposed to guilty) victims of sexual assault, and therefore what sexual behaviour is appropriate for Irish people. Secondly, national identity was inverted, in response to the X case judgment, as 'we' Irish became the oppressors, rather than the oppressed. The identity crisis that this embodied was resolved through reaffirming the value of liberal democracy, based on a sharp distinction between public and private spheres, namely the state and the family. Thirdly, the emergence of feminist protests and critique of the nation state opened up the possibilities of changing or recovering a sense of Irishness through changing abortion law, and affirming women's citizenship rights.

*Pedagogies of sexuality*
Some 'pro-life' campaigners responded to the X case by affirming a sense of pride in who 'we' are, as represented by the abortion ban.[7] The

implication is that a 'pro-life' identity is in some sense part of the national psyche, rooted in the formative experiences of the modern nation. Catholic journalist Mary Kenny, in an article in the *Irish Independent* (22 February 1992), wrote:

> The Irish anti-abortion mentality is a complex interweaving of historical and cultural phenomena. I believe at a deep level of the race memory that there is a link with depopulation. Rural Ireland, remember, has never recovered, numerically, from the famine.

This historical explanation refers to the radical cultural effect of the famine. References to the famine often work within the terms of anti-English nationalism.[8] Mary Kenny uses this major historical event to 'naturalize' her assertion that the Irish are 'pro-life'. Her particularly compelling 'pro-life' argument relies on a nationalist discourse of famine which overlaps with anti-imperialist discourses against population control.

The pedagogical effect of articulating and reconstructing a particular version of Irishness in terms of 'pro-life', anti-imperialist nationalism depends on reaffirming existing gendered identities. The key way that this is achieved is through asserting what sexual behaviour is appropriate for Irish women and men.

The way the X case reinvented a pedagogical discourse of Irishness depended on maintaining the hegemony of discourses which construct sexual identities, through the specific form that the discourse of rape took in the press. The pre-sexual identity of X was affirmed, by explicitly positioning her as a child in a family. Questions of sexual consent or intent were thus excluded (Dumaresq, 1981, pp. 56–7). X was a '14-year-old girl', someone's daughter, who was not to blame for her pregnancy, as a sexually active rape victim could be. Debate focused instead on the relationship between the state and the family. What was at stake was the state's constitutional duty to defend and protect the family as the primary unit of society.

The Irish Constitution explicitly recognizes the family (which is not explicitly defined) rather than the individual, as the primary unit of society:

> The State recognises the Family as the natural primary and fundamental unit group of Society, and as a moral institution possessing

inalienable and imprescriptible rights, antecedent and superior to all positive law.

The State, therefore, guarantees to protect the Family in its constitution and authority, as the necessary basis of social order and as indispensable to the welfare of the Nation and the State. (*Bunreacht na hEireann*, 1937, Article 41.1.1 and 41.1.2)

Rights, then, are not primarily accorded to and claimed by individual citizens, but by families. The definition of the family is implicitly patriarchal, through references to women under the heading of 'family' and in terms of her 'life within the home' upon which the 'common good' (whose good?) depends, and the state's duty to ensure that mothers are not 'obliged by economic necessity to engage in labour to the neglect of their duties in the home'. The implication is that women naturally belong in the 'home', for which read the family, and are subordinate to men and fathers, who clearly have no duties in the home which they should be prevented from neglecting by the state (Scannell, 1988, pp. 124–5). The primacy accorded to the family, rather than the individual, in the Constitution, a document which declares the fundamental rules of society and government, and which cannot be changed other than by popular referendum, is highly significant for the unequal positions accorded to women and men, both socially and politically.

X's sexual identity was erased in the press. For example, a founder member of a Limerick support group for women, Maeve Kelly, made the following comment:

This girl, as she is being called, is not a girl. She is a child and this judgement has gone against the wishes of her parents. (Cummins, 1992, p. 7)

Here we see X located exclusively in the private sphere, as a dependent child without gender or sexuality, not even a 'girl'. To recognize her as gendered, albeit within the limited conception of personhood implied by the word 'girl', would be to acknowledge her sexuality, and would introduce into the debate questions of sexuality and the family. By virtue of her position within the family, then, X was identified as the ideal worthy victim, since not only had she clearly been raped against her will, and so was not a 'guilty', as opposed to an 'innocent' victim, but her distress was explained in terms of the pain caused to her parents, not the pain she suffered herself. The family as a unit was constructed as the victim. The distress of X herself was not significant; she was submerged under the family as a whole.

## Us versus them? A collective crisis of identity

The state's action was denounced as totalitarian in the press, and the *Irish Times* editorial on 18 February 1992 condemned the state's 'descent into cruelty', comparing it with Ceauçescu's Romania and the Ayatollah's Iran. The leader of the Labour Party, Dick Spring, commented that 'girl-children' could become 'prisoners of the State' and be forced to give birth following rape. As he put it:

> the court has decided that the state is right to intervene in a situation which, in any other country in the western world, would be considered an entirely private family matter. (Spring, 1992, p. 4)

State abuse of power is associated with the actions of non-Western states, with the implication that such intrusions into family privacy are counter to the values of the civilized and enlightened West, being more typical of non-Western totalitarian regimes. The ban on abortion was thrown into question in such cases of child rape, since abortion would reaffirm the boundaries of family privacy, which had been transgressed both by the nation state and by the rape.[9]

The X case highlighted the ambiguity between the hegemonic construction of the nation state as the upholder of justice and morality, and the unjust intrusion into the private sphere which the X case illustrated. As a political issue, abortion was now problematized in the pragmatic terms of public policy, rather than in the abstract terms of an expression of fundamental moral law, as it had been during the 1980s. The ability of the state to punish the crime of rape became central. The Labour Party leader, Dick Spring, drew attention to the difficulties involved in dealing with sexual violence against women and legal minors (*Irish Press*, 19 February 1992). Effective public policy on rape and sexual violence should encourage women to report assaults to the Gardai regardless of whether they feared that they may or may not be pregnant as a result. This threw the state's position on abortion into question, facilitating the (albeit limited) eventual legalization of abortion information, and guaranteeing women's constitutional right to travel outside the state. The state's duty to recognize the family as the primary social unit was balanced with its role in protecting its citizens through the enforcement of criminal law, in a way which reaffirmed the boundary between public and private. The pivotal role of the family in legitimizing the authority of the state in this instance depended on the hegemony of discourses of sexuality based on privacy.

Many responses to the X case depicted the Irish nation state as a totalitarian regime which intruded into private family decisions, the type of state against which 'we' had previously defined who we were. Loss of certainty over who 'we' are in relation to the imperialist other can be seen in the expressions of reluctant understanding of the unionist agenda which appeared in the press.[10] Also, references to internment, for instance Martyn Turner's cartoon on the front page of the *Irish Times* on the day following the High Court decision,[11] compared the Irish state to the British state as it is constructed in Irish nationalism and republicanism, namely as a fundamentally unjust, violent regime, primarily interested in protecting and expanding its territories.

Those who did not condemn the state's intrusion into family privacy instead blamed feminists for the X case. Some 'pro-life' activists accused 'pro-abortionists' and the media of exploiting an innocent victim for their own purposes. Rather than condemning the state's actions, the Society for the Protection of the Unborn Child (SPUC) was reported as blaming 'those that refer the girls for abortion', who should suffer the brunt of anti-abortion legislation, rather than 'the girls' themselves:

> The issue is being used by the pro-abortion lobby . . . the referral trade only stopped as the result of a private case brought by SPUC . . . The ones that I would be interested in are those that refer the girls for abortion, those that don't help them find a solution here. (SPUC activists, quoted in Keena, 1992, p. 6)

Feminists were targeted by 'pro-life' campaigners as callous profiteers, who were prepared to use the circumstances of the X case for their own advantage.

The 'pro-life' movement was responding to the relative popularity that feminism achieved in response to the X case. Newspapers carried coverage of demonstrations against the injunction in Dublin, London, and New York (e.g. *Irish Times*, 17 February 1992) and feminist criticism of the state was also prominent in the national press during this period.[12] The patriarchal nature of the legal system was highlighted by newspaper coverage of the low levels of rape reported to the Gardai (police) following the High Court injunction. A spokeswoman from the Well Woman Centre made the following statement, during debate over the 'morning after' pill:

> many women who are raped are often not in a position to report it immediately and even if they do report it very quickly they face a range of physical, medical, psychological and garda interviews in addition to counselling. (Dowling and O'Keefe, 1992, p. 13)

The state's treatment of rape victims, even apart from the issue of possible pregnancy, was portrayed as prohibitively intrusive, impeding a woman's capacity to cope with rape. This is an effect of the construction of the meaning of rape, and who is constructed as a legitimate rape victim. The definition of rape depends on the absence of consent, that is, the key question in rape trials is whether the alleged rapist believed his victim was consenting to sex. The issue of consent then produces four rather than two categories, not only the guilty rapist and the innocent victim, but the innocent rapist and the guilty victim (Dumaresq, 1981, p. 57). The question of what constitutes acceptable sexual behaviour for men and women blurs the distinction between innocent and guilty, rapist and rape victim. The state's treatment of rape victims, through a barrage of examinations, explicitly defines acceptable sexual behaviour for women and men. This has serious implications in cases of rape for any woman who is deemed to have stepped outside her legally defined role, namely one of sexual passivity. The message clearly is that women's rights as citizens depend on conformity to the ideal type of 'victim' that X exemplified, i.e. a desexualized child.

Feminist protest became popular through the X case, because the immediate questions it raised about X's rights as an Irish citizen inevitably opened up the broader issues of women's citizenship rights in relation to sexuality. The very presence of feminist engagements with debates over national identity in the press point to a significant shift in the rules and conventions establishing who is authorized to speak on behalf of/to the nation, and when (Trend, 1993, p. 93). The state's strategy for managing feminist critique was built on reproducing normative family discourses. This reaffirmed power inequality, precisely because hegemonic constructions of gender and sexuality, which place women firmly in the private sphere of the family, were reinforced.

*National identity: protest and change*

The difference between 'pro-life' and 'pro-choice' discourses which constructed national identity through abortion was that 'pro-life' formulations emphasized the need to maintain the abortion ban in order to affirm 'our' identity, whereas the pro-choice position claimed that abortion law must change if 'we' are to remain the same.

Many women expressed anger that the actions of the state left them feeling alienated from the nation:

> The news that the injunction was granted to our Attorney General filled me with anger and despair – and the oppressive feeling that makes one run to pack one's bags. Not for the first time I feel an alien in my native country. (*Irish Times*, Letters to the Editor, 19 February 1992)

This woman is expressing the loss of a sense of belonging that the X case prompted. The tension experienced by many women in Ireland between belonging and not belonging, between feeling a part of the nation and oppressed by it, particularly through the workings of the state, is clear in this and other statements.[13]

A particularly explicit illustration of this tension came from one woman who recalled the pride she felt at the election of Mary Robinson (a prominent feminist, and pro-choice activist) as President in 1990, in contrast to the shame that she felt in 1992, in response to the X case:

> When Mary Robinson was elected as President of Ireland I almost burst with pride – pride in being a woman and, in particular, an Irish woman.
>
> When I learned of the judgement concerning the 14-year-old pregnant girl who has been forbidden to travel to the UK for an abortion, I feel fear, shame and revulsion – fear of being a woman in Ireland, shame of being part of a society which can pass such inhuman and intransigent laws, and revulsion towards those who simple-mindedly and smugly insist on telling us how we should live our lives. (*Irish Times*, Letters to the Editor, 20 February 1992)

This woman's pride in the election of a feminist to the position of President, the figurehead of the nation state who represents Ireland at home and abroad, was demolished by her shame at the nation state's actions against X, and her fear at the possibilities of further state actions against women. However, she also establishes a boundary between 'us' Irish, and 'those' pro-life activists and in so doing denies that the Irish are essentially 'pro-life'. She does not see the abortion law as a natural occurrence, based on the expression of 'the people's' will, but rather, as the result of those who insist on telling 'us' how 'we' should live.

Ruth Riddick, a prominent feminist activist throughout the abortion conflict, claimed that the collective will had changed in response to X. She argued that Ireland must

> right a terrible wrong. Dail deputies should know they will not lose their seats. The people are behind them now. It's a pity we've had to sacrifice a fourteen-year-old to find this out. (Culliton, 1992, p. 4)

This statement also works within populist discourse in order to effect change, using the idea of 'the people' in an attempt to avoid the divisiveness of the 1980s over abortion, by appealing to a collective conscience and collective responsibility. She emphasizes the need for 'the people' to face up to the failures of the past, by underlining the effects that popular opinions have when written into law. This discourse had significant practical consequences. Not only was the ban on X travelling for an abortion lifted on appeal by the Supreme Court, but, in November 1992, two further constitutional amendments were passed by popular referendum, on women's rights to freedom of movement and freedom of information.[14] Although abortion itself, or the 'substantive issue' as it was called at the time, was not legalized, there was at least a public acknowledgement that restrictions on abortion call women's citizenship into question.

These statements offer a more shifting and dynamic view of the nation. They do not depend on gender identities based on unequal power relations between men and women. Rather, they criticize the nation state for participating in the subordination of women, a situation which the election of Mary Robinson seemed to indicate was coming to an end. The intense alienation expressed by many women in 1992 was directly the result of the radical disjunction between having elected a pro-choice head of state and what was described in the press as 'the spectacle of Ireland as a female prison camp' (Hastings, 1992, p. 7).

# Conclusion

The debate on abortion placed feminist critique of women's position in the state more clearly in the public domain. The practical effects of this can be seen most recently in the result of the divorce referendum. Other changes have included the decriminalization of homosexuality, the establishment of a 'stay safe' programme in schools for detecting child sex abuse and protecting children, and the opening up of public debates on sexuality and the priesthood, which brought down a government in 1994.[15] However, as Ailbhe Smyth (1995, pp. 35–6) has argued, it is *women's* sexuality and reproduction that had provided the focus for the battle to maintain the *status quo*. It is difficult to argue with this in the light of the success of the 'pro-life' lobby in establishing a legal distinction between 'information' and 'referral' through the Abortion Information Act (1995), which has effectively restricted the type of support women can obtain when coping with crisis pregnancies.

The X case, then, became the focus for the ongoing battle over abortion rights in Ireland precisely because the issues involved in the case were central to the contemporary conflict over national identity. The media debate centred on the relationship between the nation, the state, the family and women. Feminists underlined the effects that pedagogies of Irishness have on women's sense of belonging to the nation, through focusing on the effects of discourses which maintain and reproduce gendered citizenship. What was at stake was women's position in the state, as defined by the relationship between sexual and national identities.

# Notes

1. Discourses which construct, reproduce and transform nations often do so through the construction of gender and sexuality, particularly by defining what sexual behaviour is appropriate (Anthias and Yuval-Davis, 1989).
2. Epstein notes the power of the media in influencing the educational agenda in schools (1993, pp. 27, 46). As David Trend has argued, 'young people are as much educated, albeit informally, through daily encounters with the media as they are in the formal environment of the school' (1993, p. 89).
3. Hereditary rights, family structure and marriage patterns changed. Women were increasingly dependent on husbands and fathers, becoming more clearly defined as a form of property, necessary for reproducing sons, and working on the farm. Maintaining the land intact depended on strict discipline of sexual activity.

4. See *Bunreacht na hEireann (Constitution of Ireland)*, 1937, Article 41.1.1 and Article 41.1.2 (quoted on pp. 198–9).

5. This visit, and other factors, including the legalization of abortion in the United States, the establishment of the Women's Right to Choose Group in the Republic and Ireland's accession to the EC in 1972, have been seen as key in explaining the emergence of PLAC, given that legalizing abortion had not been on the Irish mainstream political agenda during the 1970s (Gearty, 1992; Girvin, 1986).

6. Ailbhe Smyth (1996) contextualizes the abortion debate in Ireland in terms of the insecurity of a post-colonial national identity, particularly in relation to the uncertainties produced by Ireland's membership of the European Union, and its claim to be a modern democracy.

7. As one journalist put it: 'We must not be seduced by spurious blandishments that we become like the rest of Europe. We must have the pride and the courage to be ourselves and instead of us becoming like the rest of Europe, it is more than likely that within the lifetime of many persons now alive, Europe will want to become like us' (Des Rushe, *Irish Independent*, 21 February 1992, p.10, 'A pariah among nations? They've got it wrong').

8. This is illustrated by Sinead O'Connor's song 'Famine':

> There was no 'Famine' / See Irish people were only allowed to eat potatoes / All of the other food / meat fish vegetables / were shipped out of the country under armed guard / to England while the Irish people starved. (1994, from *Universal Mother*, Ensign)

9. Drucilla Cornell has argued against legalizing abortion only in cases of incest and rape as follows:

> there is for me an implicit moral message in these exceptions that I believe is reflective of fantasies about the sexuality of women who have abortions, whose abortions are not the result of exceptions. It is this message: women who suffer incest and rape did not choose to have sex, and therefore should not be punished with an unwanted pregnancy; those who chose to have sex should expect such a punishment. (1995, p. 81)

10. As Ronan O'Siochain, in a letter to the *Irish Times* on 22 February 1992, said: 'It is with some regret that I now understand more clearly the Northern unionist's refusal to be part of this State.'

11. '17th February 1992: introduction of internment in Ireland . . . for 14 year old girls . . . ' *Irish Times*, 19 February 1992.

12. Journalist Mary Holland wrote a damning article in the *Irish Times* entitled 'A woman's right to speak denied', focusing on the proceedings in the Dáil the

previous day, when women TDs who tried to speak on behalf of women in Ireland in the debate on the X case had been ruled out of order. Holland comments:

> There were nine women deputies in the chamber and row upon row of middle-aged men in suits. It had been agreed that four of these men, all party leaders, would speak for 10 minutes each on the case of a girl pregnant as a result of rape. Why not? It was a man who raped her, a man who put her into court, a man who handed down judgement on her future.

13. This can be seen for instance in the higher rates of emigration from Ireland for women than men, an untypical pattern among emigrant populations (Lennon *et al.*, 1988, p. 21).

14. Following the ratification of women's right to receive information on services legally available outside the state, in 1992, the 'pro-life' lobby regained ground when the Abortion Information Act was passed on 12 May 1995, having first been referred to the Supreme Court to test its constitutionality by President Mary Robinson. The Act incorporates a distinction between abortion information and abortion referral, the latter being illegal. This was a campaign strategy by the 'pro-life' lobby, and has effectively restricted the activities of abortion information providers, placing the obligation for arranging an abortion on the woman herself.

15. For details of the Fr Brendan Smyth extradition case, which led to the collapse of the government, see Ailbhe Smyth (1995).

## References

Anderson, Benedict (1983). *Imagined Communities: Reflections on the Origin and Spread of Nationalism*. London: Verso.

Anthias, Floya and Yuval-Davis, Nira (eds) (1989). *Woman-Nation-State*. London: Macmillan.

*Bunreacht na hEireann* (1937). Dublin: Government Publication Office.

Cornell, Drucilla (1995). *The Imaginary Domain: Abortion, Pornography and Sexual Harassment*. New York and London: Routledge.

Culliton, Gary (1992). '1,000 in protest at Dail', *Irish Press*, 20 February, p. 4.

Cummins, Mary (1992). 'Women's groups warn fewer will report rape', *Irish Times*, 18 February 1992, p. 7.

Epstein, Debbie (1993). *Changing Classroom Cultures: Anti-Racism, Politics and Schools*. Stoke-on-Trent: Trentham Books.

Dowling, Brian and O'Keefe, Alan (1992). 'Report rapes, teachers urge', *Irish Independent*, 20 February 1992, p. 13.

Dumaresq, Delia (1981). 'Rape – sexuality in the law', *m/f*, **5** and **6**: 41–60.

Farrell, Brian (ed.) (1988). *De Valera's Constitution and Ours*. Dublin: Gill and Macmillan.

Gearty, Conor (1992). 'The politics of abortion', *Journal of Law and Society*, **19**(4): 441–53.

Girvin, Brian (1986). 'Social change and moral politics: the Irish constitutional referendum 1983', *Political Studies*, **34**(1): 61–81.

Hastings, Tim (1992). 'Ireland "a prison camp for women" ', *Irish Independent*, 22 February 1992, p. 7.

Hesketh,Tom (1990). *The Second Partitioning of Ireland? The Abortion Referendum of 1983*. Dublin: Brandsma Books.

Hynes, Eugene (1978). 'The Great Hunger and Irish Catholicism', *Societas*, **8** (2): 132–56.

*Irish Independent* (17–22 February 1992). Daily newspaper, Dublin.

*Irish Press* (17–22 February 1992). Daily newspaper, Dublin.

*Irish Times* (17–22 February 1992). Daily newspaper, Dublin.

Keena, Colm (1992). 'SPUC slams "exploitation" ', *Irish Press*, 18 February 1992, p. 6.

Kenny, Mary (1992). 'Are we so brutal?', *Irish Independent*, 22 February 1992, p. 11.

Keogh, Dermot (1988). 'Church, state and society', in Brian Farrell (ed.), *De Valera's Constitution and Ours*. Dublin: Gill and Macmillan, pp. 103–22.

Keogh, Dermot (1994). *Twentieth-Century Ireland: Nation and State*. Dublin: Gill and Macmillan.

Larkin, Emmet (1976). 'The devotional revolution in Ireland, 1850–1875', in *Historical Dimensions of Irish Catholicism*. New York: Arno Press.

Lennon, Mary, McAdam, Marie and O'Brien, Joanne (1988). *Across the Water: Irish Women's Lives in Britain*. London: Virago.

Lovenduski, J. and Outshoorn, N. (1986). *The New Politics of Abortion*. London: Sage.

McNeil, Maureen, Fyfe, Wendy, Steinberg, Deborah Lynn, Franklin, Sarah and Randles, Tess (1991). 'In the wake of the Alton Bill: science, technology and reproductive politics', in Sarah Franklin, Celia Lury and Jackie Stacey (eds), *Off-Centre: Feminism and Cultural Studies*. London: HarperCollins Academic.

O'Reilly, Emily (1992). *Masterminds of the Right*. Dublin: Attic Press.

Pateman, Carole (1988). *The Sexual Contract*. Cambridge: Polity.

Petchesky, Rosalind Pollack (1986). *Abortion and Woman's Choice: The State, Sexuality and Reproductive Freedom*. London: Verso.

Randall, Vicky (1986). 'The politics of abortion in Ireland', in J. Lovenduski and N. Outshoorn (eds), *The New Politics of Abortion*. London: Sage.

Scannell, Yvonne (1988). 'The Constitution and the role of women', in Brian

Farrell (ed.), *De Valera's Constitution and Ours*. Dublin: Gill and Macmillan Ltd., on behalf of Radio Telifis Eireann.

Smyth, Ailbhe (ed.) (1992). *The Abortion Papers; Ireland*. Dublin: Attic Press.

Smyth, Ailbhe (1995). 'States of change: reflections on Ireland in several uncertain parts', *Feminist Review*, **50**: 24–43.

Smyth, Ailbhe (1996). ' "And Nobody Was Any the Wiser": Irish abortion rights and the European Union', in R. Amy Elman (ed.), *Sexual Politics and the European Union: The New Feminist Challenge*. Providence/Oxford: Berghahn Books.

Spring, Dick (1992). 'Frightening potential results of "new law" from Dick Spring's Dail Speech', *Irish Times*, 19 February 1992, p. 4.

Trend, David (1993). 'Nationalities, pedagogies and media', *Cultural Studies*, 7: 89–106.

Walter, Bronwen (1995). 'Irishness, gender and place', *Society and Space*, 35–50.

# 13

# Witches, Faggots, Dykes and Poofters: Moments of Danger[1] and the Realms of Subjectivity

## *Vicki Crowley*

To articulate the past historically does not mean to recognize it 'the way it really was' ... It means to seize hold of a memory as it flashes up at a time of danger ... the danger affects both the content of the tradition and its receivers. (Walter Benjamin)

You who understand the dehumanisation of forced removal-relocation-reeducation-redefinition, the humiliation of having to falsify your own reality, your voice – you know. And often cannot *say* it. You try to keep on trying to unsay it, for if you don't, they will not fail to fill in the blanks on your behalf, and you will be said. (Trinh T. Minh-ha)

knowledges are produced from and occupy particular positions that are not identical to that of their creator. (Elizabeth Grosz)

## Letters from a teacher: Letter 1

Dear D,

Let me tell you what it's like. I stand here and I want to shout back at you. Get your hands off. Step back. Take your hands off my mind. Take your mind off my body.

Why don't you let me tell you what it was like working there. You think she wanted it to be the way it was? You think I wanted it to be the way it was? You saw her arms – scarred. You saw her face – scarred. You saw her body, once bloated with alcohol, then emaciated with bulimia. Like you, I won't let them do that to me. I refuse to take that track and your name-calling sure as hell isn't going to make me.

Think about it. But of course you do. Of course you think about it. But thinking your anger onto me isn't that much removed from what has come before. We both come from histories that eradicate and efface, where ECT, incarceration and medication have been used to straighten our minds, control our ways. Our histories are not the same. But there are clues in there about what happens when we are deemed to be abnormal. There is some connection here, D, a connection across control and death. How do we now play that out? Why do you have to play that out so singularly onto me?

What was it? She disappointed you? Hmm? Is that it? What is it you think she did? What is it you think went between us, between JJ and me? Is the connection of lesbians so terrible? Is this disloyalty? Or is it so crudely that lesbians must always be lovers, can never be friends? Or is it that lecturers turn students into lesbians?

Did you know about the sexuality stuff – or was JJ straight to you? Was she straight to you? When she was 'bent', a lemon, queer, did you, did they love her and embrace her just the same as when they thought, unthinkingly, that she was straight? Tell me what is so puzzling and so abhorrent?

Yeah, I do know. They got at her 'cause she was black, female, young, body, child, the object of fetish, the at-hand object of white male desire. And they repeated centuries of the unspeakable. Stepfather, stepbrothers. And where was her stepmother? Where are we in all of this? And what is it when we women and girl children are traded across cultures and reduced to flesh for others?

So, I want to say to you, keep your hateful words off my body. They aren't new. They have long histories that we should not repeat.

I hear you cry.

It could have been you. In part it was you. But it also wasn't and isn't. So reshape those words across the worlds that she travelled – between you, history and me.

## Letters from a teacher: Letter 2

Dear K,

Ha! Say that again? Let me say it again. Let *me* say it back to *you*. I've introduced new things into my manuscript? New things like sexualities?

I hear your code.

You mean I'm talking as if I'm a lesbian. You mean in my writing I'm claiming that being a lesbian matters in this world, in conversations, in politics.

You said I've introduced new things like sexualities.

Is this an accusation?

Have I done something wrong?

What have I done wrong?

What are you saying to me?

I'll take the easy way out of this one.

'No', I say, 'no, it's been there for a long time.' In fact it's part of the first page of this manuscript. In fact it's everywhere.

I think you haven't read my work properly.

That's the easy way out of this one.

But, I now know that you don't *see me* either.

So thanks, K!


## Letters from a teacher: Letter 3

Dear N,

I sat at the desk looking at the students crowding then drifting by our enrolment table that says Gender Studies. I sit beside you, colleague. Side by side. We answer questions. No, we don't know where the philosophy people are. Yes, you'll find media studies in the room next door. We smile at each other. Colleague to colleague. You do your stuff and I do mine. And then she returns. Young woman. A young woman who retells her story of secondary school. She's interested in women in the Second World War. She told us that before. She talks to you, but includes me in her storytelling by looking at me. We also exchange smiles. And then she says, 'I wanna do gender studies but I wanna know whether, I don't wanna do, you know, what about those awful lesbians and radical feminists and women who hate men?' I look at you as I feel my face go stony and the air freeze and the world stands still in that split second. I caught your quick glance. 'Oh no', you laugh. 'We're nice', you say. I look away. The air unfreezes, the world moves on. My stony face relaxes as it changes in a split second between fire, anger, despair and the cloak of the invisible. I realize that I am invisible. I can sit here and through your reassurance of 'us', you, me and the others that teach in this course – 'we're nice'. We're not lesbians, we're not radical, we don't have a politics. I shuffle my papers and take out the invitation that I had just opened a moment earlier. I look again at the invitation to a book launch. *Lesbian Art*.[2] Rea's *Lemons # 1* graphic is on the cover. I privately thank Rea. I wish I were in Sydney. I open it up and there's two women kissing. I smile, deeply, warmly, in parts of me that you can't have. When Christina joins us I tell her about this. I open the brochure and plaster it against my chest. Like a convict number. This is me. Sister!

Lemon.

Lesbian.

## Writing contexts: letters from a teacher, Part 1

These are letters written with no intention of them ever being posted. They are letters of retort, of frustration and disturbance that spilled onto the keyboard in an explosive moment amid the need to 'unsay' (Trinh T. Minh-ha, 1987, p. 6). They speak to moments of vertigo as the imaginary works across identifications, longings and belongings. They are letters written across the politics of identity and difference in ways that both perform and transgress the unified self and unified categories. They are also letters that bring to collision issues of subjectivity experienced across antagonisms of history and identity to suggest the salience of context and contingency. They are letters from a teacher confronting her teaching self through moments that display subjectivity as it is rarely, if ever, revealed in pedagogies and curriculum especially as it is designed for schooling. They are letters about me. Still more, they are letters precariously positioned at the interstices of academic, watchful observer, researcher, commentator and spillage of the self across interior worlds 'incessantly reconstituted' (Judith Butler, 1993, p. 105) through dilemmas and confrontations of the I/we in social justice teaching or 'Affirming Diversity', as it is currently named in South Australia.[3] They speak to issues deeply in need of attention that is mindful of the histories that constitute Other and constitute teaching and schooling.

These letters did not simply emerge in a private moment of fury or despair, nor did they emerge simply out of the singular moments they might be read to represent. They are letters crafted out of a remembered past, of incidents seemingly forgotten – but moments that, for some reason, leapt to some kind of presence. They are letters crafted for an international education conference and read in contradistinction to an abstract I had scrambled together for a plenary on sexualities and education. The abstract I had put together was the story part of an anti-racism research project I had been engaged in. The paper had been titled 'Witches, Faggots, Dykes and Poofters: Assumptions of Whiteness and the Proliferation of Homophobia Through Single Factor Analysis'. It was a title that played on off-Broadway shows, the names we are called, the names we call ourselves and a discontent with the ways in which 'social issues' such as sexism, racism and now lesbian and gay oppression ('homophobia') are thought and implemented in schooling, in language policies and through teaching. This is especially so where queer identities are represented as separate and discrete issues or conversely as a universalism of implied or taken-for-granted connections across differentiated oppressions. The title borrows from the familiar and abject to suggest that theories travel, that we appropriate moments and language, performance and creativity that speak to us, perhaps not as in the intentionality of their original performance but because they connect with some part of what and who we are. I used 'Single Factor Analysis' to shadow debates about positivism, empiricism, quantitative and abstract educational research. The abstract claimed a space of concern about the ways in which sexualities – gay, lesbian, bisexual and at times even transgender identities – might appear in the school curriculum or university courses. It also flagged the need to talk about the ways in which assumptions of heterosexuality and the equation of homosexuality with whiteness continue, in Australia, to be unproblematic regimes that provide fertile ground for homophobia and lesbian hatred. It was an abstract that canvassed vast areas of incongruity, disjuncture and conjuncture across the public/private and objectivity/subjectivity bifurcations inside notions of curriculum reform.

The initial abstract was written in critique of the shape that school curriculum is currently taking in South Australia – interventions around gay and lesbian issues and homophobia are being framed in isolation from the oppressions of race, class and gender as they have been, in turn, framed as separate or as additive models in school curricula. Certainly the struggles over racism, sexism and class have assumed heterosexuality are heteronormative and almost always ignore gay and lesbian actualities and oppression. It often also seems, however, that gay and lesbian struggle assumes a universalism about whiteness or a sense of radical import that assumes (as it subsumes) the presence of difference and becomes 'one community many diversities' (as it is now being framed by the AIDS Council of South Australia; see *Adelaide GT*, 1 March 1996, p. 13).

The abstract had been safe. It could tell a close story in distant terms.

It also ignored the moments of danger, the collisions that occur in seemingly shared politics, just as it ignored a rage against incongruities that is also a frisson that fuels, and very often sharpens the edges of my political desire. It completely erased those moments of smothered confusion as one is confronted by the paucity of a politics thought to be shared, thought to be connected. I had been about to embark on a practice of distancing that would reinscribe a style of politics which Otherized and effaced the deeply conflicted complexities of the kind of life I, and perhaps other educators and teachers, lead. The erasures and effacement include worlds in which sexuality is an uneven politics, at times foregrounded, at times seemingly inconsequential, at times held closely as the interior-private, for some as the invisible in moments of passing, at other times performed in unmistakable ways for ourselves and others as it is both opposed and linked to 'the continuous "play" of history, culture, power' (Stuart Hall, 1992, p. 31).

The letters, however, suggested 'lived actualities' (Lawrence Grossberg, 1992) in which identity and subjectivity could not be seamlessly deduced from an externalized social experience as if 'experience' is not simultaneously and unevenly related and opposed to the social and cultural context (Joan Scott, 1992). The writing of the letters brought the contradiction home, and, while I would no longer have to squeeze some research moments into empirical frameworks, it meant that I would now have to 'come clean' and think through the terms, threads and moments of my critique, immersed as it is in the letters, in emotion, bafflement and the vertigo of disequilibrium. Such moments rarely make it into the tidy scripts of teaching.

## Interior spillages: letters from a teacher, Part 2

The letters course their way through a life lived not just as a white woman, or a white lesbian. I am these things, white woman, white lesbian, and in the letters I write out of the female body that is never my own to know unfettered by the words in my/our past and present mouths. It is a white body that is strangely and not so strangely named lesbian – so named through others, through me, by me. It is a white body that is in conversation across whiteness as colour-no colour, across race and ethnicity, across gender and across class – across the politics of identity, the politics of my times. Although perhaps not so readily glimpsed, in these letters, it is a white body in conversation through the history of all these things – things haunting, things forgotten, things remembered. The letters punctuate my consciousness, reflect elements of my actualities, 'seize hold of a memory as it flashes up at a time of danger' (Walter Benjamin, 1993, p. 247).[4] The danger in the letters is the twinned danger of erasure and exposure. To respond immediately is to be exposed. To be exposed in a moment of erasure is to risk histories, histories that all lesbians and gays 'know' as replete with danger. Lesbian and gay teachers, especially in schools, know very well the territory and terrors of oppression. The letters are not, however, just witness to danger as terror and fear. They are also witness to the danger and terror that lie in the traditions of reception, the content of those traditions and the scope of political frameworks.

Dear D is a letter in imaginary conversation. I had overheard what I was not meant to hear. It is a conversation I wish I had had with a friend and colleague from a university department I worked in many years ago. We shared much, but not enough. It was a department of historical significance as it was the first-ever department, in a first-ever faculty of Indigenous politics, culture and education. As with many areas of Black Studies or multiculturalism, it was fraught. Battles were fought across 'traditionalism', across essentialism and what might be termed 'roots' and 'routes', hybridity and diaspora (Gilroy, 1986, 1993). The 'problem' was an Aboriginal lesbian student. The 'problem' was that lesbianism was meant to be white, not black. There had always been discussion about 'the problem of a white lesbian lecturer' and the 'acceptability of her lesbianism to the Aboriginal community'. The connection of sexuality across an ambiguously shared space of marginality does not just interrupt the tidy scripts of essentialism – it disrupts and disturbs. Sometimes it severs.

Dear D is a letter in conversation with vexed and difficult issues. It is in part a mentioning that the tidy parameters of 'community' that provide coherence and a sense of political purpose to courses such as Indigenous Studies, become awkward and even untenable. In particular, it speaks to the spectre of the black-lesbian body, imagined as embracing, embraced, passionate with the white-lesbian body, whose history, as Barbara Creed (1995) reminds us, is that of the sodomite, the melting flesh of the witch pyre, the vampire, tomboy and tribade. What happens to an Aboriginal woman, an Aboriginal student when she publicly announces her connection? Is she still loved and embraced by the texts of Indigenous Studies and the teaching staff? How will lesbian and gay studies in the university and school curriculum say these issues? How will a project aimed at combating anti-gay and anti-lesbian beliefs and practices say these complexities? How will the white lesbian teacher connect with non-white lesbian students in ways that are simply ordinary? The notion of 'the Aboriginal lesbian' and 'the Aboriginal poofter' as Indigenous in Australia confounds the popular imaginary and plagues elements of public politics. That they might stand at times connected in a marginal space that is neither singularly black, nor singularly white, fuelled a greater animosity towards lesbians and gays in the context in which I worked. Most importantly the animosity erased the possibility for deeper knowing of histories of collision. It precluded the possibility of a more nuanced politics of identity and more open politics of struggle.[5]

Dear K is a letter in remembered conversation with a friend – a male friend who reads my work, who shares much of my politics. (I think I would only hold these imaginary conversations, write these letters to people whose lives and politics I want to share.) My friend teaches me to listen carefully about diasporas and migrancy. He is scholarly, knows philosophy, sings about racism, is an artist. He is very many things. We have conversations and debates about the problem of equivalence in oppression. We discuss at length the inescapability of the always-already raced, classed and gendered body. In the fissures of our conversation, however, are slippages that assume a transference of understanding from the raced body to the queer/lesbian body (and, no doubt, vice versa). These slippages and fissures speak, again, to the important question of how we 'do' lesbian and gay studies in the school curriculum and in university courses outside gender and other identity studies. How do we avoid the transference of frameworks from anti-sexism, from anti-racism to anti-homophobia and lesbian hatred? How do we avoid the notion of a transference of understanding about oppression because we occupy differently marginal positions? What has happened in our theorizing that suggests that differentially marginal position enables a necessary politics of intervention in Other sites?[6]

My third letter, to N, is to a former colleague. My colleague is white like me. Married. Has three kids. I was married too. But I do not have kids and I have not been married for a very long time. We briefly taught together in gender studies. Her area of expertise is schooling and gender. This reminds me of the limitations of schooling discourses and teacherly interventions. This reiterates in still other ways the questions of equivalence, and I think about the important contestation over the universalism of much second-wave feminism, especially as it has constructed itself as 'race' neutral. As early feminist interventions by bell hooks (1984) and Audre Lorde (1984) argued, and as many others since have argued, there is no universal woman. Yet the problem of universalism and equivalence of oppressions has not gone away. Does the shift from women's studies to gender studies as a broader field of study necessarily mean that the complexities are seriously core to that study? Are we to reinvent the same problems in lesbian and gay studies in schools? Is inclusive language (i.e. non-heterosexist language) in the school curriculum what issues of lesbian, gay and transgender subjectivities will be reduced to?

There is much more at stake and much more going on in the letters than I mention here. In the instance of the writing of these letters and my thinking across a conference paper about schooling and sexualities, questions spilled out about the shape of 'new curricula' in schooling in South Australia. Each letter, however, involves educators and students recognized in the imaginary as embodied subjects making meaning. Each letter is embedded in contexts of practising a politics of political freedom inside a politics that takes subjectivity, materiality and oppression seriously. Each of us inscribed in these letters attempted to position and frame our politics as one of possibility. Yet each of us reinscribes. The invisibility and marginalization of lesbians and gays are serious issues. They are issues that span the safety of passing (for those to whom it might be an available and effective strategy). They span the personal and political need to be 'out'. They span the vexed, and often dangerous, context that is schooling and education. The confrontation in the letters is that of teacher confronting her teaching self, is confrontation with assumptions about political frameworks, about contexts and contingencies, about political desire. How are these to be played out, to be content and context of teaching, as teacher, as academic, observer, researcher, commentator?

## From anti-racism to sexualities: letters from a teacher, Part 3

The letters have one more angle that is so far unsighted. They are letters not just written in retort, frustration and disturbance over the context and content of each letter. They are letters written in a fit of pique as I struggled to write the part of the research project where I had to face up to the multiple ways in which we researchers, as political activists and theorists, collude in oppression and write our own erasures. This too was a moment of danger. The research project was about the theoretical and conceptual practices of anti-racism in South Australian schools. The Education Department of South Australia had developed an *Antiracism Policy* (1990) in recognition of gender and class issues as well as the centrality of racism as it related to Indigenous peoples and issues of ethnicity. It was a policy ostensibly configured across the notion of complex identities. The research involved anti-racist activists, and in the course of the project I had become increasingly curious about the discreteness in which educators and activists thought and performed policy in contradistinction to the lives they storied in enormous complexity and richness. I had more than a passing interest in how 'sexualities' might figure in this. I waited for storying that suggested that lesbian, gay and bisexual sexualities figured in anti-racism and that identity was to be named as more than the singular categories of girls and boys, migrant, ethnic, Indigenous, white, women and men (or the mix of two). There was no mention. In desperation and out of curiosity, I asked an educator where she thought issues of lesbian, gay and bisexual sexualities figured in issues of anti-racism. My question was responded to in terms of 'paedophilia being a real problem in education'.

There are many explanations as to why paedophilia might have sprung to mind. Indeed explanations rushed by me – Adelaide is a city whose only daily newspaper has a long interest and preoccupation with paedophiles and paedophilia in the form of public outrage, whispering menace and public titillation; education departments have histories of simply moving child sexual offenders from school to school; strictures exist about talking about gay and lesbian issues in education; and a teacher union whose sympathies and support for gay and lesbian teachers have waned; why would anti-racism be understood as in any way relationally connected to sexualities, still more to homophobia? The list can go on, and as it does, popular conflagration of meaning and issues become reiterated and exponentially more confused. But the immediacy of the connection and the form of connection between issues of sexualities and paedophilia froze my insides while the vertigo of confusion and bafflement swirled. In such moments, no category or label is sufficient to claim a speaking position. At this moment anti-racism became a minefield replete with even more layers in the problems of deficit politics, schooling discourses, contexts and contingencies. Might anti-racism in schooling in South Australia not be a question of inequality but one of 'protective behaviours'? Is anti-racism presupposed and contingent upon heterosexuality in absolute terms? Still more is anti-racism, not dissimilarly to racism, a conduit for homophobia, lesbian hate, erasure and invisibility?

The response to the question about the place of lesbian, gay and bisexual sexualities in anti-racism in terms of the equivalence and immediacy of paedophilia suggests a series of oppressively determined chains of association. It is also, in Trinh T. Minh-ha's terms, a filling in of the blanks (1987, p. 6). It signals the taken-for-grantedness of racism and anti-racism viewed and thought through the normalizing gaze of heterosexuality and its myths of stability and purity. Obscured in the absoluteness of heterosexuality and its chains of association is the actuality, as Mairtin Mac an Ghaill points, that 'both gay and straight people experience their class, gender and "race"/ethnicity through sexuality' (1994, p. 165). The taken-for-grantedness of heterosexuality in the discourses of racism and anti-racism is a practice of pressing out the ruptures and discontinuities that constitute complex identities.

What became crystallized in this research moment, and as I struggled to write the valleys of its meanings and possibilities, were the depths of the problem of single-issue policies and curriculum in schooling. In this instance experience in equal opportunity, anti-racism and anti-sexism failed to provide any resources for analysing Other forms of differentiated oppression. The frameworks, attachments and associations of one form of resistance were able to reinscribe another. Indeed, the singularity of focus remained unabated and anti-racism became a policy through which homophobia and lesbian hatred could reign untrammelled.

## Bitch, witch, lemon, dyke, faghag, whore; poofter, queer, fairy, queen, and more: letters from a teacher, Part 4

All of these are names I have from time to time heard, and from time to time been called. They are also words and names of playfulness that I have used about my friends and myself. D never quite went so far as to call me names to my face. She had once told me, though, that she and her friends called each other 'lemon-slut' as a joke. Her joke was a reminder of the connections she makes in her head and also of the familiarity and ease with which lesbian hatred and homophobia slip from the tongue, across many sites, to create unity through Otherness. They are words and names, however, that schools and curriculum can readily recognize and happily deal with as if they had only simple and singular meanings, simple and singular histories; words understood and abstracted from expression and reception, uttered only in ways that are irretrievable.

The letters fall across names, naming and words of identity, identification and subjectivity. The letters in this chapter are real-life scenarios presented as theatre, a cultural performance in which sexualities, gender, class and race spill into each other as they are laden with codified meanings and meaning-making. They are presented to suggest the impossibility of an embodied politics that is, somehow, not always-already more complexly and contradictorily configured than is named and positioned through a single category such as lesbian, gay, bisexual, transgender or heterosexual. The polite term of sexualities cannot suggest the difficult fissures that fracture the lives of queer identities and subjectivities.

The axes of the enunciative subject framed in the letters and my readings of them, are a series of interconnected elements that are neither of my own making, nor moments of explicit attention to the 'real' contexts of their occurrence in actual or imaginary time. They are, however, central to identity formations, and they are the kinds of moments that witness the limits and limitations of identities and subjectivity as they are framed and elided in the practices of naming identity. They are frameworks and milieux, emphases and interests in which the 'interloper' (James Baldwin in Henry Louis Gates Jr, 1992, p. 110) is both 'said' and must 'unsay' (Trinh T. Minh-ha, 1987, p. 6).

The always-already raced, classed and gendered enunciative subject is a recombinant moment that brings the abstraction and segmentation of identity, identification and subjectivity into collision. The collision is not that of separabilities piled onto, beside or across each other. It is a collision between inseparabilities and fixity. As one element seems to take centre stage it shifts, transforms and transmutes. As one element seems to take centre stage others, rather than appear, refuse to disappear. Yet the enunciative body seen only as a subjectivity wrought on singular categories uninflected, for instance, by issues of age or intersubjectivity, is a disavowal of hybridity and bespeaks subjectivity and identity in ways that elide the milieu of iterability, the practices of discourses, the articulations of subjectivity, context and interior worlds.

The subject in this chapter, however, speaks and is bespoken. The subject speaks through the limits and limitations of available discourses and explanatory practices. The subject is bespoken through the interpretative practices of analysis, framed through the limits and limitations of available discourses and explanatory practices. As Elizabeth Grosz so significantly reminds us, 'all knowledges are produced from and occupy particular positions that are not identical to that of their creator' (1993, p. 191). The speaking and bespoken subject cannot be reduced to the enunciative acts as a crystallized moment of singularity.

The letters burst across the collision of the abstracted researcher, cultural critic and theoretician confounded by pedagogic practices that invoke the centrality of identity, subjectivity and experience as if identities are constructed outside and not within discourses. As Stuart Hall has recently written, 'we need to understand them [identities] as produced in specific historical and institutional sites within specific discursive formations and practices, by specific enunciative strategies' (1996, p. 4).

The letters, like Annette Kuhn's memory work are intended to 'demonstrate that political action need not be undertaken at the cost of the inner world, nor that attention to matters of the psyche necessarily entails a retreat from the world of collective action' (1995, p. 8). The letters are also to display the interior workings of sexuality as it might be worked in everyday contexts of teaching and a teacher's life. It is in the ordinariness of the work contexts and contingencies that sexualities, queer, lesbian and gay identities are routinely erased and remade. Working the erasures, markings and the remakings that are practised onto me and that I am complicit in are by no means resolved in this chapter. They are, however, now 'out there' for me to think about in ways in which the frisson of danger can be usefully present.

## Notes

1. This is a term borrowed, indeed expropriated, from Vron Ware's use of the Walter Benjamin quotation (see epigraph). Like Ware I am riveted by its 'vivid imagery' and the sense of 'urgency' that Ware also names as and in her project (1992, p. 116). My expropriation, however, plies the meanings of history as the irrevocably present. This is especially so as I claim but do not provide any historical trace. In the context of this chapter it is drawing an especially long bow as I write as neither historian nor literary critic.

2. See Elizabeth Ashburn (1996). *Lesbian Art: An Encounter with Power.* Roseville East, NSW: Craftsman House.

3. The Department of Education and Children's Services is currently developing a health and sexualities curriculum to address HIV/AIDS and homophobia. This includes a two-day workshop 'Training and Development in HIV/AIDS Education in Health and Physical Education, Early Childhood – Year 10; a health partnership', co-facilitated by a non-school agency. This is a particularly disturbing project because it collapses 'homophobia' into 'Health' and specifically HIV/AIDS in ways that reinscribe populist affiliations of disease and spectre as well as erasing issues that affect lesbians. Still further it is an outsourcing that ignores teachers' expertise in curriculum and is modelled on deficit models of the 1970s used to explain the underachievement of working-class children. This is a model that has travelled into the curriculum logics of

girls and schooling, multiculturalism and anti-racism. It is now being imported into issues to do with the inequalities experienced by gay, lesbian, bisexual, transsexual and transgender students, staff, parents and teachers. There has been little thought given to the context of schooling, viz. the context of 'family planning'. The latter may well be a place in which it is 'safe' to be 'out', but assumptions about safety in schools ignore their complex constituencies, their position in government structures, their histories of social and cultural reproduction and their histories of 'childhood', 'children', 'nurture' and 'shelter'. More specifically they ignore the actualities of this very moment in Australia where, for instance, the State of Tasmania has only just passed legislation to remove the criminality of homosexuality; a New South Wales inquiry into police corruption and paedophilia has led to the suspension of some 30 teachers in NSW on very questionable social justice and equity terms; and the rise of racism and homophobia where the leader of the One Nation Party believes that an Australian Republic will be presided over by an Asian, lesbian cyborg. While South Australia has not gone so far as Victoria in removing existing EO protection for teachers, the climate is such that gay and lesbian teachers are extremely vulnerable just as are gay and lesbian pupils, students, parents and care givers. Schooling does need a 'zero tolerance' policy on homophobia, just as it does on racism and other oppressive practices and structures. What it does not need is a curriculum strategy that gestures towards inclusivity in ways that further marginalize and mark difference as always and irrevocably Other.

4.  The flashes of memory I invoke are not those that a historian might take as a focus. Clearly they are flashes of recent memory, but their flash occurs in memory of histories not recorded, not known yet knowable through the presence of absence – perhaps that structure of feeling that swells in identity and identification as one brings into naming that which has been absented.

5.  Eva Johnson's play *What Do They Call Me?*, performed during the Adelaide Fringe Festival of 1988, was the first significant intervention into the politics of Aboriginality, feminism and Aboriginal lesbian identity (Eva Johnson, 1990). It is a play that among other aspects of identity speaks to the actualities that 'Being an Aboriginal lesbian can be one of the most traumatic and horrendous admissions for a woman in this country, an admission that requires affirmation in making this public cultural announcement' (Johnson in Crowley, 1993, p. 14). I use this quotation to reiterate the political contexts in which being an Aboriginal lesbian in a Department of Aboriginal Studies was, in the early 1990s, to be in the front line of pushing the boundaries of identity politics.

6.  Deborah Britzman's chapter, 'Difference in a Minor Key: Some Modulations of History, Memory, and Community' (1997), is an important intervention in the questions that underscore this issue.

# References

*Adelaïde GT*, **83**, 1 March 1996.

Ashburn, Elizabeth (1996). *Lesbian Art: An Encounter with Power*. Roseville East, NSW: Craftsman House.

Benjamin, Walter (1993). 'Theses on the philosophy of history', in *Illuminations*. Hammersmith, London: Fontana Press, pp. 245–55.

Britzman, Deborah, P. (1997). 'Difference in a minor key: some modulations of history, memory, and community', in Michelle Fine, Lois Weiss, Linda C. Powell and L. Mun Wong, *Off White*. New York and London: Routledge, pp. 29–39.

Butler, Judith (1993). *Bodies That Matter*. New York and London: Routledge.

Creed, Barbara (1995). 'Lesbian bodies: tribades, tomboys and tarts', in Elizabeth Grosz and Elspeth Probyn (eds), *Sexy Bodies*. London and New York: Routledge, pp. 86–103.

Crowley, Vicki (1993).'Aboriginality and feminism: an interview with Eva Johnson', *Social Alternatives*, **12**(1): 13–16.

Education Department of South Australia (1990). *Antiracism Policy*. Adelaide: South Australian Government Printer.

Gates, Henry Louis, Jr (1992). *Loose Canons*. New York: Oxford University Press.

Gilroy, Paul (1986). 'Steppin' out of Babylon – race, class and autonomy', in Centre for Contemporary Cultural Studies, *The Empire Strikes Back*. London: Hutchinson, pp. 276–314.

Gilroy, Paul (1993). *The Black Atlantic*. Cambridge, MA: Harvard University Press.

Grossberg, Lawrence (1992). *We Gotta Get Out of This Place*. New York and London: Routledge.

Grosz, Elizabeth (1993). 'Bodies and knowledges: feminism and the crisis of reason', in Linda Alcoff and Elizabeth Potter (eds), *Feminist Epistemologies*. New York and London: Routledge, pp. 187–215.

Hall, Stuart (1992). 'Identity', *Ten 8*, **2**(3): 24–31.

Hall, Stuart (1996). 'Introduction. Who needs identity?', in Stuart Hall and Paul du Gay (eds), *Questions of Cultural Identity*. London: Sage, pp. 1–17.

hooks, bell (1984). *Feminist Theory: From Margin to Centre*. Boston: South End Press.

Johnson, Eva (1990). 'What do they call me?', in Dale Spender (ed.), *Heroines*. Richmond: Penguin, pp. 237–56.

Kuhn, Annette (1995). *Family Secrets: Acts of Memory and Imagination*. London and New York: Verso.

Lorde, Audre (1984). *Sister Outsider*. Trumansburg: The Crossing Press.

Mac an Ghaill, Mairtin (1994). *The Making of Men*. Buckingham and Philadelphia: Open University Press.

Scott, Joan W. (1992). 'Experience', in Judith Butler and Joan W. Scott (eds), *Feminists Theorize the Political*. New York and London: Routledge, pp. 22–40.

Trinh T. Minh-ha (1987). 'Difference: a special Third World women's issue', *Feminist Review*, **25**, Spring: 5–22.

Ware, Vron (1992). 'Moments of danger: race, gender, and memories of empire', *History and Theory*, **31**: 116–37.

# Part Four

## Interventions in Sexualities

# 14

# The 'Homosexual Agenda' Goes to School

## *Mariamne H. Whatley*

**A**S A PROFESSOR at the University of Wisconsin-Madison, I sometimes think that Madison, Wisconsin, is as good as it gets in the United States for gay and lesbian educators, students and those who support them. After all, Wisconsin, which has a proud progressive tradition, was the first state to prohibit discrimination on the basis of sexual orientation. Around the same time, the legislature repealed the antiquated sex laws (about which a local minister is reported to have said that anyone who has not violated them is probably not very imaginative), the same kind of laws that still make 'sodomy' a crime in such states as Georgia. An elementary school in Madison was one of the schools featured in the film *It's Element-ary*,[1] demonstrating that it is possible to discuss gay and lesbian issues with children in a positive and non-threatening way. The same school hosted *Love Makes a Family*,[2] a photographic exhibit of a variety of gay and lesbian families. The 1997 negotiations over the Madison teachers' contract resulted in extending health-care coverage to domestic partners (a non-issue in most of the rest of the industrialized world where there is universal health-care coverage).

It may be as good as it gets, but it still is not easy. State employees who are not married, including those who work in the state's university system, cannot get health insurance benefits for their domestic partners. This cannot happen until changes have been made at the level of the state legislature and state insurance board. (This is not seen as violation of state law because it applies to all unmarried couples, whatever their sexual orientation.) When the Madison school board voted for domestic partners' health-care coverage, with only one negative vote, a state legislator proposed legislation to prevent any state funds from being used for this purpose because it is 'destroying the institutions of marriage and the family' (Lueders, 1997, p. 8). There was a nasty controversy about the exhibit of *Love Makes a Family*, though it was still shown. At the Madison première of *It's Elementary*, at which students, parents and teachers who were in the film spoke to a packed house, film-goers had to push past the anti-gay signs of a religious group's picket line. A free speech/hate speech controversy has centred on a city employee who allegedly distributed anti-gay literature at work.

Madison, Wisconsin, is not representative of the USA in general, because it is more liberal and progressive than many other places. However, the same kinds of battles are being fought everywhere. While 'multicultural education' is still seen by conservative groups as part of the menace of 'political correctness', most will still agree that it is important to study the histories, cultures and literatures of groups other than European Americans. However, this often grudging acceptance of literature by certain African Americans or the study of American Indian history does not necessarily extend to culture, history or literature of gays and lesbians, except perhaps when it cannot be avoided. That is, it is fine to teach a novel or poetry by a writer who is gay or lesbian as long as their sexual orientation is not featured in the discussion. The chapter in this volume by Maria Pallotta-Chiarolli explores this issue of where sexuality fits into multi-cultural education in an Australian context, in which the definitions of multicultural may differ from those in the USA, but in which the key issues are similar. As she points out, a flaw of some multicultural education is a lack of attention to the complexities of identity, so that gays and lesbians are denied any ethnic or racial identity, and people of colour are assumed to be heterosexual.

## Sexuality education debates

In Wisconsin, as in most of the USA, one of the most active and contested areas of education is that of school sexuality education. A colleague and I have written critiques of sexuality education curricula (Trudell and Whatley, 1991; Whatley and Trudell, 1993) and have found that, of all our work, this has probably been the most controversial, but also the most useful. Our work has had a role not only in school board decisions but also in legal decisions, as the debates about curricula have been taken to the courts. Fear-based abstinence-only sexuality education, which presents abstinence as the only appropriate behaviour outside marriage and uses fear of disease, the consequences of unplanned pregnancies and potential sexual violence as the motivating force, is being strongly promoted by a number of groups who argue against more comprehensive programmes. It is important to point out that most sexuality education in the USA emphasizes abstinence, but many of these programmes also include education about contraception and the prevention of transmission of STDs. Abstinence-only proponents object to such inclusion because, they argue, it encourages teenagers to be sexually active. This argument is not backed by research; according to peer-reviewed published research, not only do the comprehensive programmes not increase sexual activity, some have been shown to delay sexual activity (or onset of intercourse, as it is sometimes referred to; most evaluation of the success of sexuality education is very heterosexual in its focus, so that sexual activity is used to mean vaginal-penile intercourse) and to increase use of condoms and/or other forms of contraception when sexual intercourse does occur. International comparative research also supports the success of comprehensive, progressive sexuality education. For example, Epstein and Johnson (1998) cite work by Ingham which found that sexuality education in the Netherlands, compared to the UK, is more liberal, covers 'sensitive' issues often excluded in the UK or USA and begins at an earlier age. Not surprisingly, there is a much lower rate of teenage pregnancy in the Netherlands, as well as indicators that the sexual experiences of teenagers are more positive. On the other hand, no peer-reviewed published research has shown that fear-based abstinence-only programmes reduce or delay sexual activity among teenagers (Burlingame, 1997; Haffner, 1997). Plante's chapter on peer education in this volume makes it clear that even on the college level there are limitations on the kinds of sexuality education that can be done through official channels and that philosophical resistance cannot always translate into action.

Even though the debates about which kinds of sexuality education should be taught in the schools has centred around heterosexual activity, with pregnancy prevention as a major goal, one of the common strategies used to attack comprehensive sexuality education is to highlight issues related to sexual orientation. For example, a staff member at SIECUS (Sexuality Information and Education Council of the United States) reported that nearly 20 per cent of the controversies they had documented during the previous school year concerned policies about sexual orientation (Mayer, 1997). The report continues:

There were fewer controversies regarding actual curriculum content because education about sexual orientation is so rare. In Elizabethtown, PA, a heated community debate concerned a 'pro-family resolution' adopted last fall by the School Board. It stated that the 'traditional family is under relentless attack by those who want to redefine the family to include homosexual and lesbian couples and by those who want to indoctrinate children in prohomosexual propaganda against their parents' wishes.' The School Board modified the policy after objections of hundreds of community members. (Mayer, 1997, p. 25)

The good news, of course, is that there were objections by large numbers of members of the community. However, part of the bad news is that these 'pro-family' attacks on any attempts to discuss gay and lesbian issues in a positive way are very common. Another part of the bad news is the fact that there is not much in the curriculum about sexual orientation for these groups to attack. The fear of such attacks, which could demolish a sexuality education programme, can lead to self-censorship. Proponents of comprehensive sexuality education, in trying to establish or maintain their programmes in the schools, may eliminate the most controversial aspects of their programmes – discussions of gay and lesbian issues, and a balanced view of abortion.

## Government intervention in the debates

While educators are producing critiques of abstinence-only education and research is consistently showing this approach to be ineffective, the US Congress has undermined researchers and sexuality educators by earmarking $88 million in federal and matching state funds to be used toward abstinence-only education. The money was set aside by 'inserting language into welfare reform during a process reserved for corrections and technical revisions' (Edwards, 1997, p. 2), thereby precluding debate and discussion. The programmes which qualify for these funds must meet certain criteria, with a definition of an appropriate programme as one which, among other things:

- teaches that abstinence from sexual activity is the only certain way to avoid out-of-wedlock pregnancy, sexually transmitted diseases, and other associated health problems;
- teaches that a mutually faithful monogamous relationship in the context of marriage is the expected standard of human sexual activity;
- teaches that sexual activity outside of the context of marriage is likely to

have harmful psychological and physical effects. (SIECUS, 1997, p. 3)

While there is not a direct statement that prohibits positive discussions about gay and lesbian issues, the prohibition is implicit in the emphasis on marriage. Same-sex couples cannot get married in the USA (except probably in Hawaii); therefore, they cannot ever attain 'the expected standard of human sexual activity'. If gay and lesbian students were in a class that followed these guidelines, they would be taught that their sexual activity, because it is outside the context of marriage, 'is likely to have harmful psychological and physical effects'.

Federal funds are being used to support a broad national programme of sexuality education that should meet the requirements of the most conservative groups – abstinence-only, heterosexist/homophobic and marriage-centred. While a number of groups who work on such issues as teenage pregnancy prevention are holding to their principles about the need for comprehensive sexuality education and the importance of being inclusive of all students, many others, driven by economic necessity, are planning to apply for the funding. One approach is to develop programmes for young elementary age students who are probably not yet sexually active, so that many of the thorny issues can be bypassed simply by completely avoiding discussions related to sexual activity. While there are constant exposés of wasteful government spending, particularly in the military, it is still somewhat of a surprise even to the cynical among us to see $88 million devoted to a kind of educational programme that has never been shown to work.

While this funding does not prevent unfunded sexuality education programmes from being more comprehensive and inclusive of gay and lesbian issues, it can undermine the creation and support for these pro-grammes. Why, a school board might ask, should we have a programme that does not meet national standards for funding? There are still many states that do not require school sexuality education and those that do have a wide range of what is required or prohibited. For example, some states do not allow discussion of contraception or abortion or homosexuality. While there is no national policy in the USA that affects teaching gay and lesbian issues in the schools, it is, unfortunately, not hard to imagine that some conservative groups would like to move toward an equivalent of Great Britain's Section 28 of the Local Government Act 1987–88 which pro-hibits 'the promotion of homosexuality by Local Authorities by teaching or publishing material'. Under Section 28 local authorities cannot 'promote the teaching in any maintained school of the acceptability of homosexuality as a pretended family relationship' (Smith, 1994, p. 183).

## Fear of 'non-traditional' families

When legislators from any country consider such legislation, it is unlikely that they are thinking about how it might affect the lives either of gay/lesbian/bisexual youth or the children of gay or lesbians parents. Section 28 and similar policies help create the climate in which homophobia can flourish in the schools. The chapter in this section by Kathleen Quinlivan and Shane Town examines the experiences of gay and lesbian youth in New Zealand. Their interviews elucidate some of the failures of sexuality education, particularly in terms of the emphasis on anatomy/science, the heterosexual and reproductive assumptions and the mention of gay sexuality only in the context of AIDS. It is worth imagining how these stories might be different if the students had attended a school in which gay and lesbian issues were integrated into the curriculum as a normal part of human sexuality. Would their lives have been so dominated by the need for invisibility or disguise?

The fear of 'pretended family relationships' seems to be a powerful driving force, as attested to in Britain's Section 28 and the Elizabethtown School Board resolution. The question that obviously arises is why do proponents of such legislation feel that the institution of 'real' heterosexual marriage is so shaky that the mere pressure of gay and lesbian families could send it tumbling. The photo exhibit mentioned above, *Love Makes a Family: Living in Gay and Lesbian Families*, provides wonderful documentation of the families that are creating such fear. The photographs of 20 gay and lesbian families, diverse in race, ethnicity and family composition, are captioned with descriptions of the families and quotations from family members. The title clearly states the theme, which is amply demonstrated by both the photographs and the quotations, including one from Liza, aged 7, 'A family is a bunch of people, or not so many, who love each other.' Not surprisingly, such revolutionary definitions have met with strong opposition. When some schools have planned to host the exhibition, controversy has erupted, even though exhibitions were still held. I attended a workshop, arranged in conjunction with the exhibit, that was primarily for professionals in the area of early childhood development, particularly day care providers. During the workshop, the organizers had to lock the doors to prevent disruption by a homophobic religious group; when the group was unable to interrupt, members leafleted the parked cars with homophobic literature ('Do homosexuals spend eternity in heaven or hell?'). The dangerous message of the workshop they were trying to disrupt was about creating a supportive environment for young children from gay and lesbian families.

It is exactly this kind of exhibit that could help improve conditions for such students as Sibyl Fisher, the young co-author of a chapter in this section, who grew up in a lesbian household and worked to confront the homophobia she found in her school in New South Wales, Australia. Part of the response of Sibyl, her mother and a teacher was to use the 'No Fear' curriculum which was part of a larger Gender and Violence project. Using this approach helped place homophobic harassment in a broader context, which can create a less controversial and more accessible opening to encourage discussion.

## Harassment and homophobia

In US schools, sexual harassment of both boys and girls is common, and much of that harassment has a homophobic component. The American Association of University Women published the results of a major survey of sexual harassment in US schools (AAUW, 1993). One of the important findings was how widespread the problem was in the schools, with 81 per cent of students (85 per cent of girls and 76 per cent of boys) reporting that they had experienced some form of sexual harassment at school. There were some racial/ethnic differences, with African American and Hispanic girls more likely to have experienced harassment earlier in their lives compared to white girls, and with African American boys more likely to have experienced sexual harassment than white or Hispanic boys. Even though adult to student harassment was reported at a significant rate (18 per cent of those who had been harassed cited an adult as the perpetrator), most harassment was reported as student to student (79 per cent). Within this pervasive climate of sexual comments and jokes, of touching, grabbing, pinching and brushing up against someone in sexual ways, students (86 per cent) identified being called gay or lesbian as very upsetting. For many boys, being called gay was considered more upsetting than being physically abused, while 17 per cent of all students reported that this had happened to them (AAUW 1993, pp. 22–5). A survey commissioned by *Who's Who Among American High School Students* of 3,210 high-achieving high school students found that 29 per cent admitted to anti-gay prejudice and 36 per cent said most people they knew were anti-gay; this was a much higher percentage than those who said they were prejudiced against different racial and ethnic groups (*Advocate*, 1997).

As the school hallways echo with shouts of 'fag' directed at anyone to be insulted – regardless of real or presumed sexual orientation – special forms of harassment are often reserved for students who are gay or are strongly presumed to be. Wisconsin's statute prohibiting discrimination on the basis of sexual orientation is not always enforced on the local level and good legislation does not necessarily create a better climate, as one important recent case demonstrated. In 1996, one Wisconsin school district agreed to pay a former student, a gay man, $900,000 in an out-of-court settlement after a federal court found the school administrators liable for not protecting the student from anti-gay harassment and abuse. The student had reported that since the 7th grade he experienced ongoing harassment which continued until he withdrew from the school in 11th grade. His complaints included verbal harassment, a 'mock rape', and physical assaults. The physical attacks involved being kicked in the stomach a number of times by a group of students and being knocked into a urinal and then urinated on. Even though he told school officials at the time, no action was taken (*Educator's Guide to Controlling Sexual Harassment*, 1997). According to legal experts, the out-of-court settlement prevents this case from setting a precedent, but it should have the effect of pushing school districts to examine their anti-discrimination policies and to ensure that all students, including gay and lesbian students, are protected from harassment. The persistence and courage one young man showed in pursuing this case may bring about important changes in policies and attitudes. At the very least, it may shake up some school administrators who have seen the abuse of gay students as a 'normal' and inevitable part of the school environment.

## It's elementary

Policy changes are a start but clearly a lot more is necessary to create a school environment in which gay and lesbian students can reach their potential. Since changing all of society is a big task for the schools to take on, one small manageable role they can play is to implement curricula which focus on gay and lesbian issues – not necessarily in the context of sexuality education. A number of teachers around the country have been successfully introducing the topic into their classrooms. An excellent film, *It's Elementary*, by Debra Chasnoff and Helen Cohen, has documented approaches to teaching gay and lesbian issues in six different schools. The classroom scenes make it clear how open children are to these discussions and how well they can hear messages about problems with stereotypes, prejudice and discrimination in reference to any group. However, if we think that these six schools are reflective of a general trend in the USA, the Viewing Guide for the film reminds us of the ongoing struggle:

> many people who see *It's Elementary* want to know how representative the schools in the film are of schools in general. In one sense, they are not. At the time we filmed, they were the only teachers and schools that we could find in the United States willing and able to go out on a limb – not only to teach about gay people, but to give permission to publicly broadcast what they were doing, despite the risk of negative backlash.
>
> Nearly every teacher we filmed faced major obstacles in presenting the lessons we filmed. (Chasnoff and Cohen, 1997, p. 8)

The film focuses on approaches such as unlearning stereotypes, stopping name-calling, preventing violence, challenging discrimination and presenting positive examples of gay and lesbian families and individuals, and carefully avoids mentioning sexual activity. When two speakers at one school are asked about 'what they do', they make it clear both that they are not there to discuss sexual activity and that there is a lot more to a relationship than sex. It seems that the lessons presented are as uncontroversial as could be possible in presenting gay and lesbian issues positively. While not all the children seem comfortable – who could be when they are being filmed? – they seem open and responsive. However, the film has come under strong attack. For example, Concerned Women for America (CWA), a conservative group, has targeted the film:

> Characterizing the film as an 'abomination,' an 'unspeakable evil,' and a 'militant homosexual propaganda effort' aimed at 'recruiting a new generation to become homosexuals,' CWA wants to censor *It's Elementary*. Their campaign comes on the heels of similar attacks by Focus on the Family, the Family Research Council, and the Phyllis Schlafly Report. (*Off Our Backs*, 1997, p. 5)

The article above also reported that the Gay, Lesbian and Straight Educators Network (GLSEN) is offering a complimentary copy of the video to any school board member or superintendent who wants to see for themselves.

One particularly hostile review by the president of Family Friendly Libraries appeared on the website for the National Association of Research and Therapy of Homosexuality (Gounaud, 1997). In this review Gounaud attacks the documentary as a slick piece of propaganda and calls for those who oppose such approaches to counter its message. Among her criticisms are that the film is a form of indoctrination, that anti-gay criticism is equated with racism, that the film did not mention 'the scientifically proven promiscuity and disease crisis in gay male life, or the relationship between disease and anatomical unsuitability' (Gounaud, 1997). She also asserts that the film leaves out the 'explicit sex lessons' which she claims are presented in much of AIDS education for children and that it should have addressed the viewpoint that the 'reparative-therapy approach' can reverse the 'condition'.

Considering how hard it is in most schools to be explicit about sexual activity, especially when teaching children, it is unclear which sex lessons she is referring to. It also seems somewhat contradictory to suggest instruction that refers to 'the relationship between disease and anatomical unsuitability' (as if penile-vaginal sex does not transmit HIV or other disease-causing agents) while at the same time criticizing 'explicit sex lessons'. As to indoctrination, besides the fact that it is hard for teachers to convince teenagers or children to engage in any specific behaviours they want them to do such as doing homework, there is nothing in the film that in any way encourages anyone to 'become' gay or lesbian but merely asserts the basic human rights of gays and lesbians. The use by Gounaud of science, presented as neutral and objective, as a justification for anti-gay attitudes is not a new approach. Scientific 'facts' have not only been used against gays and lesbians, but have also been used historically to justify discrimination against women, many different racial and ethnic groups and religious groups.

Using science to attack comprehensive sexuality education and to support abstinence-only education is one strategy being used currently. For example, the Medical Institute for Sexual Health (MISH), a conservative group that promotes abstinence-only sexuality education, attacks the effectiveness of condoms and warns of the dangers of 'Masturbation, Mutual Masturbation, Outercourse and Dry Sex' in an article with that title (MISH, 1997). While it is useful for anyone who is sexually active to recognize the risks of any activity and to realize that safer sex is not always completely safe, this kind of information can have certain unintended consequences. Instead of convincing teenagers to avoid all genital sexual activity, this approach may convince them that nothing is safe, so they might as well do anything they want. This attitude can affect condom use, for example. Again, it is important to know that condoms, though very effective at preventing disease transmission and pregnancy, are not guaranteed 100 per cent effective. However, the incorrect and frightening messages about high failure rates can lead to the decision not to use condoms at all since teenagers may not want to bother with something they have been told does not work. Scare tactics have generally been shown to be an ineffective approach in education. For some teenagers the scare tactics may work, but they are more likely to be the ones who are not yet sexually active; for sexually active teenagers, this approach is unlikely to stop the activity. The answer MISH presents is to teach that sexual activity should occur only in lifetime faithful monogamous relationships and that unmarried teenagers should not be sexually active, a message that is particularly unhelpful for gay and lesbian teenagers.

## Conclusion

With most of the debate focused on the formal school curriculum, it can be very hard to develop, obtain approval for and implement a progressive sexuality curriculum. However, there is a great deal that individual teachers and schools as a whole can do outside the curriculum in terms of developing a positive supportive climate where discrimination and harassment in any form are unacceptable, no matter who the targets are. For example, each time a teacher interrupts a homophobic insult or joke, an important educational act has occurred.

It does seem that the school environment has improved for gay, lesbian and bisexual teenagers. However, every small step that is made in terms of policies, curricular changes and support services has required very hard work on the part of students, parents, educators. And each gain is at risk as well-funded opposition groups organize the backlash. The inspiration that comes from such sources as *It's Elementary* – from the film-makers and the teachers, students and school administrators it presents – provides fuel to keep us going as we constantly remind ourselves that we are in this for the long haul.

## 240 · MARIAMNE H. WHATLEY

## Notes

1. For information on *It's Elementary*, contact: Women's Educational Media, 2180 Bryant Street, Suite 203, San Francisco, CA 94110. Phone: 415 641-4616, Fax: 415 641-4632. E-mail: wemfilms@womedia.org
2. *Love Makes a Family* contains photographs by Gigi Kaeser and interviews by Pam Brown and Peggy Gillespie. For information about the exhibit, contact Peggy Gillespie at 413 256-0502 or E-mail: FamPhoto@aol.com

## References

AAUW (1993). *Hostile Hallways: The AAUW Survey on Sexual Harassment in America's Schools*. AAUW.

*Advocate* (1997). 'Hate in homeroom', 23 December, p. 14.

Burlingame, P. (1997). *Sex, Lies and Politics: Abstinence-only Curricula in California Public Schools*. Oakland, CA: Applied Research Center.

Chasnoff, D. and Cohen, H. (1997). *It's Elementary: Talking about Gay Issues in the School. Viewing Guide*. San Francisco: Women's Educational Media.

*Educator's Guide to Controlling Sexual Harassment* (1997). 'School district reaches settlement with former student for over $900,000', 4(5): 1–2.

Edwards, M. (1997). '88 million dollars for "abstinence-only" ', *SIECUS Report*, 25(4): 2.

Epstein, D. and Johnson, R. (1998). *Schooling Sexualities*. Buckingham: Open University Press.

Gounaud, K. J. (1997). 'It's elementary, it's slick . . . it's alarming'. http://www.leaderu.com/orgs/narth/elementary.html (NARTH website).

Haffner, D. (1997). 'What's wrong with abstinence-only sexuality education programs?', *SIECUS Report*, 25(4): 9–13.

Lueders, B. (1997). 'Cheap thrills', *Isthmus*, 22(52): 8–9.

Mayer, R. (1997). '1996–97 trends in opposition to comprehensive sexuality education in public schools in the United States', *SIECUS Report*, 25(4): 20–6.

Medical Institute for Sexual Health (MISH) (1997). 'Masturbation, mutual masturbation, outercourse, and dry sex'. http://www.mish.org/MASTUR.HTM.

*Off Our Backs* (1997). 'Reading, writing and evil?', October, p. 5.

SIECUS (1997). 'Federal definition of abstinence education', *SIECUS Report*, 25(4): 3.

Smith, A. M. (1994). *New Right Discourse on Race and Sexuality, Britain, 1968–1990*. Cambridge: Cambridge University Press.

Trudell, B. and Whatley, M. H. (1991). '*Sex Respect*: a problematic school sexuality curriculum', *Journal of Sex Education & Therapy*, **17**(2): 125–40.

Whatley, M. H. and Trudell, B. (1993). '*Teen-Aid*: another problematic sexuality curriculum', *Journal of Sex Education & Therapy*, **19**(4): 251–71.

# 15

# Queer as Fuck? Exploring the Potential of Queer Pedagogies in Researching School Experiences of Lesbian and Gay Youth

*Kathleen Quinlivan and Shane Town*

> Like . . . I would be crying some nights, just praying to God to make me straight and things because I didn't want to be gay. I guess that is how much the school and community had conditioned me . . . (Peter)

> the insistence on 'queer' – a term defined against normal and generated precisely in the context of terror – has the effect of pointing out a wide range of normalisation, rather than simple tolerance, as the site of violence. (Warner, 1993, p. xxvi)

> I can't really cope with (labels) at all . . . I don't like having to put one word to describe something that is to me so multi-faceted and mutable anyway. (Isobel)

Our research has developed out of our experience as lesbian and gay educators in co-educational high schools in Aotearoa/New Zealand. As part of postgraduate degrees we undertook separate but parallel projects exploring the perceptions of ten gay male and ten lesbian women's experiences of secondary schooling. Shane's research has focused on exploring the experiences of young gay men in schools and Kathleen's has focused on those of young lesbian women. Through collaborating from the intitial stages of our research we have been able to explore intersections of gender and sexuality.

The undertaking of the two studies has provided both the participants and ourselves as researchers with a venue within which we have been able to deconstruct our understandings of the role gender plays in constructing sexualities within binary frameworks of male/female, heterosexual/ homosexual and normal/abnormal (Sedgwick, 1993; Seidman, 1993). The experiences of the participants have led us to consider the impact of the curriculum on their perceptions of their (homo)sexuality. The treatment of sexuality within the curriculum operating around the dualism and separation of the mind/body (Sears, 1992; Fine, 1992) contributed to the participants' pathologization of (homo)sexuality and provides the frameworks for discussion within this chapter.

All of the participants to varying extents felt isolated and disempowered in their schools because there was no reflection of their emerging sexuality within the school environment. Realizing that coming out would endanger their physical and emotional well-being, they chose instead to manage their gay and lesbian identities and the implications of these by disguising them. The effects on the participants of managing their indentities in hostile schools and communities have been documented by Sears (1992b) and Trenchard and Warren (1984) as well as by ourselves: suicide ideation, depression, dysfunctional peer group and family relationships, alcohol and drug use.

Queer politics draws on lesbian feminist and post-structural perceptions of gender and sexuality as fluid, unstable and destabilizing (Jagose, 1996; Warner, 1993). The process that we, as 'queer' researchers working as teacher educators, have been involved in suggests ways in which our research reflects an emerging queer pedagogy (Britzman, 1995). 'Queer as fuck?' begins to explore what queer offers to lesbian and gay youth in challenging limited constructions of identity. Taking queer out of the realm of the academy and adult political spheres and into the world of youth and education provides opportunities for youth to move beyond the minoritizing discourses which currently frame their schooling. The final section of the chapter explores ways in which queer deconstructive processes incorporated in our research approach provided ways in which the participants could move beyond personalizing their sexuality as abnormal, deficient and unnatural.

## Framing the research process

The gendered nature of our experiences as 'queer' educators and researchers has impacted on our understandings and analysis of the perceptions the youth had of their schooling. These experiences have allowed us to focus on the nature of gendered constructions and the limitations this places on choice and possibilities for lesbian and gay youth in particular.

We both grew up in provincial New Zealand and yet came to our gay/ lesbian adult identities through quite different experiences and feelings. Shane felt that his sexual identity had been a 'part of him' from the time he was born. Kathleen had her first sexual relationship with a woman at twenty-five, coming to realize at the same time she was able to make a choice about becoming a lesbian. Both of us felt that the gay and lesbian communities which we entered were to some extent as constraining politically and socially as the 'heterosexual' worlds we had left. Kathleen's sense of justice and political ideals were strongly influenced through her involvement in feminism from an early age, while Shane's exclusion from male and masculine worlds and experience of injustice through being bullied as a gay child provided the impetus for him to adopt a political position as a gay adult.

Despite the differences we had in coming to understand our lesbian/ gay identities, as out teachers we had felt we had enough in common to form a strategic alliance. The collaboration has provided the impetus for a continuing examination of how we construct our identites and in the time in which we have been working together we have moved from gay and lesbian to perceive ourselves as queer and gay and lesbian in respect to our evolving identities.

Kathleen found tracing ten young lesbians to participate in her research a more difficult task than Shane because of the lack of formal networks available in lesbian communities in comparison with gay male communities which have been able to develop significant infrastructures through responses to the AIDS crisis. However, this difficulty is under-standable considering the silences that surround gay and lesbian issues in schools and in particular the invisibility of lesbian experience when sexual-ity issues are considered. The young lesbians range in age from 15 to 25, the young men from 15 to 21. All but one of the participants[1] in the studies identify as European New Zealanders, therefore lesbian and gay youth who experience the complex oppression of race and sexual orientation are not within the scope of these studies. Twelve of the young men and women attended schools in urban centres, four in suburban areas and four in rural/ provincial towns and districts.

Two semi-structured tape-recorded interviews were undertaken with each of the participants during 1993 and 1994. The scope of the interviews in both studies allowed the participants to explore the following areas: peer culture, social and sexual activites, teachers, curriculum, counsellors, forming lesbian/gay identities, forms of agency used by students to keep themselves safe in hostile school and family and community environments. In Shane's interviews there was also a focus on the impact of discourses surrounding HIV/AIDS.

Following the preliminary data analysis the participants had the opportunity to reflect on each of the interviews. Their responses in the form of additions and deletions were incorporated into the final analyses. Confidentiality was ensured through the voluntary use of pseudonyms.

## The mind/body binary and pathologizing (homo)sexualities

Our experience of these gendered constructions and our differing approach to the research questions helped us to acknowledge not only the silences being perpetuated by our research but also the binary frameworks and constructions in which we were operating (Sedgwick, 1993). Kathleen became aware of the limited constructions of passive female sexuality as she framed her research questions by asking the young women 'When was your first relationship?' When several of the participants expressed an interest in constructing their sexuality in more diverse ways she became interested in exploring what these prescriptions might mean for this study. This is in contrast to Shane, who asked his participants, 'When was your first sexual experience?', focusing on the constructions surrounding 'active' male roles in sexuality, rather than on notions of intimacy and emotional involvement.

Exploring the reasons for our differing approach to issues of identity within the interviews we recognized some value in making transparent the binary representations which emerged from the interview data and which the participants experienced through the delivery of the sexuality/health/ science curricula. Two of these, the mind/body split and the normal/abnormal binary through which the participants came to experience their sexuality in deficit terms form the basis of the following discussion. The participants' feelings of pathologization as a result of their experience of binary frameworks reinforced their perceptions of difference and dis/ease in relation to their sexual identities.

The binary definitions and constructions of homosexual identities and the communities that have arisen from them are seen to be responsible for creating and sustaining the conflicts which exist between gay males, lesbians and bisexuals. These conflicts prevent these groups from identify-ing commonalities, or exploring differences that would enable them to work successfully together. As Seidman states:

> gay liberation (of the 1970s) confronted a dialectic of identity and difference that revolved around straight/gay and man/woman polar-ities, currently these oppositions are multiplied a hundredfold as we introduce differences along the dimensions of race, ethnicity, gender, age, sexual act, class, lifestyle and locale. (Seidman, 1993, p. 129)

The majority of young lesbians and gay men we interviewed had learnt about sexuality within the context of the science and/or health curriculum. By focusing on anatomy, the enacted curriculum perpetuated the separa-tion of physical bodies from feelings and thoughts, which meant that issues of identity and feelings were ignored, as Andrew, a student in a provincial co-educational school suggests:

> sex education covered only the science side of things ... the mechan-ical ... talked about how you get pregnant ... how the cells divide ... only the physical attributes of the human being. (Andrew)

As Andrew points out, the information presented was reproductive and heterosexual. This reinforced the dominant heterosexist hegemony of the school environment or in the words of William, a student in a Catholic boys' school:

> I didn't learn anything except how to treat a girl right which wasn't useful at all ... (William)

William's experience of the curriculum identifies the way in which femaleness was constructed passively in relation to active male sexuality. Active constructions of female desire as Fine (1992) argued are con-spicuously absent from the sexuality curriculum. Jackie's experience in an urban state co-educational school identifies that lesbian sexuality, whether active or passive was rendered invisible:

> Homosexuality was mentioned but for men basically ... (Jackie)

One of the effects for Jackie and the participants in general of their exposure to present practices of sexuality education within schools was the reinforcement of active/passive roles within male/female binaries. For the gay male participants this resulted in them perceiving that their sexuality was something to be acted upon but not talked about; as Andrew went on to state, the only image he had of gay adulthood was found in public sex venues:

> When I was at school the gay community did not exist ... I had no knowledge of it ... the only knowledge I had was the toilets. (Andrew)

The separation of physical sexual activity from emotional intimacy and expressions of feelings was difficult for the young men and was reflected in the interview process. Expecting them to talk about their feelings proved to be a difficult exercise because they had never been provided with a venue in which to articulate their gay identity. They were expected to be pursuing more 'manly' pursuits such as sport. As Peter suggests, his experience in a traditional boys' boarding-school led him to believe:

> it would be the attitude from the executives at school that boys aren't engaging in sex at the moment ... you know ... playing rugby hard and playing cricket hard, studying hard and the sort of thing ... (Peter)

The lack of opportunity to explore feelings associated with emerging sexuality was problematic for all the gay male participants. All but two participants explored the physical dimensions of gay sexuality while at school but still found it difficult as young adults to articulate their feelings about themselves and their place as gay men in a male world. This reflects the dominant male hegemony and how it operates in schools to regulate male behaviour reinforcing the mind/body split. This suggests that males need to ensure they separate out their feelings from their public persona, which, as Zak suggested, resulted in his inability to express himself emotionally:

> It lowered my self-esteem basically ... I couldn't be myself ... I couldn't express myself to other people ... I couldn't get close to anyone ... even my close friends ... I couldn't tell them how I was feeling ... I find it hard to express my feelings now ... but then I wouldn't express them to anyone. (Zak)

The mind/body binary is also reflected strongly in the forms of sexual expression that the young lesbians saw as possible. Sexual feelings for many of the young lesbians revolved primarily around crushes and infatuations on their teachers and peers rather than actual sexual activity as it did for Melissa, who attended a provincial single-sex girls' school:

> The one I fell in love with was definitely worship from afar ... the reason that I joined the Women's Centre was to see her out of school ... I just admired her, I guess. (Melissa)

The expression of sexuality in such lofty terms often served to alienate the young women from their bodies and prevented the exploration of the physical dimensions of sexuality. Over the course of the interviews it was Isobel who experienced the alienating effects of the mind/body split most profoundly. As the research process progressed, she recognized the extent to which she had repressed the sexual side of herself and the role this repression played in affecting her ability to be sexually intimate with women:

> I've never thought of myself as a sexual person. I've always worn this really asexual androgygnous label and avoided intimate physical (contact) when I could ... I've always said that it's just not an important part of me, that I've got other ways of expressing my love and come up with these appalling excuses to avoid it. (Isobel)

The focus of the school curricula on the active/passive roles of sexuality within gendered bodies resulted in the participants' framing of their (homo)sexuality in terms of a disease. Isobel noted that the information she received about female sexuality constructed it as a problem:

> everything within sex education pathologized us. Your bodily functions are treated as problems ... problems of contraception, menstruation etc. I had a negative sensation about these functions and things that were happening to me. (Isobel)

For Isobel, the negative pathologizing messages that she received about her body as a young woman, combined with the silences that surrounded any mention of independent active female sexuality or lesbian sexuality, led her to shut down any physical expression of her sexuality:

I've felt ... it's really quite disgusting to feel physical pleasure or attraction or desire for another woman ... (Isobel)

For the young men, the implementation of HIV/AIDS education as part of the health curriculum led them to perceive their sexuality as a dis/ease. This, in conjunction with the media treatment of the crisis, resulted in Richard, a senior high school student, equating gay male sexuality with intravenous drug users and prostitution:

we were talking about AIDS and how the people who get AIDS are prostitutes, intravenous drug users and homosexuals. (Richard)

This reinforced the dysfunctional split between mind and body in the perceptions of the participants and acted in a moral sense to shut down both Andrew's and James's emerging gay male sexualities:

I was afraid of any sexual contact ... with another gay person ... it immediately put me off ... that is what scares a lot of people who are gay but haven't come out ... they see the risk ... and believe the risk is so high they couldn't possibly touch someone else. (Andrew)

I ... because I didn't know how to go about it (having a sexual relationship) because I was scared of what I was going to go through ... what would become of me ... was I going to get AIDS when I was twenty? (James)

For the young men in Shane's study this narrow treatment of sexuality led them to perceive their sexual orientation in deficit terms. In this respect, full recognition within the health curriculum of sexualities other than heterosexuality would have been helpful as would a consideration of (homo)sexualities beyond discourses surrounding the impact of HIV/AIDS.

## Queerying the research process

The interview process was the first opportunity many of the participants had to tell their stories and this proved to be an experience beneficial both for the participants and for ourselves. We have both moved from perceiving ourselves as gay/lesbian to understanding ourselves in more complex and fluid terms; Shane as 'queer and gay' and Kathleen as 'queer and lesbian', incorporating the political dimensions of our growing under-standings of sexualities and their representations in our communities. The process at the same time as providing an opportunity for ourselves to reconstitute our identities provided opportunities for the participants to reflect on the complex decisions that they had made to hide their sexual orientation during their schooling. William found that the interviews highlighted for him the extent to which he had gone to to remain invisible within his Catholic boys' school:

> reading the transcripts has helped me realize the lengths I went to to ensure I remained invisible at school and how this deprived me of an enjoyable school life ... it's taken a big blow to my confidence ... thanks for the opportunity to take part, it's been very interesting and helpful. (William)

The participants in both studies found the interview process helpful in that it allowed them to identify issues that still needed resolving in terms of their gay/lesbian identities. For Zak, the interviews helped him frame some of the reasons as to why he experienced his schooling in the ways in which he did:

> This whole interview was very enlightening and helpful for me. I finally realized what some of the problems were ... I knew I had some but I couldn't quite put a finger on what they were ... it still annoys me that my emotional development was set back 3–4 years ... but it feels so good to be myself at last and talk to others without feeling uncomfort-able. (Zak)

Lisa was able to understand the personal toll that hiding her emerging sexuality at high school took on her development as a young person:

> I am really glad to have contributed to this research ... I can look back now and know that when I was at high school I was struggling with my identity, I knew that I was a lesbian but I felt so alone and isolated that I withdrew into myself so as not to confront my feelings ... (Lisa)

The sharing of their perceptions enabled the participants to deconstruct their experience in the light of the heteronormative educational institutions they had attended. This deconstructive process is significant as it demonstrates the importance of providing venues in which youth can explore possibilities and where limitations and judgements are not imposed. It was also helpful for the participants to see their responses framed with analysis and theory to reduce their previous feelings of isolation and self-blame evoked by the schools they attended.

The deconstructive process was particularly stressful for those gay male participants who had seemingly colluded with the heterosexual 'macho' world and participated in homophobic behaviour. For Andy,[2] a member of his Catholic private boys' school 1st XV rugby team and deputy head boy, the need to 'pretend' to be heterosexual and overtly masculine led him to perceive his sexuality as a performance:

> I spent so long pretending to be a straight person that I could (now) be pretending to be a gay person. And they don't fit together at all. I don't fit into the straight community and I don't fit into the gay community . . . (Andy)

Current images of identity as represented and reinforced within schools are unfairly limiting. For Andy the opportunity to explore issues of identity as an adolescent and as an integral part of his schooling needed to be provided in an environment where one was not seen as deficient:

> There were no gay role models around, there was no one telling me it was OK to live that way. But there was a lot saying it was wrong and that it was abnormal and that it was illegal . . . it was right through school, at home, my friends, everybody was telling me that it was wrong . . . (Andy)

School communities seldom have to move beyond the personal deficit model in attempting to meet the needs of lesbian and gay youth (Quinlivan, 1996; Town, 1996). The research process enabled the young women to contextualize and understand how destructive behaviours they used in order to manage their identities in schools were responses to the constraints and limitation imposed through narrow heteronormative and gendered constructs. For example, several of the young women felt uncomfortable and guilty about the dysfunctional management strategies they employed to disguise their lesbianism. Although it was stressful to revisit these experiences, it helped Jackie recognize how much more comfortable she felt about being herself now:

It made me feel a little uncomfortable to reread . . . all that stuff I said about drinking . . . I think it feels like it happened a long time ago and if I could do it all again, it would be a really full-on smooth trip through school time. (Jackie)

The power of seeing your experiences confirmed and reinforced by others through hearing their stories cannot be underestimated. Like Jackie, Richard also felt more able to communicate his feelings and perceived he felt more comfortable with himself than when he was at school:

This manuscipt is full of emotion evoking things. I have torn myself to shreds dealing with it but that has been a good thing, I'm much more able to be myself . . . (Richard)

Reading other young lesbians' stories provided a context for Vita within which she could situate and understand her experiences in a Catholic girls' school and reinforce her emerging lesbian identity:

This was probably the first document that I've ever read that I could wholly devour with complete understanding and insight . . . Being able to share my experiences and reading those of others has helped in establishing my identity as a young lesbian and as a woman. (Vita)

The interview process also acted as a springboard for personal change in the level of self-esteem experienced by James, who had felt unable to express himself emotionally while not acknowledging his sexuality to others during his schooling:

when I went back home I saw someone from school who I hadn't seen for about a year . . . someone had told her I was gay and she said to me . . . 'you seem a lot more confident now, a lot more able to relate to people' . . . I suppose it did have something to do with the fact that I hadn't come out at school and that I did have low self-esteem there because I knew I was different. (James)

By participating in the research process, the young lesbians and gay men had their experiences legitimated. For many it represented the first opportunity in which their own stories were told and heard in a supportive environment with positive responses. This enabled the only young lesbian who was currently attending school to start a support group for young lesbians and bisexual women. With the support of sympathetic teachers, administrators and counsellors the school environment is now a much more supportive environment for her:

> The school has changed to meet my needs. (Belinda)

Similarly, participating in this study provided a catalyst for Toni to effect personal change within her own family. After moving from a small rural town to a large urban centre she became involved in establishing a young lesbian network:

> Being part of this research was a bit of an awakening . . . It gave me the strength to come out to my mother . . . and it has moved me to take positive action so that the isolation I felt need not be felt by others that follow . . . I think I got more out of this than you did. (Toni)

Several of the young lesbians in the study expressed a desire to move beyond what they perceived to be prescriptive feminisms, where identifying politically was more important than identifying sexually. Jackie expressed the need that she and her friends felt to contemplate alternative ways of being which acknowledge more active constructions of female sexuality:

> I sense an attitude of . . . wanting something . . . not quite a quick blow job but something as freeing, (getting away from) the emotional commitment they are meant to have as women. (Jackie)

Queer pedagogy offers an alternative to move beyond the limiting homo/hetero binary, a place which leaves no room for movement or change. Sexuality is then perceived as a shifting changing continuum, a place where pleasure and variety can be explored (Leck, 1995), rather than an either/or choice. Cathy, a student at an all-girls Catholic school, was interested in 'thinking the unthinkable' (Britzman, 1995), in exploring this continuum beyond the narrow confines of the lesbian label:

> At the moment I'm thinking quite seriously about bisexuality . . . I'm thinking, oh God, if they can say they are and haven't slept with any men and I've slept with men and I'm staunchly sticking to being a

lesbian, then it's just the word people are using differently rather than the actual meaning behind it. (Cathy)

Cathy's challenge to the gendered and heteronormative binaries in desiring wider definitions and possiblities of female/lesbian sexuality is significant. Schools need to address wider frameworks and representations than those that are currently reinforced by the heterosexual/homosexual binaries and played out in straight and gay/lesbian communities. Talking with young men and women about sexuality in high schools, we perceived that presenting sexuality as an either–or choice was prescribing narrow definitions of sexual expression for young women and men in schools, denying young bisexuals an opportunity to be heard and in doing so, reinforcing the barriers which prevented dialogue occurring and tolerance of difference increasing.

We have identified the limitations of equity discourses in meeting the needs of queer youth (Quinlivan, 1996; Town, 1996). Minoritizing these students under the 'at risk' label frames their 'problem as personal' and reinforces normalizing discourses of heterosexuality. In addition, school communities seldom have to acknowledge their destructive effects on queer youth of dealing with heteronormativity in schools or take action to provide safer learning environments.

Normalization processes evident in the participants' experiences of their schooling and of their entries into gay/lesbian communities were constrained by the limited representations available in both the gay/lesbian and straight communities. Their perceptions triggered a growing dissatisfaction in both our minds with prescriptively gendered and sexualized lesbian/gay orthodoxies. The pluralism of queer pedagogy has the potential to offer opportunities for students in schools including those who identify as heterosexual to consider a wider range of possibilities in defining and exploring their sexual identities. As Britzman (1995, p. 65) suggests: '*there is more to identity than meets the eye and individuals do not live their identity as hierarchies, as stereotypes, or in installments*'.

## Notes

1.  One participant, Alex, in Shane's study identified as bicultural, citing both his Maori and Pakeha backgrounds as significant in his development as a young gay man. (Maori – indigenous peoples of New Zealand. Pakeha – New Zealand 'Europeans'.)

2. Participants in Shane's study chose their own pseudonyms. Andy and Andrew are two different participants.

## References

Britzman, D. (1995). 'Is there a queer pedagogy? Or, stop reading straight', *Educational Theory*, **45**(2): 151–65.

Fine, M. (1992). 'Sexuality, schooling, and adolescent females: the missing discourse of desire', in M. Fine, *Disruptive Voices: The Possibilities of Feminist Research*. Ann Arbor: University of Michigan Press.

Jagose, A. (1996). *Queer Theory*. Dunedin: University of Otago Press.

Leck, M. (1995). 'The politics of adolescent sexual identity and queer responses', in Gerald Unks (ed.), *The Gay Teen: Educational Practice and Theory for Lesbian, Gay and Bisexual Adolescents*. New York: Routledge.

Quinlivan, K. (1994). 'Ten lesbian students reflect on their secondary school experiences'. Unpublished MA thesis, University of Canterbury, Christchurch, New Zealand.

Quinlivan, K. (1996). ' "Claiming an identity they taught me to despise": lesbian students respond to the regulation of same sex desire', *Women's Studies Journal*, **12**: 2.

Rofes, E. (1995). 'Making our schools safe for sissies', in Gerald Unks (ed.), *The Gay Teen: Educational Practice and Theory for Lesbian, Gay and Bisexual Adolescents*. New York: Routledge.

Sears, J. (1992a). 'The impact of culture and ideology on the construction of gender and sexual identities: developing a critically based sexuality curriculum', in J. Sears (ed.), *Sexuality and the Curriculum: The Policies and Practices of Sexuality Education*. New York: Teachers College Press.

Sears, J. (1992b). 'Researching the other/searching for self: qualitative research on (homo)sexuality in education', *Theory into Practice. Special Issue: Qualitative Issues in Educational Research*, **31**(2): 147–56.

Sedgwick, E. (1993). *The Epistemology of the Closet*. Berkeley: University of California Press.

Seidman, S. (1993). 'Identity and politics in a "postmodern" gay culture: some historical and conceptual notes', in M. Warner (ed.), *Fear of a Queer Planet*. Minneapolis: University of Minnesota Press.

Smyth, C. (1992). *Lesbians Talk Queer Notions*. London: Scarlet Press.

Town, S. J. H. (1995). 'Are you gay Sir?', in H. Manson (ed.), *Annual Review of Education*. Wellington: Victoria University Press.

Town, S. J. H. (1996, April). 'Is it safe to come out yet? The impact of secondary schooling on the positive identity development of ten young gay men'. Paper presented to the annual meeting of the American Educational Research Association, New York.

Trenchard, L. and Warren, H. (1984). *Something to Tell You*. London: London Gay Teenage Group.

Warner, M. (ed.) (1993). *Fear of a Queer Planet*. Minneapolis: University of Minnesota Press.

# 16

# 'No Fear' in Our School

## Lori Beckett, Mary Tweed and Sibyl Fisher

Mum and I watched the Sydney Mardi Gras on television. When I went to school the next day, a group of kids was making fun of gay and lesbian people. They said things like 'lezzos are disgusting'. I didn't know what was going on. Mum and I really enjoyed the parade, and the kids 'paid it out'. I didn't know what to say, so I kept quiet.

It happened nearly every day for two weeks. The kids kept saying the same things over and over. It made me want to cry, but I fought back the tears. I didn't know what to do, so I told Mum. She helped me understand homophobia and why some people put other people down. Now when the kids say 'you're gay', I say 'who cares'.

This is Sibyl's story about homophobia in the playground. When the first incident occurred, after the televised broadcast of the Mardi Gras parade last year, she was in grade five. The school is located in a quiet rural village on the south coast of New South Wales (NSW), Australia, not far from Robertson, where the film *Babe* was made. It is a small K–6 primary school with a population of 180 children from families who live on farms, one-acre lots and town blocks. The area can be described as mostly white, middle-class, affluent and conservative.

The experience confused and distressed Sibyl, who has grown up in a lesbian household. Thankfully, Sibyl's Mum, Lori, had 'come out' to her years ago so she has an understanding of the world beyond her years, as it were. Sibyl, who is extremely sensitive but wordly-wise, knows about difference and diversity, discrimination and gay hate. None the less, this was her first experience of vilification and she was acutely aware of the pain and embarrassment. She was also mindful of conformity and the arguments about invisibility.

The challenge for Sibyl and Lori was to counter the homophobia at a personal level and to address the matter at school. They talked through the incident and the reasons for the remarks as well as other children's home life and their experiences with homosexuality. They talked about different understandings of same-sex relationships, and different family situations. Sibyl was reminded of her own loving and secure home life, and her feelings for Ruby, Lori's long-term partner. This gave Sibyl an insightful perspective on same-sex relationships, which is not focused on the sexual aspects of a relationship nor homosexual sex.

## Approaching the school

Sibyl and Lori decided to approach Mary Tweed, the sixth grade teacher. Mary has many years' experience, with a great commitment to equity and social justice. Like other teachers in schools of this size, she has the responsibility for classroom work as well as co-ordinating the school's gender equity initiatives and student welfare programmes, including child protection, anti-racism and peer support. The NSW government, currently a Labor Government, through its Department of School Education (DSE), supports these projects with its *Social Justice Directions Statement* (New South Wales Government, 1996).

At the time, Mary was also involved in the trialling of the 'No Fear' kit, which was the set of materials produced by the Gender and Violence Project and funded by the Commonwealth Department of Employment, Education and Training. It developed out of the Commonwealth Office of the Status of Women's community education programme entitled the 'Stop Violence Against Women' campaign.

The Gender and Violence Project was undertaken in two stages. Stage one developed a position and framework on gender and violence in schools after a consideration of current literature and data collected through collaboration with educational communities across Australia. Ollis's and Tomaszewski's (1993) position paper provided an overview and evaluation of the programmes and resources then used in schools as well as a set of recommendations for the development of quality teaching and learning materials and professional development materials. Stage two involved the development of the 'No Fear' kit by Social Change Media, the successful tender who worked with teams of academics, teachers, gender equity advisers, parents, students and other interested community representatives in the drafting and trialling phases.

According to Ollis and Tomaszewski (1993), the Gender and Violence Project aimed at preventing violence by examining how the issues can be tackled in schools, which are in a unique position to educate for social change. The project was concerned with teachers' and students' attitudes and behaviours to ensure that violence is neither accepted nor ignored. The task was to educate teachers and students from pre-school to Year 12 to recognize violence in its range of forms and behaviours.

Further, the teaching and learning and professional development materials were intended to enable schools to develop management practices and organizational structures which would promote a culture where violence in schools and society would be challenged and seen as unacceptable; assist all students to understand the relationship between violence and masculinities and femininities; enable schools to identify, develop and implement policies and practices which would be effective in dealing with all aspects of violence in schools; and assist all teachers and students to understand the criminal nature of violence, the range of physical, verbal and emotional violence and the related behaviours that constitute violence against women and men, girls and boys, and the links between sex-based harassment and violence against girls and women and issues of responsibility (Ollis and Tomaszewski, 1993).

The 'No Fear' kit was published in two editions, one for primary schools (K–6) and one for secondary schools (7–12), in November 1995. It is a package of materials which consists of a leadership booklet, professional development materials, facilitator's guide, teacher's booklet and curriculum materials, plus posters and a video, one for primary and one for secondary students.[1]

## Responding to concerns

The facilitator's guide gave Mary a way of responding to Lori's and Sibyl's concerns about lesbian and gay hate and harassment. It suggested a guiding principle in that strategies for addressing violence need to be informed by an understanding of power and gender relations. This rested on Ollis's and Tomaszewski's (1993) view that violence is gendered in nature and outcome. Evidence suggests that violent offenders in society are predominantly male (see National Committee on Violence, 1992). Similarly, the evidence that is available on violence in schools suggests that men and boys are overwhelmingly the perpetrators. While other boys and male teachers are victims of violence from men and boys, it is mostly girls and female teachers who experience violence at the hands of boys and men.

Ollis and Tomaszewski (1993) also viewed violence as an expression of the power structures in Australian society, where gender-based violence is a part of the social fabric. They argued that social relations in Australia are characterized by inequality and an inequitable distribution of power which provides a structure that legitimates male violence and provides women with little protection and support. It is a fact that in Australia, women and girls continue to experience discrimination in the legal, health, welfare, employment and education systems. Moreover, they argued that beyond gender, perceptions about sexual preference, age, race and ability are factors that can place individuals and groups in relatively powerless positions.

To exemplify the situation, Ollis and Tomaszewski (1993) described the situation for homosexual men, who not only challenged the cultural representation of masculinity but experienced inequalities and discrimination on the basis of perceived and accepted cultural norms. Drawing on Connell's (1987) work, they said homosexual men have reason to fear public assault, particularly by police who are keen to uphold the accepted cultural representation of masculinity which is hegemonic. This was vindicated by a phone-in survey conducted by the Sydney Gay Hotline, which reported that in almost all instances the perpetrators of anti-gay violence were teenage boys and young men. This raised disturbing questions about the role of violence and homophobia in the construction of masculinity (see Connell, 1995).

The same thing can be said about the construction of femininity. The social relations between men and women, boys and girls, combine with the cultural representations of masculinity to forge a complementary version of femininity. Connell (1987) called it 'emphasised femininity' because most women and girls readily construct themselves in relation to men and boys and their interests and desire for romantic attention and female companionship. The dominance of hegemonic masculinity is matched by emphasized femininity, and these constructions are reinforced by the embedded nature of violence and homophobia and we would add by the negative perceptions of lesbian sexuality, which contibute not only to anti-lesbianism but lesbian invisibility (see Beckett, 1996).

The facilitator's guide also provided Mary with ideas about some possible entry points, where the 'No Fear' kit could complement the school's work on behaviour management, gender equity and equal opportunity, for example. Sibyl's exprience was a critical incident which provided the impetus for reviewing the school's procedures for dealing with homophobia. Mary decided to investigate the status of the school's 'behaviour management plan' and the school's discipline policy, which needed to be reviewed, reorganized and developed in the light of Education Minister John Aquilina's statement on *Good Discipline and Effective Learning* (NSW Department of School Education, 1996a).

At the same time, Mary and Lori continued to work together and share a commitment to the 'No Fear' kit's whole-school approach. According to the facilitator's guide, the starting point for developing a plan of action is to build a school-wide recognition that gender-based violence is an issue for the school community to address. The whole-school approach emphasizes collaboration between the school leadership, that is, the principal and the school's administration, in tandem with teachers, students, non-teaching staff, parents and the wider community. The intention is to explore what is happening in the playground, the classroom, the staffroom and the community and to work towards creating a non-violent school community.

## Getting permission

Mary and Lori approached Paul, the principal, and acquainted him with their concerns about violence in the school. Paul is both conservative and cautious. At first, he was resistant and took the view that there was no violence in our school. As principal, he was caught in a dilemma. On the one hand, he had to promote Minister Aquilina's commitment to 'safe and happy schools', which was part of the government's reform agenda called *Agenda '96*. It was a direction that schools and classrooms be secure and happy, safe from vandalism and graffiti, free from disruptive and violent behaviour and protected against security breaches (see NSW Department of School Education, 1996b). The idea of a 'safe and happy school' was also an expression of the government's and Minister's commitment to the marketization of schools, where schools are subject to the vagaries of parents' choice about public or private education and the sort of school they want for their children.

On the other hand, Paul was under increasing pressure to deliver a range of equity policies, which are promoted by the government and the Department of School Education. However, these policies and materials like the 'No Fear' kit are dependent on the staff's own initiative and goodwill. At the same time, the staff are not fully supported with adequate professional development and the necessary time for programme planning and implementation. Without support, principals, teachers and others are reluctant to, if not fearful of, addressing social issues.

In response, Lori and Mary put the three reasons for action mentioned by the facilitator's guide to Paul, who was prepared to support our project as long as it could be accommodated within *Agenda '96*. Firstly, addressing gender-based violence and exploring the incidence of violent behaviours in all their forms will contribute to improving the learning outcomes of both girls and boys. Sibyl was distracted by her experience of homophobia, which can damage young people as they struggle with matters of identity, homosocial friendships, teenage romance, sexuality, social acceptance and a sense of self.

Secondly, developing a supportive school environment will ensure the safety of teachers, students, parents and others. The effort that had already gone into making our school not only safe and free from violence and discrimination, but a pleasant place to learn and work, did not go unnoticed. The school community is justifiably proud of the school, including the caring staff, the friendly atmosphere, the learning environment and the buildings and grounds. However, a supportive school environment must also recognize that violence can be defined as any type of behaviour which can damage others. As the 'No Fear' kit's information for parents pointed out, it can include verbal harassment, bullying, physical violence and sexual harassment such as leering, touching and sexual comments.

Thirdly, our school has a legal obligation to ensure that there is no violence and discrimination. The Commonwealth Sex Discrimination Act (1984) and the NSW Anti-Discrimination Act (1977) make it unlawful for instances of harassment, discrimination and vilification to occur. Indeed, a set of 'grievance procedures' was released by the Director-General of School Education, Ken Boston, in February 1995 (see NSW Department of School Education, 1995). These provided school communities with some direction for making a formal complaint.

As it happened at our school, a formal complaint about Sibyl's experience would have been inappropriate because the young children involved did not have a knowledgeable understanding of homosexuality. They had not personalized the insults nor discriminated against a particular student. It was more appropriate to address the often invisible assumptions, values, practices and processes which underpin and perpetuate their understanding, as the facilitator's guide pointed out.

## Engaging teachers' support

Mary addressed a staff meeting and informed them of Sibyl's experience and our decision to use the 'No Fear' kit, which linked in with the school's 'behaviour management plan' and school discipline policy. She also requested that one of the so-called school development days, which are held twice yearly for professional development purposes, be allocated to the work that needed to be done for *Good Discipline and Effective Learning* (NSW Department of School Education, 1996a). The staff and the principal agreed, and Mary organized and chaired a school development day, where parents and other community members were invited to attend. In doing so, Mary cemented a consistent 'whole-school approach' to violence. As Ollis and Tomaszewski (1993) pointed out, work on school policies helps ensure a consistent identification of the problem as well as consistent responses and procedures for the school to follow.

Mary also took an opportunity to talk to parents when she addressed the new sixth grade parents at the parent–teacher night, organized during orientation week in February 1996. At the beginning of the school year, the children had been invited to articulate their reasons for being at school, what they wanted to gain from their time in Year 6 and how they would best be able to meet their goals. The children were also invited to comment on the kind of classroom and the type of school they needed for a safe, happy and effective work environment. The children identified the necessary prerequisites like co-operation and respect, for example, and they decided on measures that should be taken in the event of a breach of the teaching and learning conditions. Mary relayed these discussions to the parents, and invited comment and feedback, which provided her with support and encouragement.

By establishing a situation where teachers, students and parents can work together to determine their common goals and aspirations for teaching and learning, Mary was acknowledging the ways a non-violent school community is socially constructed. This has to do with the making of men and women, and boys and girls, taking up a range of masculinities and femininities. As Ollis and Tomaszewski (1993) pointed out, dominant masculinity, for instance, may well be defined by notions of aggression and the like, but it is not predetermined nor is it an inbuilt biological characteristic. Girls and boys make conscious and unconscious decisions about being male and female, which reflect constraints of class, race, ability and social structure. In Mary's sixth grade, they are actively involved in forging the power relations necessary for a non-violent school community as well as a more equal and just society.

## Securing parents' consent

Lori and Mary together addressed a school Parent and Citizen (P&C) meeting about the 'No Fear' kit and the results of the trialling. They recognized that the school does not exist in a social vacuum and that it was important to connect with the school's community. It was also a strategic move because the P&C is regarded as a fund-raising body, not by the parents, who acknowledge its political function, but by the principal. Significantly, because principals and teachers are cast as managers and parents as consumers by the market model of schooling, which is endorsed by Minister Aquilina, the principal's support for parent participation is not readily forthcoming.

Two incidents prompt this comment. At the P&C meeting in May 1995, Paul raised the matter of parents' concerns and requested that parents raise matters of concern with him personally rather than at the P&C meeting. In keeping with the marketization of education, he then tabled a list of 'positives around (our) School'. At the P&C meeting in February 1996, Paul actively worked against Lori's election as P&C president in view of her commitment to parent activism and to feminism, whatever that means. This sort of opposition failed to acknowledge Lori's commitment to productive partnerships, where teachers, parents and students work together on matters of mutual concern. Productive partnerships signify more equal power relationships and the capacity of men and women, boys and girls, to co-operate and work respectfully.

Two months after Mary's and Lori's joint address, Lori again addressed the P&C, and mentioned the ongoing work with the 'No Fear' kit and the different expressions of school violence. Not surprisingly, there was resistance to the idea of violence in our school. Paul, the principal, very quickly made it known to parents that our school was a safe and happy place and a haven from violence. A few parents agreed, and cited the daily incidents of violence and intimidation at other schools, which had particularly bad reputations. These schools are located in metropolitan and industrial areas where there is noticeably less affluence, government housing and unemployment.

A few other parents acknowledged the difficulties which threatened personal safety at other schools, but insisted that their children still experienced bullying and harassment in our school. The discussion that followed accommodated the resistance, which is regarded as an aspect of the change process in the 'No Fear' kit. As the facilitator's guide said, understanding the nature of the arguments against taking action is the first step in working with others to develop understandings about the complexities.

In response to the argument that there is no violence in our school, Lori teased open the definitions of violence and analysed the range of behaviours which can have damaging and destructive effects on girls and boys, women and men. The advice in the facilitator's guide to focus on the positives was sound. It is better to avoid the argument that 'the school is violent', which may only encourage resistance, and concentrate on understanding and addressing gender-based violence. Lori decided to build on the school's strengths and encourage Paul to highlight and publicize the ways the school is fostering non-violence.

Just in passing, it is important to note that Lori felt constrained by the resistance at the P&C meeting. She had dealt with Sibyl's experience of homophobia at home and wanted it dealt with at school. She had raised it with Mary and wanted to raise it with Paul and the other parents. In view of the response to the matter of gender-based violence, she opted to remain closeted and instead dealt with the matter impersonally. Although a formidable woman and outspoken in other circles, she is protective of Sibyl and does not want to do anything to jeopardize her schooling experiences and social activities.

This situation illustrated the homophobic and heterosexist culture of our school and the experience of oppression. Homophobia is not the responsibility of those who have the most to lose by speaking out. It is the joint responsibility of the school community. As Denborough (1996) intimated, this means finding ways of challenging homophobia and heterosexual dominance so that it is not left to those who are most vulnerable. It means that heterosexual adults acknowledge their privilege and question what it means to be heterosexual. It means problematizing heterosexuality by acknowledging same-sex attraction and eroticism. It also means questioning what sort of work needs to be done before gay, lesbian and bisexual teachers, students and parents can speak openly and safely about their lives.

*Enlisting support*

Lori made the suggestion that the P&C invite a guest speaker, specifically Joan Lemaire, who was then the NSW Teachers Federation's Women's

Coordinator. Joan had worked as a teacher union representative on Minister Aquilina's Gender Equity Consultative Committee and the national Ministerial Council of Employment, Education, Training and Youth Affairs (MCEETYA) Gender Equity Taskforce, and promoted the union's commitment to social justice. These two bodies respectively developed the new state *Gender Equity Strategy* and the new national framework, *Gender Equity: A Framework for Australian Schools*. Both the strategy and the national framework were informed by thinking about the ways gender impacts on girls' and boys' expectations, interests and behaviour.

Lori spoke to Joan in confidence about Sibyl's story, Mary's commitment to a whole-school approach, a concern about the school's market image, some resistance to the idea of violence in our school, and Lori's decision to remain closeted. Joan indicated a concern that while, in policy terms, the Department of School Education appeared committed to ensuring there is no discrimination in schools, they had not adequately supported this by providing appropriate training and support.

Joan approached the task thoughtfully and respectfully. She talked about the notion of gender equity in terms of power relations and work to help challenge and change inequalities. She used the extracts of students' own voices describing their own experiences from Clark's (1990) study on gender in the primary school. This helped the principal, parents and teachers connect with what happens to girls and boys in schools. It also helped explain not only the construction of masculinities and femininities, but the educational implications of rigid ideas and attitudes. The focus was on boys' and girls' experience of primary schooling, and the practices and attitudes that contribute to the production of gender difference and dominant masculinities. Joan did not comment on the specifics of homophobia in our school, but through the extracts drew the discussion around to the daily classroom practices of concern as well as those practices that can effect change.

## Politicizing the children

While this work with the teachers and parents was going on, Mary continued to work with the children, who in turn worked with parents. Taking a cue from the 'No Fear' kit, Mary concentrated not only on school policies, organizational practices and school and classroom culture, but also on curriculum programmes and teaching and learning practices. For example, Mary gave the children some scope in their individual research projects, which are due at the end of each school term, to address the twin issues of countering violence and building a safe and respectful society.

In the first project on education in the past, present and future, Sibyl was required to articulate her concerns and investigate a real-life situation, which involved using a questionnaire and interviewing family members. She explored schooling for Great-Grandma, Grandma and Mum, and demonstrated how their schooling contributed to society. She wove in a theme of anti-racism and anti-homophobia. As Sibyl wrote in her project,

> For example, Mum's history lessons were about white history not black history. Unless we learn about other ways of life we will remain ignorant and arrogant. The consequences of this are hatreds like racism, sexism and homophobia.

In the second project on social groups, Sibyl chose her family group, social group and drama group to study. In her family group work, she again wove in a theme of anti-homophobia. However, she was not inclined to name her lesbian mother because of a fear of rejection by her friends. In response, Grandma and Sibyl decided to describe the family group using a fictitous aunty to make the point about gay and lesbian family members and the ways people deal with homosexuality. In her project, Sibyl described a family argument about aunty's 'coming out'.

> My other aunty was horrified when she found out. Grandma told me this was homophobia, a hate against gay people. She said it was a problem for aunty, not the rest of us, and that she was the only one who could come to terms with it. Grandma reminded me of our family rules: love and respect for each other.

Mary took yet another opportunity to address the creation of a non-violent school community when another critical incident in the playground occurred. It involved a group of boys who had called each other 'poofters'. The boys were asked to reflect on and recount their behaviour, which was described as homophobic. They were reminded that countering domination and discrimination involved being respectful of difference and diversity. As well, the sixth grade was asked to reflect on the incidence of violence and heterosexism. Taking a cue from the facilitator's guide, Mary wanted Sibyl's classmates to acknowledge that not everyone is hetero-sexual and that lesbian and gay students do not deserve their experiences of alienation and rejection. She also wanted them to recognize that it takes strength for lesbian and gay students to attend school, and that it was the school community's responsibility to challenge homophobic attitudes.

Sibyl, Lori and Mary have made some progress towards developing a whole-school approach. The 'No Fear' kit has been an invaluable source of ideas and suggestions, although it takes courage to tackle acts of discrimination and violence in a school setting that is for the most part conservative in orientation. However, the attempt at challenging dominant cultural expressions of what it means to be a man and a woman, a boy and a girl, is well worth the effort. In Sibyl's words:

> Being gay or lesbian is part of your identity. It makes me really happy now that the kids know what it means and they stand up for people who are being hassled. We have to make it safe and happy for everyone.

## Note

1. *Creating a Non-Violent School Community: A Whole School Approach to Address-ing Gender Based Violence. The* No Fear *Kit.* Available from J. S. McMillan Outsourcing, Corner Derby and Stubbs Streets, Silverwater, NSW 2141, Australia. Tel: +61 (0)2 648 3333. Fax: +61 (0)2 648 4209. Gender and Violence – Primary Kit, A$60.00. Gender and Violence – Secondary Kit, A$60.00. Cheques to be made payable to J. S. McMillan Outsourcing. Can be paid by credit card; please supply number and expiry date. Make sure delivery address is included in order.

## References

Beckett, L. (1996). ' "Where do you draw the line?" Education and sexual identities', in L. Laskey and C. Beavis (eds), *Schooling and Sexualities: Teaching for a Positive Sexuality*. Geelong: Deakin Centre for Education and Change.

Clark, M. (1990). *The Great Divide: Gender in the Primary School*. Melbourne: Curriculum Corporation.

Connell, B. (1987). *Gender and Power: Society, the Person and Sexual Politics*. Sydney: Allen & Unwin.

Denborough, D. (1996). 'Power and partnership? Challenging the sexual construction of schooling', in L. Laskey and C. Beavis (eds), *Schooling and Sexualities: Teaching for a Positive Sexuality*. Geelong: Deakin Centre for Education and Change.

Laskey, L. and Beavis, C. (eds) (1996). 'Introduction', in *Schooling and Sexualities: Teaching for a Positive Sexuality*. Geelong: Deakin Centre for Education and Change.

National Committee on Violence Against Women (1992). *Position Paper*. Department of the Prime Minister and Cabinet, Office of the Status of Women. Canberra: Australian Government Publishing Service.

New South Wales Government (1996). *Fair Go, Fair Share, Fair Say: New South Wales Social Justice Directions Statement*. Sydney: Parliament House.

Nickson, A. (1996). 'Keeping a straight face: schools, students and homosexuality (Part 1)', in L. Laskey and C. Beavis (eds), *Schooling and Sexualities: Teaching for a Positive Sexuality*. Geelong: Deakin Centre for Education and Change.

NSW Department of School Education (1995). *Procedures for Resolving Complaints about Discrimination against Students*. Sydney: Training and Development Directorate.

NSW Department of School Education (1996a). *Good Discipline and Effective Learning: A Ministerial Statement by the Hon John Aquilina, MP*. Sydney: Student Welfare Directorate.

NSW Department of School Education (1996b). *Agenda (D4)96. A Ministerial Statement by the Hon John Aquilina, MP*. Sydney: Communications and Marketing Directorate.

Ollis, D. and Tomaszewski, I. (1993). *Gender and Violence Project Position Paper*. Department of Employment, Education and Training. Canberra: Australian Government Publishing Service.

# 17

# Sexuality and Subversion: University Peer Sexuality Educators and the Possibilities for Change

*Rebecca F. Plante*

ONE DAY IN late January, after the autumn training quarter, some peer sexuality educators (PSEs) were talking before class began. Laura Sorensen, PSE supervisor, told the students about restrictions on her and Maria Scott, the other supervisor. As campus health services professionals, their behaviour was scrutinized. As paraprofessional staff, PSEs were similarly bound. For example, every programme PSEs provided had to begin with the statement that 'abstinence is the safest sex'.

Sorensen suggested that if the PSEs wanted more freedom, they could form a group external to the organized programme. By operating as just another student group, they could plan more 'radical' activities. One PSE asked, 'But what would we do?' Another responded, 'Anything we want.' One PSE, Trixie, suggested that everyone who was interested should stay after class to discuss forming a group.

So the 'Sexual Health Information Network' (SHIN) was born, formed by what turned out to be a core group of PSEs: Debra, Jennifer, Christine, Jill, Mike, Trixie, Carlin, Samantha and Ed. Although the group was suggested by a professional in an offhand way, every step toward success or failure was taken by students. SHIN wanted to provide explicit campus sexuality education, otherwise frowned on by administrators and staff at health services. The group wanted to challenge the university, challenge the institutional version of sexuality education, challenge accepted policies about such education at the university.

## Setting the scene: programme, methods and focus

University sexuality information usually occurs via health services, academic departments or, rarely, via peer education. Trained students go into classrooms and campus housing to provide programming to their peers. However, peer education is situated in the broader context of institutionalized sexuality education, which has always been controversial.

Research on sexuality education in colleges and universities is limited to assessments of departments' teaching interventions (e.g. Brasseur, 1983; Pollis, 1986; Gingiss and Hamilton, 1989; Cohen *et al.*, 1994). One journal produced a special issue on peer education, merely detailing how to implement peer education of all types (*Journal of American College Health*, **41**, 1993). Critical analysis of peer sexuality education programmes is non-existent (Fennell, 1993).

This chapter revolves around a PSE programme (in existence since 1988) at a large, public university in the south-eastern United States. The central focus of this study, part of a larger examination, is how PSEs challenge institutionalized sexuality discourses and policies.

This university's policies about sexuality education are not written in stone. One administrator said, 'I wouldn't say that the university – whoever that is – feels like we need to do so much in the area of sex education. I think [sexuality education] could fall off the face of the earth, stop tomorrow, and nobody would notice.'

However, the three administrators I interviewed are unlikely to disturb the PSE programme unless it draws negative attention. One example, according to one administrator, would be complaints by parents, students or student (religious) groups about the content and conduct of PSE programmes:

If public opinion changed and we got a lot of letters . . . Let's say one of the PSEs does something really bizarre, we'd hear about it pretty fast. That stuff gets to the media pretty fast, and then we would have to do something.

As peer sexuality educators, students are simultaneously consumers and producers of education. Peer education casts students as subjects of institutional discourses and policies, but also as objects, able to reproduce these ideologies. Sexuality becomes an instrumental element in the social appropriation of bodies: 'Sex is located at the point of intersection of the discipline of the body and the control of the population' (Foucault, 1980, p. 125).

Based on six months of intensive fieldwork, participant observation and interviews, I analyse a smaller group of PSEs. The 'Sexual Health Information Network' I focus on was started by PSEs in February 1994, and functioned until June 1994. Nine of its ten members were PSEs (there were 25 PSEs in the larger programme). Under informed consent, participants' names are changed.

## The Sexual Health Information Network

The students surprised me that day in January. In interviews, several PSEs confessed to being disappointed by their classmates. One thought fellow PSEs would be more radical, interested in more than just sexual health. When I became a PSE in another programme ten years ago, I felt similarly. After a month, it was clear that my colleagues were only there to learn how to teach and to satisfy education major requirements.

Enthusiastic at first, SHIN organizers developed outreach and programming ideas that surpassed PSE programmes (standard fare included contraception, AIDS and gay and lesbian issues). I was also excited, because I wanted to observe how sexualities are institutionalized, and to answer two Foucaultian questions: what form could student resistance to institutional policies take, and was resistance even possible?

Although SHIN was student-organized and student-run, it had to be sanctioned through institutional channels. Various avenues in the university were closed to unofficial groups – most importantly funding. A week after the initial discussion about starting a group, Trixie addressed the PSE class: 'Anyone with activist concerns, anyone who wants campus involvement via campus channels, should join us', she said. Trixie considered herself an activist already. She worked for the local AIDS agency, delivering meals to clients and case-managing for a short time. Her classmates were used to hearing her ideas, since her soft voice often added a radical edge to class discussions.

Jennifer took charge of the steps necessary for official recognition. She was well integrated into the upper levels of the university's structure. Only a sophomore, Jennifer held a high position in student government and was vice-president of her sorority. She told the class that to petition for group formation, at least ten names and social security numbers needed to be signed to a form. 'We need to get money', Jennifer said. 'We're new, and we have to let the student affairs people know what our plans are, do a budget, and pick a group affiliation – maybe service?'

She circulated the form and some PSEs signed it, knowing their signatures did not obligate them to anything. Jennifer said the group would need an official name, a constitution, officers and a committee structure. Only Trixie realized the irony of forming a 'radical' group via official, university channels, but thought that it would be ironically appropriate to spend institutional money doing 'guerrilla sexuality education'. But the class wanted to know how this group would be different from the PSEs, and why they had to be completely separate from the programme. 'There are advantages to being perceived as a completely different entity', Trixie said.

'You could be a lot more political', Maria Scott said, implying that she and Trixie had discussed this previously. Maria and Trixie were acquainted outside the PSE class, because both were affiliated with the local AIDS group. 'Health services wouldn't approve of being political. You could be a lot more activist. As students, you can get away with it.'

'I'm attracted to controversial things', Trixie said. 'But I wouldn't want this to come down on the two of you [programme supervisors Laura and Maria]. Maybe you could just act as a steering committee.'

Maria said students have more luck changing policies than do professionals, citing student housing representatives' success in getting dormitory condom machines approved. If SHIN wanted to distribute condoms, however, it was 'sticky', Maria said, unless the group's members were all PSEs. The logic was apparently that PSEs in any context were 'experts', trained to use and distribute condoms.

After debating names like 'Sex' and 'Students Advocating Safer Sex Issues' the group called themselves 'Sexual Health Information Network'. They wanted a 'non-gendered' acronym – 'SHIN' – and agreed that a non-threatening name could attract more people. They wanted to reach those who did not get PSE programmes, whether due to schedule conflicts, living off-campus or through fear of group discussions.

The palatable, mainstream name with 'health' in it was the first of the group's many concessions. In keeping with student senate policies, they appointed officers and committee heads, in spite of their small size and desire to be egalitarian. Everyone was an officer or a committee head, but this did not equalize things. The president organized the schedule, arranged for meeting space and ran meetings. Appointed committee members had designated duties, such as public relations, making contacts in residence halls and programme development.

## Starting the group: becoming institutionally sanctioned

SHIN met on campus, in the student union of the institution whose approaches they sought to challenge. Initially, they met after class, to organize how to obtain official recognition. Once the student senate approved SHIN, core members emerged (Christine, Jill, Mike and Samantha; Debra, Ed and Carlin attended sporadically). Jennifer shepherded SHIN through the paperwork, then quit to run for student body president. She was ultimately much more interested in maintaining institutional powers and policies than in challenging them.

SHIN selected officers, in keeping with institutional mandates for funded campus groups. Debra agreed to be scribe; Jill, treasurer; and Mike, facilitator (president). Ed and Carlin volunteered to be the publicity committee. Perhaps recognizing that the group would not become an activist, subversive force, Trixie bowed out, saying that she could be an *ad hoc* 'information source', but she could not be truly involved.

Every activity SHIN envisioned needed the co-operation of campus entities, including the bus company, the student senate activities council and a dormitory. Like other campus groups (such as a political club), the student activities fund bankrolled SHIN. This fund came from fees paid by every student each quarter. Each SHIN member was essentially paying for the group's activities (while also paying to support other campus groups with less subversive goals). The university acted as treasurer and gate-keeper, ultimately determining which groups were funded.

None the less, Mike reiterated that SHIN was 'A student organization that could do things a bit more radical than what the PSEs could do, with no fallout on our advisers [Sorensen and Scott].' Mike had always felt constrained by the PSE policy of a disclaimer before every programme: 'As representatives of the health services, we advocate total abstinence as the safest sex.' He was the only PSE who departed from standard practice in his programmes – he talked openly about pleasure.

By the spring quarter, SHIN was meeting every Sunday evening. Most of their time was spent haggling over how to proceed – what kind of education to do and how and where to do it. Their goals for the spring quarter included a simple necessity – getting their name 'out to the public'. The members were surprised that I spent my Sunday evenings with them. They thought there was nothing interesting about what they were doing.

## SHIN's projects: winter quarter

SHIN members wanted to channel their 'activist concerns' into intervention and outreach that differed from the standard PSE programmes. They wanted to reach people who did not normally attend PSE programmes in dormitories or classes. Group members worked on three projects (during winter and spring quarters): informational placards on campus buses, a party/benefit at the local gay bar and a programme with the working title, 'How to Be a Better Lover'.

The idea for bus placards grew from the desire to reach students living off-campus. The campus bus service carried many students, including commuter students using satellite car parks and those travelling directly from their apartment complexes. The bus company regularly sold the space above the seats for announcements and advertisements. Everyone in SHIN was enthusiastic, citing examples of long bus rides with nothing to read, eyes searching for anything interesting to look at. But what would be printed on the bus cards? 'We should do brief, buzzword, soundbite kinds of things', said Mike, using the language of postmodern political image-makers. 'We don't want to have so much going on that no one reads them.'

Ed volunteered to talk to the bus company and find out how to get cards printed and distributed. Samantha volunteered to design the first group of cards, focused on acquaintance rape. The others chose topics: Jill, gay and lesbian issues; Debra, STDs and women and AIDS; Christine, contraception; Mike, safer sex.

Before the winter quarter had ended, SHIN had discussed their progress. Ed reported that the bus cards would cost $20 each time they were circulated on the buses. Businesses used the cards as a way to get inexpensive, wide-scale advertising, but at those rates, SHIN would only be able to make cards five times each quarter. The group thought of several ways to operationalize this. Mike suggested that each placard author write a short editorial, to be published in the independent student newspaper. The editorial would be published at the beginning of each bus 'campaign' and would relate to the topic addressed by the bus cards.

The other project SHIN began to develop in the winter was to host a party at a local gay bar. The night would include drinking, dancing and free condoms with a safer sex information card from SHIN. Mike volunteered to call condom companies, focusing on the company that had won the contract to stock the future dormitory machines. He hoped that the opportunity for relevant publicity would inspire the condom company to provide the condoms to SHIN free of charge.

No one in SHIN thought about the overall impact of these efforts in any significant way. Each strategy – bus cards, editorials and a party – had been utilized by other local groups. A local AIDS group had hosted parties and benefits at the gay club, the local rape crisis centre had bought space on the buses and individuals had written many editorials (including some protesting against the dormitory condom machines). It was unclear why the members of SHIN thought that any of these approaches were 'radical', as per the group's philosophy.

One radical suggestion, given that the audience was college students (85 per cent of whom are sexually active), was brushed aside. Carlin, who gave PSE programmes on 'intimacy without intercourse', asked why the group was doing nothing on abstinence, and Debra replied, 'Well, this is the "Sexual Health Information Network", so automatically, it's about sex . . . you know?'

## Spring quarter: nothing comes to fruition

Samantha opened the meeting by excitedly detailing the soundbites she had developed for her bus cards: 'Did you know that, legally, men cannot be raped?' and 'The average rapist rapes between 50 and 60 women before he is caught.' Samantha was a date-rape survivor and provided all the PSE programmes on rape. She also worked at the local rape crisis centre. She was very keen to get her cards onto the buses. All that remained now was for someone to design the card and submit the text, with payment, to the company which printed the cards.

No one discussed the implication of these cards, and what their connection was to acquaintance rape. What would the average reader do after digesting this information? Would the card about the number of women a 'rapist' rapes encourage a reader to view rape as something that (in reality) most often happens between acquaintances, or as something that a 'sick' minority of men do to strangers?

During this meeting, Mike broached the possibility of SHIN doing an 'interesting' programme, on sexual pleasure and techniques. The group was very excited by this idea. Samantha and Christine discussed whether they would be allowed to go into a dormitory and discuss how to be a better lover, in 'real', explicit terms. The dormitories were, on the whole, accustomed to PSE programmes, but none of these programmes specifically dealt with pleasure or doing 'technique a' with 'thing b' and 'part c'.

The possibility of moving beyond programmes with heavily factual, negatively consequential, health-related content was born. The week after Mike's suggestion, several members returned with more ideas about designing a programme on sexual pleasure and technique. Of all SHIN's projects, this programme was perhaps most closely related to their original (subversive) mandate: combining radical politics with activism, and using campus channels and resources to do so.

Each had a different idea about proceeding. Mike wanted to show excerpts from pornographic movies, to show techniques explicitly. Christine was more interested in informal discussion with programme participants, a sanctioned 'kiss and tell', where people described their best lovers and shared their techniques. Other SHIN members had no specific ideas, preferring to wait and wade through Mike and Christine's suggestions.

SHIN's programme-designing was hampered because nothing in their official curriculum had taught them how to design programmes. They also had no training specifically on 'sexual pleasure' or technique. Christine felt uncomfortable presenting herself as 'an expert' on sexual techniques. This would be the implied message if she addressed her peers, telling them how to put 'tab a' with 'slot b' in 'manner c'. Other SHIN members were worried about Mike's proposed approach as well. Samantha and Susan (the one non-PSE member, Samantha's room-mate) were wary of showing pornography, saying that it exploited women and was a 'male fantasy' of sex. At one point, they asked me what I thought.

'Do you want to risk getting arrested or seriously censured?' I said. 'Because I suspect that's the main risk you'd run if you showed explicit videos. Also, you might really offend some participants' sensibilities.' The policy on this was completely unclear. Mike said, 'But in my human sexuality class here, the professor showed some clips from these training videos, like the kind people buy from those upscale sex toy companies.' 'Did he get consent forms from you beforehand, or warn you somehow about what was going to happen?' I asked.

Mike did not remember what the professor had done. He asserted that similar clips, even from pornographic movies, would not offend someone who knowingly came to a programme on being a better lover (in other words, they would know what they were getting into before they arrived). But Mike wanted to present the programme in the lobby of one of the high-rise dormitories, to increase audience. He did not think that screening explicit sexual videos in such a public place would be problematic.

Beyond these sticky negotiations, SHIN had other planning difficulties. Mike thought SHIN members should present themselves as young Alex Comforts, offering tips, like *The Joy of Sex*, on how to improve sexual experiences. Christine was very uncomfortable with this idea, and again asked for my opinion. I said that being a good lover was more than the sum of its parts – that it was not as simple as knowing abstract techniques. I suggested they start planning by determining what their objectives were, and then design an effort that would meet those objectives.

While I was not surprised that SHIN asked my advice, I was in conflict about giving it. The footing was difficult: on one hand, I did not want to see SHIN get arrested or reprimanded for their actions, for violating university policies; on the other, I did not want to influence their behaviour or choices. But I could not plead programmatic ignorance when they questioned me, because all knew that I had led 'How to Be a Better Lover' programmes when I was a PSE.

Eventually, SHIN decided to combine some of a 'Sex and Self-Esteem' PSE programme with open discussion of technique-related activities (mostly connected to 'outercourse', oral sex and intercourse positions). Members wrote their goals for the first programme (listed verbatim):

1. Examine beliefs, attitudes, etc. that hinder good sex and try to think of attitudes that will reinforce good sex.
2. Examine whys in sex: why do you do it? why you don't? are you comfortable with sex and why or why not?
3. Figure out 'your' conditions for good sex and why.
4. Everyone is a sexual being. Piece your sexuality together in a positive way. Define.
5. Fantasies (why they're useful; they're okay to have).
6. We assume all sexual activity is OK, except with an unconsensual partner.
7. Put together a sourcebook (how to get help, think more about this).

The group wanted to accomplish these goals through various methods. Facilitators would depend heavily on do-it-yourself checklists and inventories, combined with audience participation. They considered the following: anatomy knowledge quizzes; a non-pornographic film clip;

agree/disagree statements; a discussion about masturbation; assumption statements about sexuality; and anonymous index cards with details about what makes sexual activities uncomfortable (related to attitudes, beliefs and expectations). By the time the group decided the content and object-ives, it was almost final exam study week.

The owner of the gay bar had offered to host a 'condom party' and to give some of the entry fee to SHIN, but Mike was unable to get any free condoms. No bus cards were ever printed or distributed. Attendance at SHIN meetings was low, with some members showing up for the first five minutes, reporting their lack of progress and then leaving. One week, only one person besides me attended.

A dorm had offered to promote the workshop on sexual pleasure while providing its lobby. One tentative date was cancelled because SHIN was unprepared. Rescheduling before finals week proved impossible, because of other commitments dorm personnel had made. Ultimately, the quarter and school year ended with no outward sign of SHIN's existence. The group had accomplished none of its plans, objectives or goals.

## Possibilities and changes

The peer sexuality educators in SHIN never did any radical, subversive education. They did nothing that outwardly challenged the university's policies on sexuality education in spite of the fact that SHIN developed because of policy constraints on PSE programme administrators. Can sexuality education challenge typical ideologies about such education, even when not provided by professionals and administrators? Szirom (1988, p. 56) argues that, 'Sex education as it is currently taught, rather than being a radical subject which challenges the status quo, in fact maintains the established order.' But can peer sexuality education become education that does not 'maintain the established [policies]'?

In an examination of sexuality education and policy issues in Britain and Europe, Meredith (1989, p. 3) quotes a sceptical sexuality education supporter: 'No sexually-liberating education can be provided within the context of what is in practice felt by many of its clients to be a repressive institution.' For PSEs, the 'repressive institution' is, in one sense, the university. Foucault asserts that specific knowledges are central to normal-izing social life and institutions, including the knowledges produced by, in and around education. The possibilities for new languages and challenges are innately constrained by 'institutional practices, power relations' (Ball,

1990). The possibilities for PSEs are restricted by the institutional and political contexts in which their efforts occur. PSEs are thus impeded from doing anything other than maintaining the *status quo*.

According to Szirom (1988, p. 134), '[Sexuality education] continues to maintain an "objective" or "value free" position, which neither examines such issues as power within relationships, nor the sociopolitical context in which such relationships occur'. Some might argue that peer educators can operate outside this context, producing knowledges devoid of the influence of official discourses and policies. But my case suggests that context is too central; SHIN was officially sanctioned, was subject to university policies for group formation and budgeting and was operating fully within institutional confines. Ultimately, SHIN challenged no policies, did nothing 'radical' in public.

In this case study, subversion did not happen on an institutional scale. SHIN accomplished nothing except the reinscription of certain health promotion discourses and other sexuality discourses (specifically, the libertarian 'pleasure is the answer'). The group began and faded without notice; no one on campus ever knew what SHIN was. Why?

There are two strands of answers: institutional constraints and individual constraints. Funded by student activity fees, approved by the student senate and forced to appoint committees and officers, SHIN was subject to institutional policies. Even as a subversive response to the PSE programme, SHIN occurred within the confines of this system. SHIN was organized by PSEs after their training into the discursive strategies of health promotion and sexuality education. These disciplinary and institutional constraints impeded both the PSEs and SHIN.

Ultimately, though, it is probably impossible for peers to educate outside the borders of the institution. The history of university peer education in the United States includes underground, illegal student efforts (in the 1960s and 1970s), which were quickly quashed by and/or reappropriated by administrators (Sloane and Zimmer, 1993). What the peer educators were doing and not doing, and could and could not do, is contextualized by individual constraints via socialization into sexuality – through education, peers, family, media and religion.

But subversion on a small, individual scale did happen. Some individuals bucked socialization by becoming PSEs in the first place. Although Foucault would argue that we have not been repressed in talking about sexuality, many of the PSEs describe parental sexual silences. For them, training to talk about sexuality (in public, no less) was subversive. For most of the PSEs, the most subversive act was discarding socialized heterosexism during training. Some had never met gays, lesbians or bisexuals before the class.

So what form would resistance to institutional policies take? In terms of sexuality, resistance might be a turning away, a renouncing. Resistance might be refusing to believe that 'sex' is a universal, that 'sex' is pleasure, that 'liberated sex' can exist. Resistance would be a form of atheism: 'I do not believe in sexual pleasure; it does not exist.'

There is no room for atheism in peer sexuality education. There is only room for truths. Perhaps PSE is flawed because it is not really about sexuality or 'sex'. It is about health, 'facts', and 'problems with solutions'. Peer sexuality education operates within this context but also outside this context. Ultimately, peer sexuality educators are object and subject simultaneously.

## References

Ball, S. J. (1990). 'Introducing Monsieur Foucault', in S. J. Ball (ed.), *Foucault and Education: Disciplines and Knowledge*. London: Routledge, pp. 1-10.

Brasseur, J. (1983). 'An anonymous peer counseling system for use with pregnant students', *Journal of American College Health*, **32**: 88.

Cohen, G., Byrne, C., Hay, J. and Schmuck, M. L. (1994). 'Assessing the impact of an interdisciplinary workshop in human sexuality', *Journal of Sex Education and Therapy*, **20**(1): 56–68.

Fennell, R. (1993). 'A review of evaluations of peer education programs', *Journal of American College Health*, **41**: 251–3.

Foucault, M. (1980). *Power/Knowledge: Selected Interviews and Other Writings 1972–1977*. New York: Pantheon.

Gingiss, P. L. and Hamilton, R. (1989). 'Teacher perspectives after implementing a human sexuality education program', *Journal of School Health*, **59**(10): 427–31.

Gould, J. M. and Lomax, A. R. (eds) (1993). 'The evolution of peer education: where do we go from here?' [Special issue], *Journal of American College Health*, **41**.

Meredith, P. (1989). *Sex Education: Political Issues in Britain and Europe*. London: Routledge.

Morris, R. W. (1994). *Values in Sexuality Education: A Philosophical Study*. Lanham, MD: University Press of America.

Pollis, C. A. (1986). 'Sensitive drawings of sexual activity in human sexuality textbooks: an analysis on communication and bias', *Journal of Homosexuality*, **13**(1): 59–73.

Sloane, B. C. and Zimmer, C. G. (1993). 'The power of peer health education', *Journal of American College Health*, **41**: 241–5.

Szirom, T. (1988). *Teaching Gender? Sex Education and Sexual Stereotypes*. Sydney, Australia: Allen & Unwin.

# 18

# 'Multicultural Does Not Mean Multisexual': Social Justice and the Interweaving of Ethnicity and Sexuality in Australian Schooling

*Maria Pallotta-Chiarolli*

## Mestizaje: the interweaving of 'lifeworlds'

> As people are simultaneously the members of multiple lifeworlds, so their identities have multiple layers, each layer in complex relation to the others ... We have to be proficient as we negotiate these many lifeworlds – the many lifeworlds each of us inhabit, and the many lifeworlds we encounter in our everyday lives. (Cope and Kalantzis, 1995, pp. 10–11)

This chapter will explore dilemmas, concerns and strategies in placing 'multiculturalism' on the 'multisexual' agenda and placing 'multisexuality' on the 'multicultural' agenda in Australian education. To what extent do Australian pedagogic discourses, school policies and programmes create or deny space for the realities that involve the crossing of ethnic, gender and sexual boundaries? In making Australian schools places of 'safety and social justice', as many policies declare, does this practice construct artificial homogeneity within categories such as NESB (non-English-speaking background), gay and lesbian, and a lack of interweaving between the categories?

Mestizaje theories, as expounded by Chicana cultural theorists of the United States such as Anzaldúa (1987) and Lugones (1994), and other post-colonial writers such as Trinh (1991), explore the interweaving of and the living on borders of sociocultural groupings based on ethnicity, gender, sexuality and other variables of personal identity. They attempt to articulate 'a reality that involves the crossing of an indeterminate number of borderlines, one that remains multiple in its hyphenation' (Trinh, 1991, p. 107). Mestizaje theories 'create new categories of identity for those left out or pushed out of existing ones' (McLaren, 1993a, p. 142). The border is a space where one can find 'an overlay of codes, a multiplicity of culturally incribed subject positions, a displacement of normative reference codes, and a polyvalent assemblage of new cultural meanings' (McLaren, 1993b, p. 121; see also Trinh, 1991). Using the metaphor of egg white and egg yolk, Lugones (1994) explains the positions of *metissage* or *mestizaje*. The intention of separation and classification is to separate the white from the yolk, to split the egg into two parts as cleanly as one can. She adopts *mestizaje* as a name for the impurity of living within many worlds and the ensuing interlocked, intermeshed oppressions such as those of racism, sexism and heterosexism:

I think of the attempt at control exercised by those who possess both power and the categorical eye and who attempt to split everything impure, breaking it down into pure elements (as in egg white and egg yolk) for the purposes of control ... Mestizaje defies control through simultaneously asserting the impure, curdled multiple state and rejecting fragmentation into pure parts. (Lugones, 1994, p. 460)

Thus, impurity and intermixture can be powerful sites of resistance and political activism (see also Bhabha, 1990).

These theories are very useful in framing educational policies, programmes and practices as they examine human chameleons, individuals with multiple identities and/or mixed cultural backgrounds, positioning them as sites of confluence and intermixture, rather than as having to assimilate to one 'world' at the expense of another, nor 'intersecting' within oneself two or more neat and homogenous 'worlds' with distinct chasms between them. Mestizaje theories acknowledge the differences *within* as well as *between* categories and the word 'interweaving' presents a more apt metaphor of fluidity, boundary-blurring and the diversity of strategies individuals use to negotiate, manoeuvre and resist the codes and identities of various categories.

## Australian educational policies in relation to ethnicity and gender

Since the early 1980s in Australia, educational materials and policies have been produced which acknowledge that being of non-English-speaking background does not mean being split or torn between two worlds, but means negotiating and drawing upon the many to inform the one, being able to live in many worlds within the one, being aware of the interweaving of many categories such as ethnicity, gender and class rather than construct an artificial research model and educational practice where categories are dealt with as separate and not impinging upon or being influenced by the others (see Angelico, 1989; Ministry of Education, 1989; Sloniec, 1992a, 1992b). The work of educationists such as Tsolidis (1986) interweaving ethnicity, class and gender, and of Connell (1995) in relation to homophobia, masculinities and class, have provided theoretical frameworks and extensive data for the development of national and state educational policies and practices for social justice (see also Gilbert and Gilbert, 1994, 1995).

However, despite the pedagogical discourses of social justice, access and equity for all students to all educational resources, and inclusive curricula used in all government and independent religious school policies to frame curriculum and student welfare programmes and practices, the interweaving of *sexuality* with categories such as ethnicity, gender and class is largely lacking. Australia requires educational research such as the exploration of sexuality, race and masculinity undertaken by Mac an Ghaill (1994) in British schools, and more personal accounts of growing up mestiza as in the poetry of Chinese–American bisexual Colligan (1991). Examples of inclusivity that incorporate sexuality are also required, such as the London school reported by Patrick and Sanders that holds assemblies to mark 'International Women's Day, Martin Luther King's birthday, May Day, Nelson Mandela's release from prison and Lesbian and Gay Pride Week' (1994, p. 119).

There appear to be three approaches – exclusion, indirect incorporation, direct and specific incorporation – none of which attempts directly to address this mestizaje or multiple lifeworlds of students which incorporates the diversity of sexualities.

1. *Exclusion*: Sexuality, homophobia and heterosexism are deliberately excluded from a list of social and personal development curriculum and student welfare concerns.

One recent example of this is the *Equity in Schooling* policy from the Department of Education and the Arts (1995), Tasmania, which states that 'In a fair and egalitarian society in which all people are considered to have equal worth and equal rights, a commitment to principles of educational equity is essential' (1995, p. 7). It explains that schools 'should provide a learning environment that is free from harassment, bias and discriminatory practices and one that promotes personal respect and physical and emotional safety' (1995, p. 9). It then proceeds clearly and in great detail to discuss the 'target groups' in separate categories with some reference to the blurring of boundaries between these categories in many students' lives. The 'target groups' are: Aboriginal, Disabilities, NESB (non-English-speaking background/ethnicity), Poverty, Geographical Isolation, At Risk (e.g., homelessness, victims of child abuse, teenage mothers), Gender.

Sexuality and homophobia do not appear anywhere in this 84-page document. Given that only in late April 1997 has the Upper House voted that all laws penalizing sex between men be removed from Tasmania's legal system after a nine-year campaign which involved the United Nations, Amnesty International, the Australian Federal Government and High Court, this exclusion is hardly surprising but is already being contested (see Studdert, 1997).

A second example is *ESL (English as a Second Language) Provision Within a Culturally Inclusive Curriculum Guidelines* from the Catholic Education Office (1997), Melbourne. This states that 'culture' is meant to be interpreted broadly 'to include not only concepts of race and ethnicity, but also to take account of the range of intersecting elements that shape cultural identity including gender, class, religious background, socio-economic status, age, ability and disability' and that all 'individuals are simultaneously members of many overlapping social and/or cultural groups and there is as much diversity *within* social and/or cultural groups as there is *between* them' (1997, p. 10).

Sexuality and homophobia do not appear anywhere in this 112-page document. From my work with some of the educators responsible for producing this policy and guidelines, it appears that they are often aware of the exclusions, are often uncomfortable with the exclusions, but feel real and/or imagined surveillance, regulation and possible punishment from a panopticonic educational and/or religious institution within which they work.

2. *Indirect incorporation*: The policy, usually directly addressing gender issues, is worded in such a way as to be open to interpretation and use as including homosexuality, homophobia and heterosexism. However, this is never explicitly stated in order not to antagonize those in power who may be homophobic and possibly sabotage the whole policy.

An example of what could be called 'inclusion by omission' is the *Gender and Equity Policy* from the South Australian Catholic Commission for Catholic Schools (1992). Directly addressing guidelines for implementing gender reform, the Policy refers to the framing 'Gospel values (love, justice and reconciliation)' that require Catholic educators to 'demonstrate the equality, dignity and full humanity of each person' and 'promote each person's gifts and talents, foster self-esteem and self-acceptance' (1992, p. 4). As the Gender and Equity Officer at the time responsible for developing and implementing the Policy in consultation with a Working Party of principals, parents and Catholic Education Office administrators, I was aware of how many educators assumed issues of racism and homophobia would also be addressed within this policy. However, because of homophobic reactions coming from some school and Church Office administrators who refused to support the Policy if it was seen to 'promote homosexuality', it was left to individual schools to determine to what extent the Policy would be interpreted as inclusive of homophobia in relation to masculinities and gender issues.

Within this non-specific inclusivity, the application of mestizaje interweaving is not addressed.

3. *Direct and specific incorporation*: The policy directly and specifically addresses homophobia as an issue to be addressed in schools. The national *Gender and Equity: A Framework For Australian Schools* from the Ministerial Council for Employment, Education, Training and Youth Affairs (MCEETYA) (1996), and the Specific Focus Programs Directorate of the New South Wales Department of School Education (1996) *Girls and Boys at School: Gender Equity Strategy 1996–2001* are significant steps forward in their situating sexuality and homophobia alongside other categories throughout the documents.

*Gender and Equity: A Framework for Australian Schools* states that understandings of gender construction 'should include knowledge about the relationship of gender to other factors, including socio-economic status, cultural background, rural/urban location, disability and sexuality' (1997, p. 8). Although it should have been given a section unto itself alongside other specific groupings such as Aboriginality, disability and ethnicity to illustrate its equal importance, homophobia is addressed in several sections of the *Framework*, particularly in relation to hegemonic masculinity, and to violence in schools.

Similarly, *Girls and Boys at School* states that societal beliefs about gender, 'interacting with factors such as ethnicity, Aboriginal and Torres Strait Islander cultures, socio-economic status, sexuality and disability, can be linked to patterns of girls' and boys' participation in education and to their post-school outcomes' (1996, p. 2). It also specifically asks schools to consider what 'mechanisms are in place to ensure staff and students recognise sex-based harassment, homophobia, bullying and other forms of violence, treat it seriously and actively work towards its elimination' (1996, p. 5).

Again, these policies raise awareness of the interconnectedness of many sociocultural categories although still dealing with the issues separately rather than developing mestizaje awareness and strategies.

## Interweaving sexualities with ethnicities and genders

As the above policies and guidelines illustrate, Australian classrooms have become locations for the exploration of ethnic and gender sociocultural constructs involving the deconstruction of and resistance to racism, ethnocentrism and sexism (e.g. Sloniec, 1992a; 1992b). Non-heterosexual sexualities and homophobia are also finally beginning to be acknowledged and addressed in some Australian schooling systems as significant components of schools' social justice and equity frameworks (Pallotta-Chiarolli, 1995a). As I have said, my concern with much of this practice, including my own, is its construction of artificial homogeneity within the categories and a lack of what I call 'interweaving' between the categories (Pallotta-Chiarolli, 1996a, 1996b).

As Trinh writes:

Multiculturalism does not lead us very far if it remains a question of difference only between one culture and another ... To cut across boundaries and borderlines is to live aloud the malaise of categories and labels; it is to resist simplistic attempts at classifying; to resist the comfort of belonging to a classification. (1991, pp. 107–8)

In other words, identity may still be defined as signifying only *one* label, *one* category. Thus, an individual may be perceived to be *only* Italian, or *only* a woman or *only* gay, depending upon which social context the person is located at a particular point in time. Hence, in our educational policies and programmes, we may be addressing only racism *or* sexism *or* homophobia without finding ways of exploring the lived realities of our multicultural society of combinations of racism *and* sexism *and* homophobia. How can we overcome this splitting through classification?

In relation to gay, lesbian and bisexual students from culturally diverse backgrounds, multicultural and inclusive education policies and programmes need to develop a greater awareness of socioculturally constructed boundaries and borderlines in relation to gender and sexuality by considering the following:

- what is the *range* of knowledges, assumptions and expectations within a particular ethnic culture in relation to gender and sexuality?
- what is the *range* of assumptions and expectations about gender and sexuality among diverse ethnic cultures uncomfortably lumped together as non-English-speaking background, and often presented as in total opposition to the other uncomfortable classification of Anglo-Australian?
- how do children born into these cultures live out their realities and make their decisions about gender and sexuality?
- how do we engage students in literacy practices and other learning strategies that provide access to debates and examples of a *range* of lived realities of gender and sexuality that incorporate ethnic diversity without resorting to the 'poor little ethnic kid' cultural deficit paradigm which can alienate and silence students?
- as educators, how can we utilize existing texts and call for a greater *range* of representations of gender and sexuality issues in culturally diverse texts, in media representations of ethnicity and of course the incorporation of a diversity of ethnicity–gender–sexuality issues into mainstream texts and representations?

In two recent Australian anthologies on multicultural writing, one of them specifically about ethnicity and gender, my contributions have been the only ones addressing non-heterosexual sexualities. They are now being used in some schools (Pallotta-Chiarolli, 1992, 1994). My own books were two of the first to address ethnicity and homosexuality (Pallotta-Chiarolli,

1991, 1998). In two recent significant Australian anthologies for adolescents and young adults on gay, lesbian and bisexual sexualities, there is minimal writing about cultural diversity (Macleod, 1996; Pausacker, 1996). Australian writers for adolescents and young adults need to be encouraged to explore the crossing of borderlines and expanding of boundaries in relation to ethnicity, sexuality and gender. One such novel, *Loaded*, by Christos Tsiolkas (1995), a day in the life of a Melbournian 19-year-old 'queer' young man of Greek background, has achieved much success among young adult readers, although it has been criticized by some readers and teachers of non-English-speaking backgrounds for its perpetuation of the 'poor little ethnic gay boy' stereotype.

## Strategies and guidelines for mestizaje practice in Australian schools

I will now briefly outline some guidelines and strategies for how the interweaving of ethnicity, gender and sexuality can be addressed in curriculum programming and teaching practice. Based on Pam Gilbert and Rob Gilbert's (1994) four flaws with the cultural conflict/deficit model's situating students into categories of 'disadvantage' according to constructs such as ethnicity and gender, I have constructed five strategies that seem to frame usefully the development of policies, programmes and practices through an informed approach to diversity and multiplicity in our student populations. Many educators seem to believe that the way to deal with ethnicity and sexuality has to be somehow extremely different, extremely unheard of, extremely difficult, as contrasted to strategies used to engage students with other sociocultural issues. Many of these strategies are the same basic pedagogic, critical awareness and critical literacy skills used in other social studies and minority group studies.

*Intracategory heterogeneity*
This means avoiding the disguising or denying of intragroup and individual experience through homogenizing practices such as stereotyping and essentialism. Students can be presented with a diversity of lived realities within and between communities and individual identities based on ethnicity, gender and sexuality, and the impossibility of making universal statements that will summarize the experiences of all members of a particular group such as an ethnic group or sexuality group (Wille, 1995; Pallotta-Chiarolli, 1998).

Pettman (1992) states that categories and boundaries need to be contested without denying the validity of identities based on shared experiences and common social location, and the discursive power of individuals to challenge such situatedness. Hence, it is racist and ethno-centric to dismiss whole ethnic communities as homophobic without acknowledging the diversity and the significance of other factors apart from ethnicity that encourage homophobia among NESB people in Australia (Pallotta-Chiarolli, 1992; 1995c). Likewise, as part of this encouraging of students to think beyond homogenizing categories, it is important that our discussions of sexuality are also not limited to the heterosexual/homosexual oppositional discourse but consider issues such as bisexuality, transgenderism and sexual fluidity.

Matteo, a gay man of Italian background, is a character in *Someone You Know* who explores the successful interweaving of ethnicity, gender and sexuality in his personal identity, albeit at the cost of having chosen not to come out to his parents.

> It's harder for gay men and lesbians from Italian backgrounds to come out. I love my parents and don't want to hurt them. I say things like 'Of course I'll get married one day, I'm just waiting for the right girl.' How can two old people who'd need to have the word 'homosexual' explained to them ever come to terms with their gay child? They'd think it was something we'd picked up from Australian friends. They've lived through poverty, war, hunger. They come to a country where they have to start again in everything. They make a thousand sacrifices for the kids they cherish. After all that, I haven't got it in me to break their hearts. (Pallotta-Chiarolli, 1991, p. 23)

Students can discuss the impact of the following on his parents: a lack of education and familiarity with sexual diversity, war, poverty and migra-tion, and constructions of gender role in relation to masculinity.

Some migrant parents need to be portrayed as non-homophobic in order to represent the diversity within any ethnic group:

> I would often stand back and watch my parents talking to Jon and Kevin over the front fence, their cheerful voices carrying across the road . . . My father discussed his vineyard and winemaking with Jon, an interested listener, unlike his own children, who wouldn't drink his wine . . . My mother would invite them to come over any time and take

eggs from the chickens because her daughter rarely cooked decent meals and they'd rot. (Pallotta-Chiarolli, 1991, pp. 23–4)

*Interweaving of categories*
This includes drawing attention to the relationships between various conditions and constructs such as ethnicity, class, gender, sexuality, religion, geographical location and education.

The poem 'Conversations with My Grandmama', by Annie Ling (1992) provides a powerful and positive example for students of the experiences of belonging to many 'worlds'. The title of Ling's anthology is *Mei Tze Is Also My Name*, indicative of her claiming of her Chinese–Malaysian identity alongside her Chinese–Australian identity. She transcends both the traditional world of her grandparents in Sibu, Malaysia, and the Chinese–Australian world of her parents in Sydney, Australia. Simultaneously, she claims her dowry, 'I want my gold as in Chinese tradition', and talks about her 'lesbian existence'. She challenges her grandmother's gender and lesbian constructs and challenges Western society's constructs of ethnicity, gender and lesbian sexuality. She draws from all sociocultural constructions to devise a multiple or mestizaje identity that cuts through any stereotype of homogeneity within any one category. She can connect across time, geography and cultures to voice her particular identities with both her significant and societal others.

Students can be asked to 'map' Annie Ling/Mei Tze's identity and list the influences of history, geographical location, language, cultural traditions, 'urban' lifestyles and 'modern' concerns such as HIV/AIDS. Students can also 'map' the different 'selves' of the character: the 'self' of the first (ethnic)culture, the 'self' of the second (Australian) culture, the gendered 'self', the lesbian 'self', the 'self' in grand/parent–child relationship, the adult 'self' in love and friendships. What are the expectations of the different 'worlds' and 'codes'? Where are the points of connection and points of conflict?

Similarly, in a short story called 'Lesbos' which interweaves three generations of women in a Greek family both in Greece and Australia, Karaminas (1998) interrogates the multiple meanings of 'Lesbos' and 'Lesbians' that interweave in the understanding of her own sexual, ethnic and gender identity. These include: Lesbos as island, Lesbos as home of ancient Greek lesbian poet Sappho, Lesbos as a late-twentieth-century tourist attraction for international lesbians, Lesbos as an industrial centre, Lesbos as the site for Greek–Australian lesbians and Greek diasporic lesbians to reclaim a cultural ancestry and identity, Lesbians as inhabitants of Lesbos, lesbians as a sexual and political identity.

*Connecting marginalities*

This means making links between many forms of prejudice and oppresson such as racism, sexism and heterosexism/homophobia under a common framework of equity, social justice and personal development.

As the MCEETYA (1996) and Specific Focus Programs Directorate (1996) policies illustrate, anti-heterosexism needs to be included and incorporated into existing policies, practices and perceptions alongside anti-racism and anti-sexism. We need to encourage students to situate homophobia within the parameters of human experience of oppression and marginalization rather than positioning these prejudices as outside or deviant from the 'usual' prejudices and thus being able to detach them-selves from these 'alien' people (Misson, 1995).

*Me Mum's a Queer* by Catherine Johns is about an Adelaide girl, Manny, who decides to tell her schoolfriends that her mum is a lesbian. The consequences of Manny's decision provide ample material for con-necting the landscapes of marginality as the similarities between racism, sexism and homophobia are clearly presented through the characters from diverse cultural backgrounds. Manny's Aboriginal friend, Joanne, says to her:

> Now you got somethin' to stick up for and fight for too, eh? . . . Well, I've taken all sorts of shit all me life too. Boong this, and Abo that, . . . I guess you're lucky that your mum ain't a black lesbian. (1994, p. 45)

Although meticulously striving for such balance in most of the text, the ethnic family of the Greek–Australian boy Milos is constructed as sexist and homophobic, and there is no other ethnic representation to counter-pose this. Stereotypes such as arrranged marriages, the housebound, unhappy Greek mother ignorant of contraception and of the English language, are presented without alternative images presented alongside. Nevertheless, these ethnic stereotypes are useful in giving students posi-tions from which to consider and research alternative realities within the category 'Greek–Australian'. It may also be a useful exercise in illustrating how challenging one prejudice in a text may be counteracted by the possible perpetuation of another.

In the NSW Department of School Education (1993) video kit *MATES* about HIV/AIDS and homophobia, the leading highly respected and popular male figure who has to come to terms with his friend's homosexuality and possible HIV-positive status is Vietnamese. An example that would be very useful with students in connecting anti-racism and anti-homophobia occcurs when Tran comforts his younger sister who has been racially harassed at school for being Vietnamese. In explaining the causes of racism to her, he makes the connection to his homophobic harassment of Steve, and remembers the taunting he received as a young child because of his ethnicity.

*Contextualization*
This renders definitions, identities and sociocultural values and attitudes as in constant processes of shifting and fluxing rather than static by exploring diverse historical and international sociocultural constructions of gender and sexuality.

It is important to explore the impact of migration on attitudes in regard to gender roles and non-heterosexual sexualites. Encouraging students to interview parents and conduct family projects can assist in opening communication at home and for students to understand the background to parental attitudes and behaviours which may seem 'strange' if viewed only from the context of Anglo-Australian or Western culture.

Students can be asked to consider whether because a prejudice or exploitation is 'common' or 'accepted' in Australian society, it automatically means that it is 'normal' or 'all right'. They can draw a line between two points designated as 'normal' or 'queer' and map where various prejudices were 100 years ago, 50 years ago, 20 years ago, today and at various predicted points in the future. For example, to be racist was considered quite 'normal' and 'acceptable' 100 years ago in Australia but not so today. What about sexism? Homophobia? Classism? Australian history and data, such as the support of the 'White Australia Policy' of the early 1900s, the gradual development of multicultural attitudes and policies, equal opportunity policies and the women's movement, and the development of indigenous policies in relation to shifting attitudes to racism, are useful in illustrating historical processes and shifting sociocultural and political constructions (e.g. Richards, 1988; Castles *et al.*, 1992; Pettman, 1992). Providing cross-cultural anthropological, historical, religious and cultural codes and meanings in relation to sexualities allows students to have a broader base of knowledge within which to situate contemporary Western, Christian constructions and to acknowledge the shifting qualities of sociocultural constructs based on concerns such as political power, economics and adaptation (e.g. Ratti, 1993; Lim-Hing, 1994).

*Self-ascription and personal agency*
This means to acknowledge the subjective perceptions, definitions and agency of the persons who have been assigned labels and slotted into categories, and their efforts at negotiation through ongoing and shifting processes of resistance, compliance and transcendence. We need to ensure that we are presenting persons of NESB as not only end products of various political, cultural and social processes, thereby rendered solely as passive victims, but also as having various amounts of agency, such as resisting, negotiating, manipulating borders and boundaries, and identifying and claiming spaces (Pallotta-Chiarolli, 1992; 1995a; 1996b).

Two very powerful examples of Australian adolescent school students of non-English-speaking backgrounds who are publicly resisting the homophobic harassment they have been subjected to in their schools are heralding in a new phase in Australia of student and parental anti-homophobic activism. Both cases also reflect the impact of Australia's multicultural and immigration policies of the last 40 years in producing a generation of adolescents born to migrant parents and negotiating their multiple lifeworlds, resisting external racist and homophobic ascriptions which they perceive as linked, and claiming their particular mestizaje spaces within their schools and within the wider Australian society.

This interweaving of multicultural and multisexual realities as end products of historical and political forces and policies has resulted in a situation of great historical relevance in Australia in its pioneering successful legal challenge to homophobic vilification in schools. This confluence is embodied in Christopher Tsakalos, a 14-year-old student from a Greek background and identifying as gay, who has made national and international headlines as well as appearing with his mother, Vicky Tsakalos, on Australian television programmes such as *Sixty Minutes* in a segment entitled 'Pride and Prejudice' (23 March 1997).

At a meeting on 19 March 1997 with the New South Wales Assistant-Minister of Education, George Green, and attended by members of GALTAS (Gay and Lesbian Teachers and Students Association), Ms Tsakalos clearly explained that she likened the homophobic harassment her son was receiving to the racist harassment she had received as a child migrant in Australian schools in the early 1960s. However, she and her family had felt powerless to challenge the school's blatant mono-culturalism and silent condonement of the harassment due to their poverty, poor English language skills and unfamiliarity with legal and educational policies and student rights. By contrast, Ms Tsakalos had approached GALTAS to assist her three-year demand that the NSW Education Department live up to its anti-homophobic policies because she did not want her son to continue to experience the powerlessness she had felt as a child and which had already resulted in three suicide attempts by Christopher. She insisted in the meeting and in subsequent media inter-views that what had been achieved in relation to anti-racism in schools needed to be replicated in relation to anti-homophobia. She and her son could not see any differences between the types of harassment Christopher had been subjected to and racist harassment except in the different labels by which such violent behaviours were classified.

Over the next couple of weeks, mainstream media and the gay media documented the daily progress of this pioneering legal action against Christopher's school for failure to protect him against extreme anti-gay vilification, including death threats and violent assaults (e.g. Passey, 1997; Pollard, 1997a). His victory in the Supreme Court on 11 April was the successful end of the first case of its kind in Australia, establishing a precedent for school liability for gay students who are vilified under their care.

This activism was immediately taken up by more parents and students in New South Wales, such as the family of James Brilley suing the Catholic Education Office in Sydney for two years of homophobic abuse while attending a single-sex boys' school, resulting in suicide attempts and psychiatric treatment (Pollard, 1997b). This case is also challenging the Catholic Education Office's exemption from the NSW Anti-Discrimination Act which covers homosexual vilification and discrimination.

Simultaneously, in Victoria, a 16-year-old gay student from a highly respected single-sex Catholic boys' school wrote a letter to the Melbourne-based gay and lesbian newspaper *BrotherSister* and signed it 'Angry VCE [Victorian Certificate of Education] Student'. He explained he had been taking action at his school with 'lay staff and ministers and chaplains . . . to stand up for who I am and my society of people, and to do something about the current level of homophobia' (1997, p. 7). He had named his activism the 'Campaign Eradicating Homophobia' and it included writing in school publications and organizing a student group within the school. His letter ended with 'I urge that people like me in high school start taking some sort of action' (1997, p. 7).

Upon my contacting him, 'Luciano' told me he was from an Italian background and his 'Campaign' had the full support of his parents. His responses in an interview with me in relation to his ethnicity, gender and sexuality clearly express mestizaje understandings and comfort in his multiple lifeworlds:

> I'm not just Italian, and I'm not just gay. I have had people tell me 'You're Italian and you're gay? Why are you still alive?' . . . people say that being Italian and gay is pretty much asking to be crucified. I just laugh at stupid comments as these . . . I will not give up my ethnicity, nor my sexuality, because of stereotyping . . . I love my big family. I especially love the friendly and casual atmosphere . . . and the way we are so 'cultural' . . . also our food of course.

He believes there are similarities between his Italian family and the 'gay scene'. Both are 'fun', both are places where people 'stick together' and 'stand up for their rights and for what they believe in'. He feels that racial discrimination toward him has decreased at school over the years as 'a lot of people see it as "cool" to be Italian'.

'Luciano' is aware of particular factors he believes have contributed to his parents' understanding of his sexuality. They are relatively young and well educated, and in professional careers. They are not as traditionally Catholic as some other Italian families he knows, and this means they are not significantly affected by Church views on homosexuality.

'Luciano' intends to increase his political activsim, demanding anti-homophobic policies and programmes in Catholic and state Victorian schools through his own 'Campaign' and membership to Context, a gay and lesbian teachers' group to which he intends to introduce student activism. Likewise, his mother has begun attending P-Flag (Parents, Family and Friends of Lesbians and Gays) to support her son further and undertake public activism with other parents.

## 'Multicultural *does* mean multisexual'

The above two examples of resistance to homophobic harassment in schools by non-English-speaking background students and their families, either in response to the inadequate implementation of existing policies as in the NSW Department of School Education, or in calling for the development of policies as in the Catholic Education system of Victoria, reveal how culturally diverse persons can connect racist and heterosexist discrimination as well as live mestizaje lives that interweave categories such as ethnicity and sexuality.

Young people of diverse sexualities and diverse cultures are cultural negotiators. Schools and teachers can act as cultural mediators between student and family/community, student and mainstream society and student and social services/organizations/community groups that cater for their ethnic, gender and sexual identities. At the time of writing, Australia is witnessing both confluence and conflict as the end products of historical forces and policies in relation to multiculturalism and homosexuality are beginning new inscriptions and resistances to long-standing discriminatory institutions such as education and Church.

Thus, while Pauline Hanson, herself an end product of feminist activism for women's equal participation in politics and the rights of single mothers, launches and promotes her One Nation political party which is blatantly racist and homophobic, such as calling for the end of Asian immigration to Australia and a reinstatement of homosexuality as 'unnatural' and 'abnormal', she is being challenged by second-generation non-English-speaking background academics and activists such as Dr Andrew Jakubowicz (1996–97) of Polish–Jewish background and a lesbian of Chinese background, Dr Happy Ho (1997). Likewise, migrants and their lesbian, bisexual and gay descendants such as Ling, Karaminas, Tsiolkas, Tsakalos and 'Luciano' are coming forth/coming out as key agents in eroding long-standing exclusions and silences in relation to multicultural multisexuality in Australian institutions such as education.

Educators can play vital roles in encouraging this recognition and emergence of multiplaced persons in educational policies and programmes. Our education systems are responsible for and accountable to students in accessing resources, knowledges and skills to negotiate their multiple 'lifeworlds'. And an important component of this learning is education that is *not* undertaken within an exclusionary, homogenizing and assimilative model that denies and separates. To continue to ignore the relevance and importance of the interweaving of sexuality and ethnicity is to continue to allow lesbian, gay, bisexual and transgender students of non-English-speaking backgrounds in Australia to suffer from silence, isolation and verbal, emotional, psychological and physical violence, or, as in the case of Christopher Tsakalos and 'Luciano' and their families, it is to launch bravely their own activism with minimal systemic support and thus deal with the added harassment and vulnerability of public and school community scrutiny and vilification.

As educators failing to mobilize within our systems we are standing back and allowing the lived multiple realities of members of our schools to be excluded, distorted and trivialized, even while as educators we participate in our systems' hypocritical engagement in the discourses of anti-discrimination, equal opportunity, pedagogic responsibility.

> as long as the complexity and difficulty of engaging with the diversely hybrid experiences of heterogenous contemporary societies are denied and not dealt with, ... the creative interval is dangerously reduced to non-existence. (Trinh, 1991, p. 229)

## Acknowledgements

Some of this material forms part of my PhD thesis. My gratitude to the support of my supervisors, Dr Jeannie Martin and Dr Andrew Jakubowicz. Also, my ongoing appreciation to the many friends and colleagues who allow me to tell their stories, such as Matteo, and of course to Jon who is still teaching with me. My thanks also to Mei Tze for access to her writing. I also wish to thank 'Luciano' and his family, and Christopher and Vicky Tsakalos, for giving me the privilege of supporting their pioneering actions. And my appreciation to teachers and students, including my own, who have discussed or written to me about their approaches, ideas and strategies. Finally, my ongoing appreciation to the personal and professional support and encouragement of Michelle Rogers, Wayne Martino, Alan Stafford and Robert Chiarolli.

## References

Angelico, Teresa (1989). 'In search of "wholeness"', Diversity, 7(1): 8–10. Melbourne: Catholic Education Office.

Angry VCE Student (1997). 'Generation why?', BrotherSister, 20 March, p. 7.

Anzaldúa, Gloria (1987). Borderlands/LaFrontera: The New Mestiza. San Francisco: Spinsters/Aunt Lute.

Bhabha, Homi (1990). 'The third space', in J. Rutherford (ed.), Identity: Community, Culture, Difference. London: Lawrence & Wishart.

Castles, Stephen, Cope, Bill, Kalantzis, Mary and Morrissey, Stephen (1992). *Mistaken Identity: Multiculturalism and the Demise of Nationalism in Australia.* Sydney: Pluto Press.

Colligan, Sharon Hwang (1991). 'One ... ', in L. Hutchins and L. Kaahumanu (eds), *Bi Any Other Name.* Boston: Alyson Publications.

Connell, B. (1995). *Masculinities.* Sydney: Allen & Unwin.

Cope, Bill and Kalantzis, Mary (1995). 'Why literacy pedagogy has to change', *Education Australia*, **30**: 8–11.

Department of Education and the Arts (1995). *Equity in Schooling.* Hobart, Tasmania: DEA.

ESL (English as a Second Language) Education Officers (1997). *ESL Provision Within a Culturally Inclusive Curriculum.* Melbourne: Catholic Education Office.

Gilbert, Rob and Gilbert, Pam (1994). 'Discourse and disadvantage: studying the gender dimensions of educational disadvantage'. Paper presented to the Annual Conference of the Australian Association for Research in Education, Newcastle, 27 November–1 December.

Gilbert, Rob and Gilbert, Pam (1995). *What's Going On? Girls' Experiences of Educational Disadvantage.* Canberra: DEET.

Harris, Simon (1990). *Lesbian and Gay Issues in the English Classroom.* Buckingham and Philadelphia: Open University Press.

Ho, Happy (1997). 'The Hanson factor', *Sydney Star Observer: Gay and Lesbian Community Weekly Newspaper*, **352**, 1 May, p. 14.

Jakubowicz, Andrew (1996–97). 'Fear and loathing in Ipswich: exploring the "race debate" in contemporary Australia', *Australian Rationalist*, **42**: 6–13.

Johns, Catherine (1994). *Me Mum's a Queer.* Stirling, South Australia: Epona Press.

Karaminas, Vicki (1998). 'Lesbos', in M. Pallotta-Chiarolli (ed.), *Girls Talk: Young Women Speak Their Hearts and Minds.* Lane Cove, Sydney: Finch Publishing.

Lim-Hing, Sharon (ed.) (1994). *The Very Inside: An Anthology of Writing by Asian and Pacific Islander Lesbian and Bisexual Women.* Toronto: SisterVision Press.

Ling, Annie (1992). *Mei Tze Is Also My Name.* Sydney: PMT Publishing.

Lugones, Maria (1994). 'Purity, impurity, and separation', *Signs: Journal of Women in Culture and Society*, **19**(2): 458–79.

Mac an Ghaill, Mairtin (1994). '(In)visibility: sexuality, race and masculinity in the school context', in D. Epstein (ed.), *Challenging Lesbian and Gay Inequalities in Education.* Buckingham: Open University Press.

McLaren, Peter(1993a). 'Multiculturalism and the postmodern critique: towards a pedagogy of resistance and transformation', *Cultural Studies*, **1**: 118–43.

McLaren, Peter (1993b). 'White terror and oppositional agency: towards a critical multiculturalism', *Strategies*, 7: 119–33.

Macleod, Mark (ed.) (1996) *Ready or Not: Stories of Young Adult Sexuality*. Milsons Point, Sydney: Random House.

Ministerial Council for Employment, Training and Youth Affairs (MCEETYA) Gender Equity Taskforce (1996). *Gender Equity: A Framework for Australian Schools*. Canberra: Department of Education and Training (DEET).

Ministry of Education (1989). *Equal Opportunity for Girls in Education*. Melbourne: Victorian Ministry of Education.

Misson, Ray (1995). 'Dangerous lessons: sexuality issues in the English classroom', *English in Australia*, 112 (July): 25–32.

New South Wales Department of School Education (1993). *Mates*. Sydney: Health Media for the New South Wales Department of School Education.

Pallotta-Chiarolli, Maria (1991). *Someone You Know: A Friend's Farewell*. Adelaide: Wakefield Press.

Pallotta-Chiarolli, Maria (1992). 'What about me? A study of lesbians of Italian background', in K. Herne, J. Travaglia and E. Weiss (eds), *Who Do You Think You Are? Writings by Second Generation Immigrant Women in Australia*. Sydney: Women's Redress Press.

Pallotta-Chiarolli, Maria (1994). 'Roses', in P. Moss (ed.), *Voicing the Difference*. Adelaide: Wakefield Press.

Pallotta-Chiarolli, Maria (1995a). 'Only your labels split me: interweaving ethnicity and sexuality in English studies', *English in Australia*, 112: 33–44.

Pallotta-Chiarolli, Maria (1995b). ' "Can I write the word GAY in my essay?": challenging homophobia in single sex boys' schools', in R. Browne and R. Fletcher (ed.), *Boys in Schools: Addressing the Issues*. Lane Cove, Sydney: Finch Publishing.

Pallotta-Chiarolli, Maria (1995c). ' "A rainbow in my heart": negotiating sexuality and ethnicity', in C. Guerra and R. White (eds), *Ethnic Minority Youth in Australia*. Hobart: National Clearinghouse on Youth Studies.

Pallotta-Chiarolli, Maria (1996a). 'Inclusive education is more than multicultural education', *Independent Education*, 26(1): 23–5.

Pallotta-Chiarolli, Maria (1996b). ' "A rainbow in my heart": interweaving ethnicity and sexuality studies', in C. Beavis *et al.* (eds), *Schooling and Sexualities: Teaching for Positive Sexualities*. Melbourne: Centre for Education and Change, Deakin University, Deakin University Press.

Pallotta-Chiarolli, Maria (ed.) (1998). *Girls Talk: Young Women Speak Their Hearts and Minds*. Lane Cove, Sydney: Finch.

Passey, David (1997). 'Gay pupil's victory – now it's back to school', *Sydney Morning Herald*, 12 April, p. 3.

Patrick, Paul and Sanders, Susan A. L. (1994). 'Lesbian and gay issues in the curriculum', in D. Epstein (ed.), *Challenging Lesbian and Gay Inequalities in Education*. Buckingham: Open University Press.

Pausacker, Jenny (ed.) (1996). *Hide and Seek: Stories about Being Young and Gay/ Lesbian*. Dingley, Victoria: Mandarin.

Pettman, Jan (1992). *Living in the Margins*. Sydney: Allen & Unwin.

Pollard, Ruth (1997a). 'Landmark case: student sues', *Sydney Star Observer: Gay and Lesbian Community's Weekly Newspaper*, **348**, 3 April, pp. 1, 3.

Pollard, Ruth (1997b). 'Another school faces gay abuse charges: Catholics sued', *Sydney Star Observer: Gay and Lesbian Community's Weekly Newspaper*, **352**, 1 May, p. 1.

Ratti, Rakesh (ed.) (1993). *A Lotus of Another Color: An Unfolding of the South Asian Gay and Lesbian Experience*. Boston: Alyson Publications.

Richards, John (1988). *Australia: A Cultural History*. Melbourne: Longman Cheshire.

*Sixty Minutes* (1997). 'Pride and Prejudice', 23 April. Television Network 10.

Sloniec, Elizabeth (1992a). *Schooling Outcomes of Students from Non-English Speaking Backgrounds: An Overview of Current Issues and Research*. Adelaide: Education Department of South Australia.

Sloniec, Elizabeth (1992b). *Supportive School Environment: Report of Research Project on Cross-Cultural Tensions and Student Interaction in School*. Adelaide: Education Department of South Australia.

South Australian Commission for Catholic Schools (1992). *Gender and Equity Policy*. Adelaide: Catholic Education Office.

Specific Focus Programs Directorate (1996). *Girls and Boys at School: Gender Equity Strategy, 1996–2001*. Sydney: NSW Department of School Education.

Studdert, Fiona (1997). 'Gay law reform in Tasmania: it's over', *Melbourne Star Observer: Gay and Lesbian Weekly Newspaper*, **364**, 2 May, pp. 1, 4.

Trinh T. Minh-Ha (1991). *When the Moon Waxes Red*. New York: Routledge.

Tsiolkas, Christos (1995). *Loaded*. Sydney: Vintage.

Tsolidis, Georgina (1986). *Educating Voula*. Melbourne: Ministerial Advisory Committee on Multicultural and Migrant Education.

Wille, Annemarie (1995). 'Affirming diversity', *On the Level*, 3(3): 3–9.

# Index